THE TRANSHUMAN
ANTIHERO

The Transhuman Antihero

*Paradoxical Protagonists
of Speculative Fiction from
Mary Shelley to Richard Morgan*

Michael Grantham

McFarland & Company, Inc., Publishers
Jefferson, North Carolina

LIBRARY OF CONGRESS CATALOGUING-IN-PUBLICATION DATA

Grantham, Michael, 1986–
    The transhuman antihero : paradoxical protagonists of speculative
fiction from Mary Shelley to Richard Morgan / Michael Grantham.
        p.   cm.
    Includes bibliographical references and index.

    ISBN 978-0-7864-9405-7 (softcover : acid free paper) ∞
    ISBN 978-1-4766-1955-2 (ebook)

    1. Science fiction, English—History and criticism.   2. English
fiction—History and criticism.   3. Antiheroes in literature.
4. Monsters in literature.   5. Literature and science.   I. Title.

PR830.S35G72 2015
823.009'352—dc23   2015027519

BRITISH LIBRARY CATALOGUING DATA ARE AVAILABLE

Cover images © 2015 Blend Images/Thinkstock

Printed in the United States of America

McFarland & Company, Inc., Publishers
  Box 611, Jefferson, North Carolina 28640
  www.mcfarlandpub.com

Table of Contents

Preface

Advances in science and technology no longer change how we, as individuals, live; they determine it. And if the promises of transhumanism are to be believed, such technoscientific developments will, at some point, provide individuals with the capacity to become smarter and stronger, and to live longer, healthier, and more productive lives. But to what end?

Speculative fiction, as anyone with an interest in the genre will know, presents readers with a plethora of transhuman beings—protagonists whose strengths, intelligence, or skills and abilities mark them as superior to everyday individuals. Often, these protagonists are antiheroic in nature and openly reject the normative moral and social conventions of their social reality. In most cases, these protagonists enact or espouse undoubtedly immoral and/or extremist ideologies, thereby challenging, if not positioning readers to accept, though not necessarily condone, what they might otherwise condemn.

This book offers a reading of selected examples of the antiheroic transhuman in speculative fiction and examines the duality—transhuman, yet also antiheroic—by which they are rendered paradoxical. What becomes evident is that in spite of their apparent superiority, the paradoxical protagonists, like traditional antiheroes, are plagued by personal insecurity and are as susceptible to vice, violence, and petty motivation as ordinary individuals. Ultimately, what the paradoxical protagonist comes to demonstrate is that while technoscientific development might enable us to transcend the limitations imposed upon the human condition, it won't enable us to transcend human nature.

The paradoxical protagonist emerged as a result of my preoccupation with speculative fiction, antiheroes, and the concept of transhumanism. This book based upon my doctoral thesis, is a product of my personal views and observations, structured around my own social reality and the genre to which I have dedicated much of my life.

1

Introduction:
The Paradoxical Protagonist

Many protagonists in speculative fiction represent a paradoxical mix of human and transhuman. This book argues that these paradoxical protagonists, especially when considered in the context of the social realities in which they are depicted and the issues by which they are confronted, offer an alternative medium for the exploration of the dynamic and complex relationship between individuals, society, and technoscientific development. They reflect the ways in which changes in scientific understanding and new or emerging technology are affecting existing normative moral and social convention. Further, these characters also offer new insight into the modern crisis of identity, along with the generalized fear and anxiety surrounding the emergence of transhuman theory and the possibility of transhuman beings.

Much like the hybridized image of "machine and organism" described by Donna Haraway in "A Cyborg Manifesto" (1991, p. 149), many of the protagonists of modern speculative fiction represent what might be interpreted as a threat to existing categories, often serving as a mechanism for the deconstruction (or even complete removal) of the differentiation between polarized concepts such as biology and technology, human and animal, human and machine, reality and illusion. Further, the antiheroic nature of these protagonists, as will be demonstrated throughout each chapter, serves to challenge previously established notions of morality and social convention, inevitably blurring the line between right and wrong, morality and immorality, thus providing new insight into broader concepts such as good and evil and how they have come to be perceived.

In order to demonstrate such a claim, this study traces the origins of the antiheroic transhuman back at least as far as Mary Shelley's *Frankenstein* (1818) and follows its development through key works such as Olaf

Stapledon's *Odd John* (1935), Alfred Bester's *The Stars My Destination* (1956), William Gibson's *Neuromancer* (1986), Alan Moore's and Dave Gibbons's *Watchmen* (1986–1987) and contemporary narratives such as Richard Morgan's Takeshi Kovacs trilogy (*Altered Carbon* [2002], *Broken Angels* [2003] and *Woken Furies* [2005]) and *Black Man* (2008). The narratives examined throughout this book have been recognized as having made a significant contribution to the development of speculative fiction and—with the exception of Richard Morgan's Takeshi Kovacs trilogy and *Black Man*, discussed in the final chapters—have been the subject of scholarly inquiry (for example, Lopes, *Demanding Respect* [2009, pp. 111–158]; Broderick, *Reading by Starlight* [1995, pp. 80–174]; Stableford, *Science Fact and Science Fiction* [2006, pp. 4–558]; Cavallaro, *Cyberpunk and Cyberculture* [2000, pp. 14–209]). Equally significant is the fact that the protagonists depicted within these narratives not only reflect the paradoxical mix of human, antihero, and transhuman that is the foundation of this study but are also developed and complex characterizations which allow for in-depth analysis, especially when entering into discussions that draw on concepts such as Nietzschean philosophy and the distinction between right and wrong, good and evil.

At the most basic level, the paradoxical protagonist is an amalgam of two primary concepts: the antihero and the transhuman. As a literary concept and character archetype, the antihero has been in circulation since the translation of Fyodor Dostoevsky's *Notes from Underground* in 1864. The emergence of the antihero has had a significant impact upon the development of western literature, specifically in relation to its exploration and depiction of the human condition, the fallibility of the individual, and his susceptibility to vice, corruption, violence, and perversion. As the concept may suggest, the antihero is essentially the antithesis of traditional modes and models of heroism such as those described in-depth by Joseph Campbell's *The Hero with a Thousand Faces* (1949). In "The Madman as Hero in Contemporary American Fiction," Michael Woolf argues that the traditional heroic figure has for some years now been mostly "inappropriate," especially in relation to "contemporary culture" (1976, p. 257). Woolf argues that the "concept of the anti-hero reflects the nature of reality much more obviously" (1976, p. 257). Brombert, in his study *In Praise of Antiheroes*, makes a similar observation regarding the presence of the antihero within contemporary literary fiction, which he views as becoming increasingly crowded with "weak, ineffectual, pale, humiliated, self-doubting, inept, occasionally abject characters—often afflicted with self-conscious and paralyzing irony" (1999, p. 2). Brombert contends that it is the limitations of the antihero, particularly his limited capacity to effect change and his "self-conscious and paralyzing irony" (1999, p. 2), which separate him from more traditional heroes.

Elaborating upon the unique mode of action (or perhaps, more appropriately, inaction) expressed by the antihero, Woolf perceives anti-heroic literary fiction as populated by protagonists who have no "special powers" by which they are distinguished from others (1976, p. 258) and who also do not have the capacity "to act as a dynamic factor in the evolution of a given fictional system" (1976, p. 258). According to Woolf, the limitations by which the antihero is afflicted are indicative of the issues and concerns plaguing postmodern society, inevitably producing environments wherein the individual's capacity to elicit change is "severely limited" (1976, p. 258). This environment, Woolf concludes, is one that has become devoid of any "accessible logic" and is thus no longer "hospitable" to the individual (1976, p. 258).

The emergence of the antihero is significant both psychologically and philosophically. According to Brombert, the antihero challenges personal values and assumptions and calls into question broader facets of social and moral convention through the direct juxtaposition of individual and subject (1999, pp. 2–4). Brombert argues that the antihero, as a hero of negative value, "more keenly perhaps than the traditional hero, challenges our assumptions, raising anew the questions of how we see, or wish to see ourselves" (1999, p. 2). As Brombert points out, the antihero more often than not fails, "by a deliberate strategy of their authors, to live up to expectations still linked to memories of traditional literary or mythical heroes" (1999, p. 5), thus calling into question, if not subverting, notions of the heroic ideal.

In "Anti-heroic Literature," Andrew Daniel builds on Brombert's claim, suggesting that "just as the antihero represents a defiance of the social tradition and its most cherished values so, too, the authors themselves appear to be resisting tradition by creating works which protest, rather than affirm the norm" (1994, p. 2). What both Woolf and Brombert inevitably conclude, however, is that in spite of their limited capacity to effect change, the antihero reflects a unique form of courage, one that is perhaps more accurately suited to contemporary social reality (Woolf, 1976, p. 257: Brombert, 1999, p. 5).

Woolf claims that such protagonists are largely the result of historical experience, through which individuals have come to realize that their "capacity to effect change or to control the direction of [their] own experience was severely limited" (1976, p. 257). For Woolf, antiheroes might simply be interpreted as heroes of inaction, already defeated by the social reality in which they exist and their own incapacity to effect change:

> They do not, for example, significantly change the prevailing social conditions. They do not possess superhuman powers, nor, in a world generally imagined to be without God, do they communicate with deities … they pursue some projection of an ideal despite the fact that the pursuit of the ideal is doomed to failure [1976, p. 262].

In *Heeding the Antiheroine's Call*, Cynthia Lyles-Scot adopts a feminist perspective, arguing that antiheroes of today are indeed a product of postmodernism; they are indicative of internal rather than external conflict, whose struggle is manifest within themselves, rather than derived from oppositional forces (2007, p. 1).

While the definitions offered by these critics provide an initial foundation for coming to understand the antiheroic protagonist, each fails to acknowledge the significance of speculative fiction in shaping the development of contemporary literature. These definitions describe what this study will refer to as the traditional antihero.[1] However, in focusing upon the paradoxical protagonist, the following chapters will demonstrate that many of the antiheroes presented in speculative fiction cannot be described as "weak" or "ineffectual" as Brombert claims, nor are they devoid of superpowers or special abilities or limited in their capacity to effect change, such as those characters described by Woolf.

Unlike the traditional antihero, the paradoxical protagonist of speculative fiction is depicted as having gained skills, powers, abilities, and attributes that far supersede those of everyday individuals. More often than not these extraordinary attributes are derived from technoscientific[2] developments in areas commonly associated with transhumanism. In spite of this transhuman status and having surpassed the limitations imposed upon ordinary individuals, these protagonists, as a result of their antiheroic nature, are not completely unrecognizable from traditional antiheroes. More often than not they are imperfect individuals, displaying a number of flawed characteristics and susceptibility to vice, selfish desire, and violence. This study will focus particularly (but not exclusively) upon the issue of violence, for violence becomes almost synonymous with the paradoxical protagonists discussed. Primarily, the paradoxical protagonist can be seen employing violence as a means to an end, and while the violent acts may be considered immoral in the social reality[3] inhabited by both reader and protagonist, such actions can usually be justified in relation to the situation or issues by which the protagonist is confronted. This link between real-world violence and violence depicted in literature is examined by a number of critics. In *Violence and the Limits of Representation*, for instance, Matthews and Goodman argue that violence is one of the most important issues facing contemporary social reality and that it needs to be considered in context of the values by which it is framed (2013, p. 1). Britt, on the other hand, in discussing the role of violence in speculative fiction, argues that the genre needs violence because violence is an undeniable component of the social reality inhabited by the reader and "in order to be effective fiction, [speculative] fiction has to comment on the real world" (2011). While violence is a mode of action employed by many, if not all, of the protagonists examined throughout the following chapters, it should not be thought of as being strictly typical of the transhuman depicted in speculative fiction. A number of works (including Frederick Pohl's *Man Plus* [1976] and Greg Bear's *Blood Music* [1985]) depict transhuman beings who seldom, if ever, use violence.

Paradoxical protagonists not only have the capacity to more accurately reflect the human condition, but—as a result of their transhuman status and the social realities in which they exist—also offer unique insight into the potential consequences, issues, and concerns derived from technoscientific development and its impact upon both the individual and social reality.

The terms transhuman and posthuman are often used interchangeably, resulting in a level of ambiguity. Transhumanism refers to an area of critical investigation concerned with improving and ultimately perfecting the human condition, physically and cognitively, through the use of science and technology. The transhuman is a concept first employed by critic and futurist FM-2030 as an abbreviation for "transitional-human" which refers to the individual subject as being in a state of transition (1989, p. 42). According to FM-2030, the "transitional-human" or "transhuman is representative of the earliest manifestation of new evolutionary beings" (1989, p. 42). As perceived by FM-2030, the transhuman evokes a sense of progress, whereby the human will become surpassed by the transhuman and, inevitably, the transhuman (in reaching a logical evolutionary conclusion) will be surpassed by the posthuman. Thus the transhuman can be interpreted as an individual in the process of reducing imposed limitations, whereas the posthuman is, theoretically, an individual who is no longer bound by physiological constraints such as sickness, aging, fatigue, or even death. Thus, the transhuman should be seen as the individual subject separating the polarized opposition of human and posthuman. Therefore the posthuman, unlike the transhuman, reflects the final stage of human evolution, whether biological or directed. According to transhuman theorist Nick Bostrom, the posthuman might be interpreted as a human descendent

> who has been augmented to such a degree as to be no longer a human.... As a posthuman, your mental and physical abilities would surpass those of any unaugmented human. You would be smarter than any human genius.... [Your] body [would] not be susceptible to disease and it will not deteriorate with age, giving you indefinite youth and vigour. You may have a greatly expanded capacity to feel emotion and to experience pleasure and love and artistic beauty. You would not need to feel tired, bored or irritated about petty things [1999, p. 3].

Although the transhuman is often associated with empirical areas of science and technology, in *How We Became Post Human*, Katherine Hayes argues that there is also the potential for fluidity and that the term is essentially an "amalgam, a collection of heterogeneous components, a material-informational entity whose boundaries undergo continuous construction and reconstruction" (1999, p. 3), specifically in relation to the dynamics of the human experience.

The notion of transhumanism conjures images of the cyborg, wherein biology and technology become integrated into a single subject, thereby blurring the boundaries separating organism from artifact or machine. While the cyborg is the most prolific and the most recognized image relating to the possible shapes of transhuman evolution, it is not the only possibility. Hayes, for example, stresses the significance of subjectivity, arguing that it is the "construction of subjectivity that will be the defining characteristic of the transhuman, rather than the presence of non-biological components" (1999, p. 4). Speculative fiction, as will be shown throughout the following chapters, presents a number of transhuman beings who have overcome the limitations imposed upon the human condition in a variety of ways. Further, the antiheroic protagonists of speculative fiction, as will be demonstrated, become inseparable from images of the transhuman: the monster presented in Mary Shelley's *Frankenstein* (1818) is created using science and technology and thus granted strength, speed, intellect, and survivability that far surpass those of everyday individuals; Gully Foyle, the protagonist of Alfred Bester's *The Stars My Destination* (1956), is so driven by revenge that he undergoes augmentation and later obtains almost god-like power; in Richard Morgan's *Altered Carbon* (2002), the protagonist Takeshi Kovacs is a psychologically conditioned and physically augmented super-soldier whose lethal skills are available to anyone willing to pay.

This, however, is not to suggest that examples of transhuman beings, or even the paradoxical protagonist as explored throughout this study, cannot be identified in other works of speculative fiction. Ian M. Banks's Culture series, beginning with *Consider Phlebas* (1987), Greg Bear's *Blood Music* (1985), Pat Cadigan's *Synners* (1991), Frederik Pohl's *Man Plus* (1976), Kameron Hurley's *Bel Dame Apocrypha* (*God's War* [2011], *Infidel* [2011], and *Rapture* [2012])—along with narratives by Greg Egan including *Permutation City* (1994) and *Diaspora* (1997)—explore a variety of issues pertaining to transhumanism. Given limited space, it has not been possible to explore the complete range of transhuman beings presented in speculative fiction, and precedence has been given to those works sharing the particular preoccupation with violence.

There are also several films—including Wally Pfister's *Transcendence* (2014), Josh Trank's *Chronicle* (2012) and Vincenzo Natali's *Splice* (2009)— that depict various forms of transhuman evolution and the issues that inevitably arise as a result of their existence. That said, cinematic representations of the paradoxical protagonist fall beyond the boundaries imposed by this book and would be best examined in a separate study.

It is perhaps worth noting that with the exception of Shelley's *Frankenstein*, the narratives examined throughout this book are predominately by male authors. This, it should be pointed out, is not an oversight but a deliberate strategy of focus. It should not be seen as disregard for writers such as Pat Cadigan, Lisa Mason, Syne Mitchell, Elizabeth Moon, Lyda Morehouse, and Melissa Scott; to the contrary, this is a strategy that accepts the need to look separately at female and feminist incursions into territory that was once seen as a males-only domain.

A number of commentators on transhumanism—critics such as Justin Johnston (*The Prosthetic Novel and Posthuman Bodies* [2012]) and Marquard Smith and Joanne Morra (*The Prosthetic Impulse* [2006])— identify prostheses (such as prosthetic limbs and bionic substitutes such as cochlear implants) as being significant in the discussion of the transhuman. But others disagree: Pete Moore, for instance, suggests that enhancement or augmentation enables the individual "to do something no other human can" or achieve something that would be "impossible for a vast majority of human beings" (2008, p. xi). Similarly, but in a more general approach, John Harris argues that enhancements, as they are currently situated, can only be defined as such if they have the capacity "to make us better people" (2007, p. 2). For the purposes of this study, transhumanism is taken to be primarily concerned with improvement, following the arguments of Moore and Harris.

In spite of critics such as Moore and Harris advocating transhumanism as being essentially designed for the betterment of human kind, views are divided. Those who support the movement believe that technoscientific progress will inevitably lead to the singularity[4] and the abolition of global economic, social, cultural, and environmental concerns. Elaine Graham contends that individuals who look favorably upon transhumanism believe that it will inevitably lead to the creation of a "techno scientific utopia assisted by smart drugs, prosthetics, genetic modification and computer assisted communication" (2002, p. 154). Opponents of the movement, such as Francis Fukuyama, argue that it is the "world's most dangerous idea" (2004). According to Graham, opponents to transhumanism perceive it as being a perversion of the natural order, and instead of aiding humanity, technoscientific development "will bring about alienation and dehumanization, the erosion of the spiritual essence of humanity" (2002, p. 6). Fukuyama argues that transhumanism will lead to vast inequality between modified and unmodified individuals, specifically for those opposed to the idea or unwilling to undergo voluntary augmentation, resulting in greater political, moral, and economic concerns (2002, pp. 155–160). In a more extreme statement, Annas, Andrews, and Isasi argue that should transhumans come to exist, they will, more than likely, perceive ordinary humans as violent, ignorant, un-enlightened savages, only "fit for slavery or slaughter" (2002, p. 162).

The first chapter traces the origins of the antiheroic transhuman back to Mary Shelley's *Frankenstein* (1818) and draws parallels between the image of the monster and the transhuman. In examining the relationship between Victor and his monster, this chapter not only highlights some of the potential consequences resulting from unethical technoscientific development, but also examines how the implementation of violence, while still immoral, cannot be considered as unjustified, thus blurring the boundary between right and wrong.

Shifting from the monsters derived from science and technology presented in Chapter One, Chapter Two focuses on the idea of natural transcendence as providing an alternative to the integration of biology and technology in the development of the transhuman. This chapter argues that the notion of natural (though not necessarily biological) transcendence can be traced back to German philosopher Frederick Nietzsche's *Thus Spake Zarathustra* (1885), which advocates the rise of the Übermensch, a being described as the intellectual and moral successor to existing individuals. Nietzsche's conception of the Übermensch, as will be demonstrated, is largely informed by his broader philosophical theories, specifically the will to power, self-overcoming, and sublimation. To explore this idea, this chapter focuses on representations of the Übermensch in three works of speculative fiction: Olaf Stapledon's *Odd John* (1935), Theodore Sturgeon's *More Than Human* (1953), and Alfred Bester's *The Stars My Destination* (1956).

Chapter Three shows how the social reality presented in a given narrative has the capacity to position readers to accept, while perhaps not condone, actions or ideologies they would otherwise have condemned, thereby effectively altering their perception of right and wrong, good and evil. This argument is demonstrated through the chapter's examination of Alan Moore and David Lloyd's *V for Vendetta* (1982–1989), which confronts readers with a dystopian reality in which the protagonist's only reasonable course of action is through the implementation of violence, rebellion, and anarchy.

Chapter Four looks at the deconstruction of the superhero in Alan Moore's and Dave Gibbons' *Watchmen* (1986–1987). In considering Victor Brombert's claim that the "negative hero" or antihero "more keenly perhaps than the traditional hero, challenges our assumptions, raising anew the question of how we see, or wish to see ourselves" (1999, p. 2), this chapter argues that the characters in *Watchmen* present the reader with a more realistic, humanized account of the traditional superhero. Building on Michael Woolf's identification of two iconic forms of insanity commonly manifest within the antiheroic protagonist, this chapter also contends that the protagonists depicted throughout the narrative display a third form of insanity that is derived from their deeper insight into the human condition and recognition of its savage nature. Further, this chapter argues that Moore's deconstruction of the superhero offers an alternative perspective on the possible ramifications stemming from the existence of transhuman individuals.

Chapter Five asserts that the protagonists presented in the cyberpunk subgenre reflect an early interpretation of the possibilities resulting from the integration of biology and technology. To put it bluntly, this is to suggest that many of the protagonists depicted in cyberpunk are cyborgs.

Through an examination of William Gibson's *Neuromancer* (1984), George Alec Effinger's *When Gravity Fails* (1986), and Neal Stephenson's *Snow Crash* (1992), this chapter explores the influence of the punk rock counter-culture of the 1980s upon the development of cyberpunk and its celebration of anarchy, nihilism, anti-establishmentism, and self-destruction. It will be argued that it is the protagonists' adoption of punk ideology that determines and reinforces their antiheroic nature.

Chapter Six focuses on Richard Morgan's Takeshi Kovacs trilogy— *Altered Carbon* (2002), *Broken Angels* (2003) and *Woken Furies* (2005)— which provides insight into the crisis of identity evoked by the emergence of transhuman theory through its reinterpretation of canonical cyberpunk.

Chapter Seven argues that the image of the monster is particularly important in considering the fear and anxiety surrounding technoscientific developments in areas commonly associated with transhumanism such as genetic or biological engineering. The chapter discusses Richard Morgan's *Black Man* (2008), which confronts readers with a social reality in which developments in the fields of genetic research have led to the existence of several man-made variations upon the human genome.

ONE

The Transhuman
and the Monster

The figure of the monster, specifically those monsters depicted early speculative fiction, provides the foundation for the development the paradoxical protagonist because of the monster's affinity with the tra shuman. Both the monster and the transhuman reflect alternative mod of being, beyond that of the human experience. These alternatives n only broaden the notion of developmental (though not necessarily natur or biological) corporality but also detract from, if not remove altogethe the space separating previously polarized concepts such as human and nonhuman, biology and technology, organism and artifact. Frequently, the monster is a paradox whose illicit nature and unnatural existence force it into obscurity and to engage in actions far outside moral and social convention, which then determine their status as antiheroes. To support this claim, this chapter will focus on Mary Shelley's *Frankenstein* (1818) and also examine Robert Louis Stevenson's *The Strange Case of Dr. Jekyll and Mr. Hyde* (1886) and Oscar Wilde's *The Picture of Dorian Gray* (1890).

Monster and Transhuman

The monster is the embodiment of social, cultural, theological, and (today) technoscientific fear and anxiety. In *Representations of the Post/ Human*, Elaine Graham argues that the anxiety evoked by monsters is derived from their representation of the fragility of axiomatic boundaries separating human from nonhuman, biology from technology, and organism from artifact (2002, pp. 11–12). This notion is supported by Margrit Shildrick, who explains that the monster's very existence is a force of destabilization whereby previously accepted boundaries (such as those dis-

cussed by Graham) are forced into question (2002, pp. 8–10). As a result, the monster usually connotes something that is evil, wrong, or unnatural; a grand, albeit frequently grotesque, subversion of normative value, representing the potential for physical, spiritual, or psychological harm. As Andrew Hook-soon Ng points out, the monster is "traditionally (and still) objectified as the threatening other" (2004, p. 12). The threat such beings pose is that of destabilization. According to Georges Canguilhem, for instance, the monster is dangerous because it represents the subtraction of natural logic, stability, and reason; the very possibility of the monster's existence "throws doubt on life's ability to teach us order" (1962, p. 27). Thus the monster is perceived as a figure existing within, but simultaneously reducing, the space separating polarized concepts such as human and nonhuman, organic and inorganic.

For Ilya Wick, the monster in its conceptional sense reflects a "reaction against what is presumed to be outside the limits of the human, of what the human conceptualizes as itself" (2006, p. 20). Monsters can thus be interpreted as developing in response to social, moral, and ideological evolution. While mythology and the medieval imagination, for instance, were populated by a variety of hybridized creatures such as the chimera, minotaur, and centaur, contemporary popular culture has today become saturated with artificial intelligence, robots, cyborgs, and the misbegotten products of genetic engineering.[1] Elaine Graham observes the correlation between the evolution of the monster and social development, suggesting that just "as the monster of the past marked out the moral and topographical limits of their day, so today other similar strange … creatures enable us to gauge the implications of the crossing of technological boundaries" (2002, p. 39). As will be discussed later in the chapter, the latter refers to the monster as a metaphor, which serves as a direct, often critical, reflection of social reality and, to some extent, facets of the human condition. This apparent contradiction is clarified by Graham, who explains that more definitive "accounts of human nature may be better arrived at, not through a description of essences, but via the delineation of boundaries" (2002, p. 11). Scott Niall, offering a historical reading of the monster's development alongside social reality, affirms this when arguing that the monster is essentially one of the most "significant creations serving to reflect and critique human existence" (2007, p. 1). Richard Kearney comes to a similar conclusion in relation to postmodern social reality, claiming that monsters "emerge as the self-fulfilling prophecies of modernity," representing what he describes as a "return of the repressed" (2001, p. 97).

Physically, the monster is often depicted as grotesque or hideous. The ugliness of its aesthetic properties solidify its identity as other than human and serves to reinforce its ability to evoke sensations of fear and anxiety. This fear, according to Jasia Reichardt, stems from the monster's capacity to subvert individual or social expectations (1994, p. 139). The result, Reichardt claims, is always explosive: "We react violently when what appears natural proves not to be, and to some extent vice versa" (1962, p. 139). The monster's body, as it were, nevertheless remains a site of curiosity and disgusted fascination. As Reichardt rightly observes, it is only the "human being or humanoid" monster that is capable of possessing those qualities necessary to render its existence truly monstrous, as no "monstrous cupboard, chair, plant or teapot could engender real fear, horror and fascination all at once" (1962, p. 139). In conforming to Masahiro Mori's theory of the "uncanny valley" (2007), Reichardt argues that monstrosity is strictly reserved for the organic, as there can be no such thing "as a mineral monster" nor even a "mechanical monster" (1962, p. 28). What Reichardt concludes is that the monster is an organic or "living being of negative value" (1962, p. 28).

In literature, the monster is commonly indicative of an identity in crisis, derived from its unnatural origins and perpetuated by its continued existence. On one hand, the monster is a corporeal artifact and a physical manifestation that stands testament to the fragility of logic and the natural order. On the other, the monster, as will be shown later in this chapter, is often underpinned by some moral or metaphoric value. Cohen makes a similar observation, stating that the monster is seldom, if ever, devoid of meaning: "It exists at metaphoric crossroads, as an embodiment of a certain cultural moment—of a time, a feeling, and a place" (1996, p. 4). As Lykke and Braidotti observe, this reinforces the monster's paradoxical nature, in that it inevitably exists as both human-like and nonhuman and is thus "neither a total stranger nor completely familiar" (1996, p. 141). Wick agrees, yet moves to emphasize the degree to which the monster is largely a product of social understanding: "At the extremes, the monster is what the human desires it to be, is seen as the human needs it to be seen, and is reshaped in a negative image of the human, in contrast to, yet insistently and intimately related to it" (1996, p. 2).

The crisis of identity experienced by the monster, as a facet of its paradoxical nature, comes to be expressed through its appearance. This, as will be demonstrated in the following, is especially true in relation to the humanoid monsters depicted in early speculative fiction. In Shelley's *Frankenstein*, for instance, the paradox and crisis of identity evoked by the monster emerges from his creation. Comprised of organic matter acquired through grave robbery by his creator, Victor Frankenstein, the monster, though human-like in appearance, is given life through the application of some unknown scientific method. In this, the monster can be interpreted as both human and nonhuman, alive and dead, organic and inorganic. As Graham rightly observes, the monster depicted in Shelley's narrative "confuses many of the boundaries by which normative humanity has been delineated" (2002, p. 62).

Within the narrative itself, the paradox of the monster is first seen through the response of Victor. He had originally selected the monster's features "as beautiful" (1818, p. 58), but once animate, however, this beauty is suddenly subverted:

> His yellow skin scarcely covered the work of muscles and arteries beneath; his hair was of a lustrous black, and flowing; the teeth of pearly whiteness; but these luxuries only formed a more horrid contrast with his watery eyes, that seemed almost of the same color as the dun-white sockets in which they were set, his shriveled complexion and straight black lips [1818, p. 58].

Through this sudden subversion, the creature, which had represented Victor's greatest accomplishment, comes to be identified as a "miserable monster," a "demonical corpse," and a thing "such as even Dante could not have conceived" (1818, p. 59).

A similar theme can also be observed in Stevenson's *The Strange Case of Dr. Jekyll and Mr. Hyde* (1886). Here, the subversion of natural beauty is conveyed through the sense of deformity evoked by Mr. Hyde, Dr. Jekyll's alter-ego. Once again the monster has been created with the purest of intentions, for Dr. Jekyll has tried to craft a potion that would separate the individual from his primal instincts. Later, believing that he has perfected the technique, he ingests a quantity of the formula and is instantly transformed. The result, however, is not the complete suppression of evil impulses as he had hoped, but rather the emergence of a second, wholly deviant, and immoral alter-ego: Mr. Hyde. Those who encounter this monstrous alter-ego describe him as being grotesque or repellent but are unable to explain why. Mr. Enfield—who has witnessed Mr. Hyde's accidental, albeit unsympathetic assault on a young girl—explains that the assailant is not an easy man to describe and there seemed to be something fundamentally "wrong with his appearance; something displeasing, something downright detestable" (1886, p. 10). Enfield, like everyone who crosses paths with Mr. Hyde, is instantly affronted, stipulating that he had never met someone he had so disliked and yet could neither explain nor remember why (p. 10). He goes on to say that Mr. Hyde must be "deformed somewhere" as he "gives a strong feeling of deformity" (1886, p. 10). Utterson has a similar reaction, describing the former as being "pale and dwarfish" and, in accordance with Enfield, speaks of an impression of deformity without any nameable malformation: "he had a displeasing smile ... and spoke with a husky, whispering, and somewhat broken voice" (1886, p. 19). Significantly, Utterson concludes that "the man seems hardly human!" and might be considered more "troglodytic, shall we say" (1886, p. 19).

Subverting the trend set by the two previous narratives, Oscar Wilde's *The Picture of Dorian Gray* (1890) presents a subtler version of the monster. In Wilde's narrative, the young Dorian, having recently moved to accept his inheritance, comes to the attention of Basil Hallward, an artist who, becoming somewhat infatuated with the youth, asks the latter to sit for a portrait. Dorian agrees and through Basil meets Henry Wotton (Harry), who introduces him to the idea of a new hedonism.[2] Essentially, it is though his exploration of the ideology underpinning hedonism that Dorian becomes a monster. Dorian's transformation is initiated when he is first shown Basil's finished portrait: "When he saw it he drew back, and his cheeks flushed for a moment.... A look of joy came into his eyes, as if he had recognized himself for the first time"[3] (1890, p. 25). His transformation is driven by his commitment to Harry's philosophy of a new hedonism, dedicated to experience all life's pleasures in earnest, unaware that he had already consigned his soul to the portrait. Subverting the trends of former protagonists such as Frankenstein's monster and Mr. Hyde—monstrosity largely informed by grotesque appearance—Dorian remains physically unchanged and charismatically beautiful. The progress of Dorian's transformation is displayed by the portrait, which reflects his monstrous and immoral actions:

> Looking now at the evil and aging face on the canvas ... now at the fair young face that laughed back at him from the polished glass. The very sharpness of the contrast used to quicken his sense of pleasure. He grew more ... enamored of his own beauty and more ... interested in the corruption of his own soul. He would examine with minute care, and sometimes with a monstrous and terrible delight, the hideous lines that seared the wrinkling forehead, or crawled around the heavy sensual mouth, wondering sometimes which were the most horrible, the signs of sin or the signs of age [1890, p. 113].

The similarities between the monsters presented in the narratives examined within this chapter and the transhuman can be identified upon both an aesthetic and ideological level. As Shildrick suggests, the monster, at the very least, "destabilizes the grand narrative of biology and evolutionary science and signifies other ways of being in the world" (2001, p. 10). The transhuman similarly acts to destabilize previously accepted models of categorization and to blur the boundaries separating the human from the other or non-human. According to Graham, technoscientific areas of research and development often affiliated with the transhuman movement such as "new reproductive technologies, cloning and genetic modification" will fundamentally alter what it means to be human as "the boundaries between humanity, technology and nature will be ever more malleable" (2002, p. 3).

Patricia MacCormack observes the link between the monster and the transhuman as stemming from their otherness. The fundamental element that defines a monster, she contends, is that "they are not monsters, not us, not normal" (2012, p. 303). In this, monsters are defined not simply because of their aesthetic but because they defy existing modes of categorization. When the monster is created through human intervention or from "human matter," it is "never entirely independent from the human form," MacCormack argues (2012, p. 303). Such monsters are problematic due to their "uncanny redistribution" of those elements which individuals define as human into "aberrant configurations" (2012, p. 303). It is these human elements existing in "proximity with a part with which it should not sit side by side" that makes the monster "monstrous" (2012, p. 303). Taking this into consideration, it is easy to see how the transhuman, as a being with recognizably human characteristics juxtaposed with (for example) technological components or a sophisticated prosthesis, might be interpreted as being a monster. Even if the proximity of human characteristics to seemingly unnatural objects is hidden or completely metaphysical—as in the application of a technoscientific method to produce a human or human-like being—it nonetheless underpins that being's existence, thus identifying him as a monster.

At its most basic level, the affinity between the monster and the transhuman is expressed in their reinterpretation of the human condition. In presenting alternative modes of being, beyond those of human experience, both the monster and the transhuman challenge the very notion of what it means to be human. Paradoxically, however, in challenging the idea of what it means to be human, the monster and transhuman, at the same time, offer new insight into the human condition. This perspective is one shared by Graham, who argues that a more accurate sense of human nature might be "better arrived at not through a description of essences, but via the delineation of boundaries" (2002, p. 11). MacCormack makes a similar observation, claiming that in exploring the monster or the transhuman, neither should be considered as coming either before or after the human subject, but instead should be perceived as an "interrogation of the myths of human integrity, biologically and metaphysically" (2012, p. 303). What constitutes or defines a being as transhuman, however, is a matter of degree and, as will be demonstrated, is essentially reliant on having, in one way or another, overcome those limitations imposed upon human individuals.

Examples of the Transhuman Monster in Early Speculative Fiction

The monsters depicted in each of the three narratives examined throughout this chapter demonstrate abilities far beyond those achievable by ordinary individuals. These abilities, as will become evident in later chapters, have made a significant contribution to the development of speculative fiction, as a whole, as well as the paradoxical protagonist.

Shelley's *Frankenstein* depicts an artificially created being whose superiority to both his creator and other individuals is manifest in a number of different ways. The most obvious, however, can be seen in the creature's speed, strength, survivability, and endurance:

> I suddenly beheld the figure of a man, at some distance, advancing towards me with superhuman speed. He bounded over the crevices in the ice, among which I had walked with caution; his stature, also, as he approached seemed to exceed that of man [1818, p. 101].

Further, in the conversation that takes place between the monster and his creator, the former speaks of his ability to thrive in extreme conditions and exist in environments that ordinary individuals would find inhospitable. His diet, he explains, is much simpler than that of any human individual. He does not need to "destroy the lamb and kid" to sate his hunger as "acorns and berries afford … sufficient nourishment" (1818, p. 148).

While the monster's physical superiority is clearly evident, his intellectual capacity also seems far greater than that of other individuals. His intellectual abilities allow him to learn quickly, independently, and with little trouble. The monster first learns to speak, for example, by observing the De Lacy family; as he explains to Victor, through imitation he quickly mastered "the names that were given to some of the most familiar words of discourse" (1818, p. 115). The monster's increased learning capacity is effectively described when the De Lacy family welcomes Safie, a young Arabian girl, into their home. As he tells Victor, the family went to great efforts to tutor their guest in spoken English:

> My days were spent in close attention, that I might more speedily master the language; and I may boast that I improved more rapidly than the Arabian, who understood very little and conversed in broken accents, while I comprehended and could imitate almost every word spoken [1818, p. 121].

Although devoid of life experience and without early socialization, the monster is nonetheless revealed to be highly intelligent and capable of both maturity and reasoning. This capacity for logical reasoning is expressed during the monster's encounter with Victor in the mountains. At first, Victor reacts violently. The monster, however, in drawing his creator's attention to his physical superiority, responds not so much as to threaten, but to reason:

> Be calm! I entreat you to hear me, before you give vent to your hatred.... Have I not suffered enough, that you seek to increase my misery. Life, although ... only an accumulation of anguish, is dear to me, and I will defend it. Remember, thou hast made me more powerful than thyself; my height is superior to thine, my joints more supple. But I will not be tempted to set myself in opposition to thee [1818, p. 102].

Considering his physical, mental, intellectual, and to some extent emotional, superiority, the monster depicted in *Frankenstein* is, in spite of his grotesque appearance, a being that has transcended many of the limitations imposed upon ordinary individuals.

Much like Frankenstein's monstrous creation, the monster depicted in Stevenson's *The Strange Case of Dr. Jekyll and Mr. Hyde* is similarly a being created through the application of a technoscientific method and imbued with abilities beyond those of ordinary individuals.

Again, the monster is described as having superior physical strength. A witness to Mr. Hyde's sudden and unprovoked attack upon a passer-by, for instance, gives some indication as to the feats of strength the monstrous alter-ego is capable of achieving:

> Mr. Hyde broke out of all bounds and clubbed him to the earth. And next moment with apelike fury, he was trampling his victim under foot and hailing down a storm of blows, under which the bones were audibly shattered and the body jumped upon the road [1880, p. 27].

Although Mr. Hyde shares with Frankenstein's monster superior agility and endurance, he is also described as having almost animal-like instincts. For example, when suspected of murder, Dr. Jekyll willingly transforms into Mr. Hyde, knowing the latter's chance of avoiding capture to be far greater than his own:

> I have more than once observed that, in my second character, my faculties seemed sharpened to a point and my spirits tensely elastic; thus it came about that, where Jekyll perhaps might have succumbed, Hyde rose to the importance of the moment [1890, p. 92].

While both the monsters depicted in Shelley's *Frankenstein* and Stevenson's *The Strange Case of Dr. Jekyll and Mr. Hyde* have abilities far exceeding those of ordinary individuals, especially in a physical sense, the monster made of the protagonist in Wilde's *The Picture of Dorian Gray* is altogether more subtle. Although Dorian lacks both the physical strength and heightened cognitive function of Frankenstein's monster and the keen senses and animalistic instincts of Mr. Hyde, he is nonetheless transhuman as a result of the immortality bestowed through the unnatural connection he shares with the portrait. Immortality, as discussed by a number of transhuman critics including Max Moore, Ray Kurzweil, Nick Bostrom, and Aubrey de Grey, is a fundamental aspect of the transhuman.

Each of the three protagonists examined throughout this chapter reflects alternative modes of being, beyond that of the human experience, made possible through human intervention. Each narrative thus offers new insight into the relationship between the individual, society and artifact, specifically in context to technoscientific development and the potential that may emerge resulting from the existence of transhuman beings. Further, each narrative also offers insight into the potential disparity manifest between humans and transhumans. This insight is often revealed through the moral, metaphorical, or allegorical value underpinning the narrative as a whole.

Morals, Metaphors and the Dehumanization of Frankenstein's Monster

As mentioned previously the monster, as the threatening other, is often positioned by its physical aesthetics. According to Hock-soon Ng, the monster is "largely interpellated by the symbolic gaze which prescribes certain significances to particular bodies, rendering them monstrous" (2004, p. 2). Alternatively, however, as Michel Foucault has argued, there is no reason to believe that the monster is of a different nature "from the species themselves."

> We should believe that the most apparently bizarre forms... belong necessarily and essentially to the universal plan of being; that they are metamorphoses of the prototype just as natural as the others, even though they present us with different phenomena; that they serve as means of passing to adjacent forms; that they prepare and bring about the combinations that follow them, just as they themselves were brought about by those that preceded them; that far from disturbing the order of things, they contribute to it [1971, p. 57].

However, due to the monster's identity as the threatening other, such possibilities are seldom, if ever, considered prior to its destruction and the inevitable dehumanization of those responsible. This is largely significant when considering the potential application of technology and science to alter, if not completely re-shape the human form.

In Shelley's *Frankenstein*, the monster serves two primary moral and metaphorical functions: on the one hand, as Victor's creation, he serves to reflect the potential dangers of unchecked scientific progress and the dehumanization derived from the increasing industrialization of social reality. On the other, the monster also reflects a sense of causality, showing how an individual's experience—in this case, negative—can later determine his actions.

As Graham rightly points out, the monster's "hideous being, with its physical oddities, places him beyond the pale of human culture" (2002, p. 64). Thus the monster's nonhuman attributes exist not to attest to potential exploration and expansion of existing cultural knowledge, but rather as an unnatural testament to the evils of the scientific method. Nevertheless, *Frankenstein* is not simply a narrative detailing the negative ramifications of unchecked technoscientific development. The novel draws the reader's attention not only to the monster's more human qualities, but also to the tragedy of his experiences and the inequalities manifest between human and nonhuman, which ensure his alienation from human society. This notion is supported by Graham, who states that in giving the monster an authorial voice equal to that of Robert Walton and Victor Frankenstein, "Mary Shelley implicitly challenges" the monster's "nonhuman status" (2002, p. 65). The monster is itself a metaphor, and within the narrative, both metaphor and morality are thus closely linked. This is supported by Percy Shelley, who explains:

The crimes and malevolence of the single Being, though indeed withering and tremendous, are not the offspring of any unaccountable propensity to evil, but flow irresistibly from certain causes fully adequate to their production. They are the children ... of Necessity and Human Nature.... Treat a person ill and he will become wicked. Requite affection with scorn;—let one being be selected, for whatever cause, as the refuse of his kind—divide him, a social being from society, and you impose upon him the irresistible obligations—malevolence and selfishness [2007, p. 65].

The moral to which Shelley refers in the latter is perhaps most effectively demonstrated through the process of the monster's dehumanization, which begins immediately following his creation, when he is abandoned by Victor. Here Victor realizes, perhaps for the first time, that the immorality of his actions are clearly reflected in the monster's aesthetic: "Oh! No mortal could support the horror of that countenance. A mummy again could not be so hideous as that wretch" (1818, p. 59). The tragedy for Victor is that he had selected the parts that were to contribute to his monster as beautiful and had worked for two years "for the sole purpose of infusing life into an inanimate body," but upon beholding the creature itself, "the beauty of the dream vanished and ... disgust filled my heart" (1818, p. 59). This is but the monster's first encounter with rejection, which, as he explains to Victor during their encounter in the mountains, is something he experienced many times.

When he first enters the woods, for example, he comes across a small hut which he enters to find an old man who, upon seeing the monster, shrieked loudly and "quitting the hut, ran across the fields with a speed of which his debilitated form hardly appeared capable" (1818, p. 108). Later, he enters a small village, appraises a series of small houses, and enters the one he believed to be the most attractive, but as he later explains to Victor,

I had hardly placed my foot within the door before the children shrieked, and one of the women fainted. The whole village was roused; some fled, some attacked me, until, grievously bruised by stones and many other kinds of missile weapons, I escaped to the open country and fearfully took refuge in a low hovel [pp. 108–109].

From the hovel, the monster sees the figure of a man in the distance but tells his creator, "I remembered too well my treatment the night before, to trust myself in his power" (1818, p. 109). During his time in the hovel, the monster becomes aware of the De Lacey family living in the adjoining cottage, whom he observes through a window, describing them as "a lovely sight, even to me, poor wretch! Who has never beheld aught beautiful before" (1818, p. 110). Further, the monster explains the family had evoked "sensations of a peculiar and overpowering nature" (1818, p. 111). This, the monster discovers, is his own desire for companionship, and he decides that he will reveal himself to the family in due course. However, the monster finds the aesthetic contrast between himself and the De Lacey family a source of anguish. He tells Victor,

> I had admired the perfect form of my cottagers—their grace, beauty, and delicate complexions: but how was I terrified, when I viewed myself in a transparent pool! At first I started back, unable to believe that it was indeed I who was reflected in the mirror; and when I became fully convinced that I was in reality the monster that I am, I was filled with the bitterest sensations of despondence and mortification [1818, pp. 116–117].

The monster chooses to reveal himself to Mr. De Lacey, who is blind, believing that without his sight, the old man will have no reason to fear, while his children, Alex and Agatha, along with their guest, Safie, are out walking. The monster introduces himself and strikes up a conversation with the old man, but when he hears the children returning, he throws himself upon the old man's mercy, begging for protection. Nevertheless, the monster is again rejected, as he explains to Victor:

> Who can describe their horror and consternation on holding me? Agatha fainted, and Safie, unable to attend to her friend, rushed out of the cottage. Felix darted forward and with supernatural force tore me from his farther, to whose knees I clung: in a transport of fury, he dashed me to the ground and struck me violently with a stick. I could have torn him limb from limb, as the lion rends the antelope. But my heart sunk within me as with bitter sickness, and I was refrained [1818, p. 137].

The monster is furious, later telling Victor: "I, like the archfiend, bore a hell within me, and finding myself unsympathised with, wished to tear up the trees, spread havoc and destruction around me, and then to have set down and enjoyed the ruin" (1818, p. 138). This marks a significant facet in the monster's dehumanization. Another occurs during his search for Victor when, passing through the woods, he sees a young girl slip into a river. The monster dives in, pulls her to shore and "endeavored, by every means ... to restore animation" (1818, p. 143). Moments later, they are discovered by a young man, who, upon seeing them together, darts forward and tears the girl from the monster's arms before leading her deeper into the forest. The monster follows them and attempts to explain what had happened, but when the man realizes, "he aimed a gun, which he carried, at my body, and fired" (1818, p. 143). In spite of his previous treatment, for the first time the monster acknowledges the disparity and injustice by which he is separated from other individuals. "I had saved a human being from destruction and as a recompense I now writhed under the miserable pain of a wound which shattered the flesh and bone" (1818, p. 143). The "ingratitude" of the injuries the monster had received further "augmented" his suffering (1818, p. 143).

The monster continues to seek his creator, whom he encounters within the mountains. After presenting an account of his experiences, the monster pleads with Victor to construct a second monster, so that he might have some semblance of companionship:

> I am alone and miserable; man will not associate with me; but one as deformed and horrible as myself would not deny herself to me. My companions must be of the same species, and have the same defects. This being you must create [1818, p. 146].

When Victor refuses, the monster attempts to justify his request, explaining that he is malicious "because I am miserable. Am I not shunned and hated by all mankind?" (1818, p. 146). The conversation that follows alludes to two separate moral metaphors underpinning the narrative as a whole. First, the monster, when pointing out to Victor that the latter would not "call it murder, if you could precipitate me into one of those ice-rifts, and destroy my frame, the work of your own hand" (1818, p. 147), highlights the inequality manifest between human and nonhuman. Second, by suggesting that Victor is the primary source of his sorrow and excess of emotion, the monster raises the question of responsibility: specifically, to what end is Victor, as his creator, responsible for his creation's actions, experiences, and place within social reality?

While still reluctant, Victor, when faced with the monster's logic, agrees, but on the provision that the monster and his mate quit the world, never to be seen by human eyes. Victor begins working on a second creation, but when he considers the potential ramifications resulting from the existence of a second monster, he ceases and destroys the partially complete monster, fearing that from the monsters' union, "a race of devils would be propagated upon the earth, who might make the existence of the species of man a condition precarious and full of terror" (1818, p. 171). Prior to the latter event, which symbolizes Victor's final rejection of his creation, the monster, for the most part, had been a kind and benevolent being which found beauty in the world and sought only to be accepted, as will be demonstrated in the following section.

Ultimately, it was the suffering experienced that contributed to his dehumanization and the destruction of the second monster that marked his final transition from nonhuman to monster. At this point, the monster is forced to acknowledge, if not accept, as will be shown in the following section, his monstrous nature, which, in turn, establishes and reinforces his identity as an antihero.

The Monster as Antihero

The transformation undertaken by Victor's creation from benevolent being to revenge-seeker determines the monster's antiheroic identity.

As previously mentioned, the monster had been kind and sensitive; a "benevolent" being whose "soul glowed with love for humanity" (1818, p. 103). He finds joy in the natural world by which he is surrounded: "I was delighted when I first discovered that a pleasant sound, which often saluted my ears, proceeded from the throats of the little winged animals who had often intercepted the light from my eyes" (1818, p. 106). He finds a similar joy in the appearance of other individuals: "The silver hair and benevolent countenance of the aged cottagers won my reverence while the gentle manner of the girl enticed my love" (1818, p. 110). The monster's benevolent nature is further reflected during his first night staying in the hovel adjoined to the De Lacey family's cottage. He steals some of the latter's store to sate his hunger, but as he explains to Victor, "when I found that in doing this I inflicted pain upon the cottagers, I abstained, and satisfied myself with berries, nuts and roots, which I gathered from the neighboring wood" (1818, p. 114). Further, he explains that during his observation of the De Lacey family, he discovered new means "through which I was enabled to assist their labors" (1818, p. 114). Noticing, for example, the time spent collecting firewood, the monster would venture out during the night and return with "firing sufficient for the consumption of several days" (1818, p. 114).

Following numerous rejections, as shown in the previous section, the monster is forced to accept his isolation from human individuals but is unwilling to completely abandon his hopes for companionship. In his request for a mate, the monster tells Victor that should his request be granted, neither he "nor any other human being shall ever see us again" and that he would quit the civilized world, vanishing into "the vast wilds of South America" (1818, p. 148). Further, he explains that with a mate, the "evil passions" derived from the cruelty of others will have fled and that in spite of his abandonment, "during my dying moments I shall not curse my maker" (1818, p. 149).

At this point it is important to note that the monster has already been responsible for the death of two individuals in an attempt to hurt his creator. After recovering from the gunshot he received after saving the young girl from the river, he continues his travels and happens across a young boy. Thinking that the boy, still possessing the purity of youth and innocence, may not judge his physical appearance, the monster attempts to make contact. When the boy screams, however, the monster snatches him up and tells him to be silent, afraid of being discovered. The boy demands to be released, telling the monster that his father is a "syndic—he is M. Frankenstein" and "he will punish you" (1818, p. 144). Upon further inquiry, the monster discovers that the boy is William Frankenstein, Victor's younger brother. Realizing that the boy's death will bring pain to his creator, the monster proceeds to strangle the boy, and before quitting the scene, he steals a locket containing the portrait of a "most lovely young woman" (1818, p. 144). Later, the monster enters a barn to discover a sleeping girl who is later revealed to be Justine Moritz, who came to live with the Frankenstein family following the death of her mother. He contemplates waking her, but fears that if she should scream, it would call unwanted attention to his presence. Instead, he plants the locket which he had stolen from William in the girl's pocket, knowing that when she is discovered with the article, she will become the most likely suspect for the boy's murder (1818, p. 145). Inevitably, the monster's scheme comes to fruition as the girl is arrested and later executed for the death of William Frankenstein. Even so, he returns to rationality, as evidenced through his attempts to reason with Victor for the creation of a second mate. It is only following Victor's destruction of the partially completed creation that the monster forgoes what remains of his humanity and adopts those attitudes which determine his antiheroic identity.

Upon witnessing the breaking of Victor's promise—reflected in his destroying the monster's mate—the monster appears before his creator and demands: "Do you dare to break your promise? I have endured toil and misery... do you dare destroy my hopes?" (1818, p. 172). In an effort to take responsibility for his prior transgression against the natural order and to minimize the threat the monster's existence poses to other individuals, Victor responds in the affirmative, telling him that never again shall he make another "equal in deformity and wickedness" (1818, p. 172).

Overcome with rage, the monster, for the first time, acknowledges and draws upon his superiority in order to threaten his creator:

> Slave, I before reasoned with you, but you have proved yourself unworthy of my condescension. Remember that I have power; you believe yourself miserable, but I can make you so wretched that the light of day will be hateful to you. You are my creator, but I am your master—obey! [1818, p. 172].

The monster then tries to reason, imploringly: "Shall each man ... find a wife for his bosom, and each beast have his mate, and I be alone?" (1818, p. 172). Victor, unmoved, ignores the monster's plight and tells him to be gone from his sight, prompting the monster to warn:

> You can blast my other passions, but revenge remains—revenge, henceforth dearer than light or food! I may die, but first you, my tyrant and tormentor, shall curse the sun that gazes on your misery. Beware; for I am fearless, and therefore powerful [1818, p. 173].

Seen as an exasperated final response to shunning and betrayal, the vow to take revenge and destroy his creator's happiness marks the point where the monster takes up his antiheroic identity.

The first action undertaken by the monster, in his efforts to ensure that his creator suffers as he has suffered, is to kill Henry Clerval (Victor Frankenstein's best friend), whose body is found the following day, washed up on the beach, lacking "sign of any violence, except the black marks of fingers on his neck" (1818, p. 178). The monster's greatest victory over his creator and what might be identified as the pinnacle of his revenge occurs upon the day of Victor's wedding to Elizabeth, during the cruise the couple had planned for their honeymoon. Remembering the monster's promise to destroy his happiness, Victor leaves Elizabeth in their cabin and steps out with a mind to confront the monster, believing that he would be the latter's target. While waiting, however, Victor is roused by a scream which causes him to return to his cabin, only to discover that Elizabeth had been murdered, her body "lifeless and inanimate, thrown across the bed, her head hanging down, and her pale and distorted features half covered by her hair" (1818, p. 199). Victor grieves, but—fearing that the monster might still take revenge upon his remaining friends and family—returns to his home in Geneva and is happy to find his father still alive. The latter, however, quickly succumbs to ill-health upon receiving news of Elizabeth's death, and over time those closest to Victor are "snatched away, one by one" (1818, p. 201).

With little else to live for, Victor vows to hunt down and destroy his creation. As he later confides in Captain Walton,[4] "revenge alone endowed me with strength and composure; it molded my feelings, and allowed me to be calculating and calm, at periods when otherwise delirium or death would have been my portion" (1818, p. 205). Victor's pursuit of the monster takes him around the world but inevitably concludes in the Arctic, where, after telling the captain of his experiences, he dies alone in his cabin, his desire for revenge left unfulfilled. When the captain comes to check on Victor, however, he is shocked to find the monster standing over his deceased creator. The monster tells the captain that he had orchestrated the chase simply to prolong Victor's suffering.

In spite of his experiences, having murdered at least three people and been responsible for the execution of another, the monster is still depicted as having retained much of his humanity, as revealed when explaining to the Captain:

> That is also my last victim.... In his murder my crimes are consummated; the miserable series of my being is wound to a close! Oh, Frankenstein! Generous and self-devoted being! What does it avail that I now ask thee to pardon me? I, who irretrievably destroyed thee by destroying all thou lovedst. Alas! He is cold, he cannot answer me [1818, p. 221].

He also tells the captain that he "pitied Frankenstein" and "abhorred" himself for his crimes (1818, p. 222), but when he learned that Victor was to marry Elizabeth and gain the very happiness he had been denied, he was instantly filled with an "insatiable thirst for vengeance" (1818, p. 222). As a result, the monster thus determined to carry out the threat of destroying his creator's happiness. He knew, however, that he was preparing himself for "deadly torture" but was "slave" not "master" to an "impulse" which he "detested yet could not disobey" (1818, p. 222). Yet, when he succeeded in killing Elizabeth, he was, for some moments, able to cast off all "feeling," subdue all "anguish" and thus revel in his crime: "Evil thenceforth became my good" (1818, p. 222).

For the monster, murdering Elizabeth was the point of no return and the logical conclusion to his transformation. As he explains, "Urged thus far, I had no choice but to adapt my nature to an element which I had willingly chosen. The completion of my demoniacal design became an insatiable passion" (1818, p. 222). During his encounter with Captain Walton, following Victor's death, the monster summarizes the causality underpinning his transformation from a kind, benevolent individual to an antiheroic monster, explaining,

Once I falsely hoped to meet with beings who, pardoning my outward form, would love me for the excellent qualities which I was capable of unfolding. I was nourished with high thoughts of honour and devotion. But now crime has degraded me beneath the meanest animal. No guilt, no mischief, no malignity, no misery, can be found comparable to mine. When I run over the frightful catalogue of my sins, I cannot believe that I am the same creature whose thoughts were once filled with sublime and transcendent visions of the beauty and the majesty of goodness. But it is even so; the fallen angel becomes a malignant devil. Yet even that enemy of God and man had friends and associates in his desolation; I am alone" [1818, p. 223].

Further, he goes on to explain that having come to recognize the disparity manifest between himself and ordinary individuals and his inability to effect change, compounded with the guilt of having slain individuals whom he had known to be wholly innocent (aside from their association with Victor), the monster has become pensioned by his crimes "and torn by the bitterest remorse" (1818, p. 224). His only remaining salvation is the promise of self-destruction: "I shall collect my funeral pile and consume to ashes this miserable frame, that its remains may afford no light to any curious and unhallowed wretch who would create such another as I have been" (1818, p. 224). Although the monster's death is tragic—as is the death of any emotionally sensitive being—it is not necessarily unwarranted. Graham comes to a similar conclusion, suggesting that the monster's death seems more "despairing than heroic or even sacrificial" because while the text's emphasis upon the monster as "wronged victim is powerful" and the corruption of his character is undeniable (2002, p. 68).

In the monster's self-destruction, the last irony underpinning Shelley's narrative is revealed: although Victor was determined to discover the means by which life might be prolonged, he created only death and despair. Further, the monster has been shown to be kind and sensitive, whereas Victor, by abandoning his creation and rejecting its human status, is thus revealed to be cruel and uncaring. The monster's violent behavior may be reprehensible, but it is a heroic decision to oppose injustice and intolerance. His behavior marks him as an antihero, just as his transhuman status marks him as paradoxical.

Two

Antiheroes and Overheroes

Shifting from the unnatural monsters derived from science and technology discussed previously, this chapter addresses the notion of natural transcendence as an alternative to the integration between technology and biology in the development of the transhuman. This will be facilitated through an examination of the protagonists presented in three key narratives: Olaf Stapledon's *Odd John* (1935), Theodore Sturgeon's *More Than Human* (1953) and Alfred Bester's *The Stars My Destination* (1956). As will be illustrated, the notion of natural transcendence can be traced back to German philosopher Frederick Nietzsche's *Thus Spake Zarathustra* (1885), which advocates the rise of the Übermensch as the natural successor to existing individuals. As will be shown through the application of Nietzsche's theories, similarities between the protagonists presented in the works of Stapledon, Sturgeon, and Bester are clearly evident. Further, this chapter also shows Nietzsche's conception of the Übermensch to be informed by his broader philosophical theory, especially in context to the death of God, self-overcoming and the rejection of accepted moral and social convention. Often, as will be demonstrated throughout the examination, it is the protagonist's adoption of such notions that informs and at times determines his antiheroic identity.

The Übermensch in Context

The following discusses the core concepts pertaining to Nietzsche's vision of the Übermensch, a being superior to existing individuals, outlined in *Thus Spake Zarathustra*, the significance of the author's broader philosophical theories upon its conception, and their relevance when viewed in relation to literary depictions of the transhuman.

Technoscientific progress has become the central focus of transhumanism as both an intellectual movement and area of investigation. The significance of technoscientific development within the field of transhumanism is clearly illustrated in its definition as a cultural movement that seeks to reduce the limitations imposed upon the human condition by "making widely available technologies to eliminate aging and to greatly enhance human intellectual, physical, and psychological capacities" (Bostrom, 1999). Even so, the notion of transcending the limitations imposed by the human condition is not a contemporary theory. The idea of becoming something more than human, of self-overcoming, can be traced back to Nietzsche's *Thus Spake Zarathustra* (1885). The relationship between Nietzsche's broader philosophical theory and his conception of the Übermensch in *Thus Spake Zarathustra* is affirmed by Mrs. Forester-Nietzsche, Nietzsche's sister, who, in Thomas Common's translation (1999), explains that it was Nietzsche's most "personal work" and that "Zarathustra's views, as also his personality, were early conceptions" of her "brother's mind" (1999, pp. 7–8).

The narrative focuses on the prophetic Zarathustra, who, following a period of contemplative hermitage, returns to society to address the people and advocate the coming of the Übermensch. Zarathustra argues for the rejection of religious conventions, dismissing these as outdated, untenable doctrines to which the individual clings for fear of change and which distract the individual from what Zarathustra considers to be the ultimate goal of any living thing; namely self-overcoming and remaining true to the earth: "I entreat you, my brothers, *remain true to the earth*, and do not believe in those who speak to you of superterrestrial hopes" (1961, p. 42). According to Zarathustra, the sole purpose of the individual is to prepare the earth for the coming of the Übermensch, before participating in his own down-going[1]: "What is great in man is that he is a bridge and not a goal … he is a *going-across*[2] and a *down-going*" (1961, p. 44). Like the . Darwinian notion of survival of the fittest, Nietzsche sees the process whereby one organism comes to be superseded by another as in accordance with the law of nature. Zarathustra affirms this during an early address in which he tells the people that "man is something that should be overcome" before elaborating: "All creatures hitherto have created something beyond themselves" (1961, p. 41). As if to punctuate this argument and acknowledge its accordance with Darwinian theories of evolution, Zarathustra asks "What is ape to man?" (1961, p. 42). He suggests that the individual's simian forbears are "A laughing-stock, or a painful embarrassment" and "just so shall man be to [Übermensch]" (1961, p. 42).

Nietzsche criticizes individuals for their stubbornness and willful resistance to considering alternative modes of thought or being, claiming "You have made your way from worm to man, and much in you is still worm. Once you were apes, and even now man is more of an ape than any ape" (1961, p. 41).

The latter statement is of special significance for its double metaphor: on the one hand, in referring to existing individuals as still being "worm," Zarathustra accuses them of cowardice; while on the other hand he alludes to the savagery of human nature and its propensity toward unnecessary violence in stipulating that the individual remains "more ape than any ape" (1961, p. 41). That is to suggest that the individual, in spite of its evolutionary progression from ape (seen here as the savage ancestor) to human, remains inexplicably savage, perhaps more so than its evolutionary simian counterpart. It will be demonstrated later in the chapter that this is a major concern addressed by the protagonist of Stapledon's *Odd John*, who likewise acknowledges the evolution of *Homo sapiens*, yet remains cautious about their naturally aggressive disposition.

For Nietzsche, the Übermensch does not simply reflect a being superior to existing individuals, but rather one willing to consider alternative modes of moral and social consciousness and whose life is dedicated to the development and progress of social reality. Magnus makes a similar observation, claiming the Übermensch represents an idealized mode of being (rather than an idealized individual) who is governed by self-overcoming, sublimation, creativity, and the desire to achieve self-perfection so as to contribute to the development of society (1986, p. 633). On the other hand, Walter Kaufmann sees the Übermensch as an individual who has surpassed the animalistic elements of the human condition and "sublimated" his impulses, desires, and passions so as to focus on self-perfection through the process of self-overcoming (1974, p. 312). Irrespective of how the concept of the Übermensch is interpreted, several facets remain indispensable to Nietzsche's original conception of the idealized individual, primarily self-overcoming, self-perfection, the ability to consider alternative modes of being, and perhaps, if applicable, the rejection of moral and social conventions and the will to power.

At this point it is important to point out that the Übermensch was not the only model Nietzsche presented in relation to the potential evolutionary development undertaken by existing individuals. Zarathustra also warns the people of the dangers presented by the letzte mensch,[3] the antithesis of the Übermensch. During his address, Zarathustra encourages the people to plant the seed of their "highest hope" as the soil is still "rich enough for it" yet warns that in time it will become too "poor and weak" to support such things[4] (1961, p. 46). Soon the time will come when individuals possesses neither capacity nor desire to "shoot the arrow of [their] longing out over mankind" and the "string of [their] bow will have forgotten how to twang"[5] (1961, p. 47). The letzte mensch is a mode of being devoid of individuality and thus indicative of herd mentality: "Everyone wants the same thing, everyone is the same: whoever thinks otherwise goes voluntarily into the madhouse" (1961, p. 46). This same argument is used by the protagonist of *Odd John*, who describes individuals as having "a sameness of intellectual and moral taste which makes them fundamentally all alike in spite of their quite blatant superficial differences" (1961, p. 65). Thus the idea of the letzte mensch can be summarized as an individual who has abandoned notions of self-improvement (self-overcoming) and creativity in favor of the comfort and security offered by routine and intellectual nihilism. Further, when corrupted by nihilism, the letzte mensch can thus be seen as an individual who has slumped into apathy and is no longer concerned with the outside world or the development of society. Irene Price suggests that through the letzte mensch, Nietzsche sought to reflect his fears regarding the potential "degeneration of humankind to a point where passivity and risk avoidance are considered the greatest good on both a personal and societal level" (2004, p. 103).

The disparity between the Übermensch and existing individuals underpins Nietzsche's *Thus Spake Zarathustra*. This same disparity is also a core element explored in the works of Stapledon, Sturgeon, and Bester, each of which offers a vision of the Übermensch. Further, in their reflection of the potential ramifications resulting from the existence of superior beings, the narratives can be interpreted as testing Nietzsche's theories, specifically those pertaining to self-overcoming and sublimination.

Representations of the Übermensch

The protagonists depicted in the works of Stapledon, Sturgeon, and Bester are paradoxical. They are, on the one hand, human in both form and origin, while on the other they are beings who have transcended the limitations imposed upon the human condition. Each represents a unique interpretation of the transhuman, and it is this amalgamation of human and transhuman that promotes their paradoxical identities.

34

As discussed in the previous chapter, there is a close affinity between the monster and the transhuman. Even though the term monster is never used directly to describe the protagonists, in the selected works by Stapledon, Sturgeon, and Bester, each retains or comes to reflect some element of monstrosity, whether aesthetically, metaphorically, ideologically, or morally.

Easily the strangest character examined in this chapter is the protagonist of Stapledon's narrative, who, as the title suggests, is affectionately referred to as *Odd John* by both his mother, Pax, and his love interest, Lo. Through John and his fellow colonists, Stapledon introduces the concept of Homo Superior in reference to a race of superior beings who have naturally evolved to transcend the limitations imposed by the human condition. The novel is told from the perspective of an unnamed narrator whom the protagonist names "Fido," seeing him as his faithful hound (1935 p. 42). John's perception that *Homo sapiens* are no more evolved than beasts underpins Stapledon's message and alludes to those arguments presented by Zarathustra in reference to the evolution of ape to human.

Although only one of several examples of Homo Superior presented in the novel, John remains individual. His superiority to everyday individuals is manifest, primarily in his intellectual capacity. At the age of six, for example, John took an interest in mathematics, until one day he suddenly declared that he had "finished numbers" and that he now "[knew] all there is in that game" (1935, p. 12). John explains that he had not simply grown tired of mathematics, but had done everything that was possible in the field. To emphasize the point, John and his mother are visited, at the insistence of John's father, by two world-renowned mathematicians, one of whom explains to Pax that it is John's "imaginative power that is so amazing. He knows none of the jargon and none of the history, but has *seen* it all already for himself" before concluding that the child, somehow, has the capacity "to visualize what can't be visualized" (1935, p. 11). Confounded by John's insight, the two mathematicians are later found outside the university grounds "sitting under a street lamp ... at 2 a.m. drawing diagrams on the pavement and disputing ... the curvature of space" (1935, p. 12). As a result of his extraordinary intellectual capabilities, John might simply be interpreted as a prodigy. However, as Roy Swanson notes, even a prodigy "is something both monstrous and prophetic" (1982, p. 285).

John reflects both Nietzsche's prophetic character, Zarathustra, and his vision of the Übermensch. Like Zarathustra, who retires from the world to contemplate his task, John too seeks refuge in nature when he turns to the mountains, later explaining to the narrator he needed to escape because he felt "spiritually contaminated by contact with the civilization of *Homo sapiens*" (1935, p. 77). In alluding to Zarathustra's avocation of remaining true to the earth, John abandons "all his clothes, including his shoes" so as to test himself both physically and mentally and to prove that he could stand and exist completely independent of the "primitive and debased creatures" which currently "dominated the planet" (1935, p. 77). During his hermitage, John relies on nothing but his hands and what tools might be constructed from the materials made available by the mountain. Nevertheless, John remains aware of his superiority to existing individuals and the futility reflected by their continued existence: "The thought of the agony of this world of nightmare-ridden half-men crushed him as nothing else had ever done" (1935, p. 83). It is during his time spent in the wilderness that John first becomes aware of his own powers, later explaining that he had come to learn all manner of things about himself. For example, "by a kind of telepathy" he was able to remain in contact with his mother and "could sometimes feel" what the narrator is thinking, yet, as John explains, the latter's intellect was far too "dull to catch [John's] messages and respond" (1935, p. 84). Also, when discovered by two climbers, McWhist and Norton, whom John had briefly encountered earlier, he explains to the narrator that he was able to "read the whole of their past lives in their faces" and that he "saw how thoroughly sound they both were within the limitations of their kind" (1935, p. 84). In order to ensure their silence, John performs a "miracle" by lifting away the large rock that had formed the roof of the cave in which he had been living, so as to show them the stars (1935, p. 84). Later, when John is accused of showing off, he explains that "exercising one's power is healthy" and that children enjoy "learning to walk" as an artist enjoys "painting pictures" (1935, p. 85).

The similarities between Zarathustra and John can also be identified in their inevitable conclusions regarding the nature of individuals and the human condition. For Nietzsche's Zarathustra, the greatness of the individual lies in the knowledge that he is a "going-over" rather than a destination, a beginning and not an end. Similarly, for John, though the human individual is undeniably "a spirit of a higher order than any beast" they are nonetheless "obtuse, heartless" and "unfaithful to the best in [themselves]" (1935, p. 83). Here, Stapledon's allusion to Nietzsche's argument regarding the stubbornness of the individual, his inability to consider alternatives, and reluctance to participate in what John considered to be their ultimate goal is undeniably apparent. Further, like Zarathustra, who loathed individuals for their stubbornness and inability to consider alternatives yet loved those who possessed qualities he saw as admirable, John's own feelings toward the species are equally contrary. As the narrator explains, John's feelings for humans, which "as a species, he heartily despised" are "a strange blend of contempt and respect, detachment and affection" (1935, p. 35). On one hand, "he despised us for our stupidity and fecklessness," while on the other he "respected us for our occasional efforts to surmount our natural disabilities" (1935, p. 35). As John later tells the narrator, however, in spite of his affection for *Homo sapiens* as a whole, he is forced to acknowledge that he is up against "a savage race which would never tolerate me or my kind, and would sooner or later smash me with its brute weight" (1935, p. 83). John's acknowledgment of his assured destruction inevitably leads to the revelation that he and his fellow Homo Superiors reflected no more than "just a little self-important microbe making a fuss over nothing" (1935, p. 83).

As is the case with Nietzsche's Übermensch, John feels compelled to contribute to the development of the world and the species as a whole, telling the narrator that even if he were to be destroyed, even if his existence was completely insignificant, "the things I could *do, the beauty* I could make, and the *worship* that I was now beginning to conceive, did most emphatically matter, and *must* be brought to fruition" (1935, p. 83). In accepting the inevitability of his own demise, John unknowingly acknowledges that in some instances even an Übermensch, or a transhuman (by affiliation), might, at some point, be forced to set about his own down-going. Swanson makes a similar observation, claiming it to be Stapledon's suggestion that every species, even those seemingly superior, is predestined for self-destruction through its need to transform or develop into higher, more advanced life forms: "Invertebrates must become vertebrates, animals must become human, humans must become gods, gods must transcend their divinity" (1982 p. 285).

In *More Than Human* (1953), Theodore Sturgeon offers a vastly different depiction of the Übermensch in the form of *Homo gestalt*,[6] a being composed of not one, but a number of individuals.

Sturgeon's narrative introduces a number of characters who are, as individuals, little more than alienated "freaks" existing on the fringe of social reality, yet together compose a being that is suggested to mark the next stage in human evolution. The first of these is the fabulous idiot (1953, p. 1) who later adopts the name Lone, following his interaction with Mr. and Mrs. Prodd, who nurse him back to health following a near fatal beating (1953, p. 20). Like Zarathustra and John, Lone initially seeks comfort in the isolation provided by the wilderness. Unlike the former, however, who move to reject their animalistic nature, Lone lives like an animal ("a degrading thing to be among men") and is described to exist in a "black and gray world, punctuated by the white lightning of hunger and the flickering of fear" (1953, p. 2). Similar to the beauty Zarathustra finds in the snake and the eagle, or the elegance John sees reflected in the stag, there is an elegant simplicity to Lone and his animalistic life: "As an animal in the woods, he moved like an animal, beautifully. He killed like an animal, without hate and without joy" (1953, p. 2). Like the Homo Superior of Stapledon's *Odd John*, Lone is transhuman because he possesses unique abilities which allow him to read and manipulate the thoughts of others, bending their actions to suit his needs. When introduced, Lone is depicted using his abilities to meet his basic needs: "He fed himself when he could, he went without when he could. When he could do neither of these things he was fed by the first person who came face to face with him. The idiot never knew why, and never wondered" (1953, p. 1). Later, he uses his power to force Alicia Kew, Evelyn's sister, to gather information about a variety of topics, primarily biology, which he then plucks directly from her mind.

The construction of *Homo gestalt* can be identified in the events surrounding Lone's chance encounter with a young girl, Evelyn Kew, who awakens something in his mind. When Evelyn's deeply religious father finds them together, however, he attacks Lone, wounding him almost fatally, before killing his daughter and then himself. Lone, under the care of Mr. and Mrs. Prodd, is taught to speak and in turn helps out on the farm.[7] When Mrs. Prodd becomes pregnant, Lone decides it is time to leave and once again, returns to the wilderness. Accustomed to the comforts afforded by the Prodds' house, Lone builds himself a shelter and is soon joined by three runaway children—Janie and the twins, Bonnie and Beanie—who are other components of what will eventually be the *gestalt*. Janie is telekinetic, able to manipulate physical objects by thought alone (1953, p. 24), whereas the twins, though unable to communicate with others, have the ability to teleport to any destination they choose— leaving their clothes behind in the process (1953, p. 26). Before long they are joined by the sixth member of the group, Baby, who is described as being like a living computer, able to solve any problem so long as he possesses the necessary foundational knowledge (1953, pp. 55–60). With Lone acting as the head, Baby the brain, Janie the mouth and the twins as arms and legs, the gestalt is complete. The gestalt, however, is restricted due to Lone's intellectual limitations; as Baby explains: "We can do practically *anything* but we most likely won't. He says we're a thing, all right, but the thing is an idiot" (1953, p. 60). Aware of his impact upon the group, Lone thus seeks to discover a new head, which he finds in Gerry, whose experience as an orphan has shaped his contempt for society and other individuals:

> Hatred was the only warmth in the world, the only certainty. A man clings to certainties, especially when he has only one.... Then he ran away from the state orphanage, to live by himself, to be the color of gutters and garbage so he would not be picked up; to kill if cornered; to hate [1953, p. 21].

Following Lone's death and Gerry's succession, the group settles into its newly acquired identity as *Homo gestalt*, unaware that the gestalt is not yet complete. The gestalt does not obtain perfection until the novel's conclusion, when the group is joined by Hip, hinted to be Gerry's long-lost brother, who represents the ethics *Homo gestalt* requires in order to interact with society and other individuals. Once the gestalt obtains perfection, the group suddenly becomes aware of the existence of other gestalts spread throughout the universe, each holding a non-aggressive power that could be used only for the benefit of life as a whole:

> Their memories, their projects and computations flooded in to Gerry, until at last he knew their nature and their function; and he knew why the ethos he had learned was too small a concept. For here at last was power which could not corrupt; for such an insight could only be used for its own sake, or against itself. Here was why and how humanity existed, troubled and dynamic, sainted by the touch of its own great destiny. Here was the withheld hand as thousands died, when by their death millions might live... not an exterior force, nor an awesome Watcher in the sky, but a laughing thing with a human heart and reverence for its human origins, smelling of sweat and new-turned earth rather than suffused with the pale odor of sanctity [1953, p. 186].

Although each of the characters presented in Sturgeon's narrative possesses unique powers and abilities, thus informing their individual identities as transhumans, it is only the gestalt itself which might be interpreted as a reflection of Nietzsche's Übermensch. As the final paragraph reveals, the gestalt, as with the Übermensch, rejects the notion of God as some "awesome Watcher in the sky" and not only makes reference to the implementation of a power which could "not corrupt" but one which has a "human heart" and is derived from natural "new-turned earth rather than suffused with the ... odor of sanctity" and "human origins" (1953, p. 186). As with Stapledon's John, the protagonists of Sturgeon's narrative come to reflect a being that so supersedes the human condition as to be rendered incomprehensible by other individuals and nonhuman by comparison.

The third interpretation of the Übermensch is reflected in Gully Foyle, the protagonist of Alfred Bester's *The Stars My Destination* (1956). Unlike the other protagonists examined in this chapter, Gully is not born with unique abilities. On the contrary, his development can be traced from everyday individual through to becoming transhuman and finally to becoming posthuman, when he is depicted as obtaining almost godlike powers.

At the start of the narrative, Gully could be seen as Nietzsche's notion of the letzte mensch, an individual who has slipped into apathy and no longer seeks self-overcoming; he is described as "Gully Foyle, the oiler, wiper, bunkerman; too easy for trouble, too slow for fun, too empty for friendship, too lazy for love" (1956, p. 11). The initiation of Gully's transformation takes place when the ship, *Nomad*, aboard which he serves, is destroyed. Through sheer tenacity, he survives: "He was one hundred and seventy days dying and not yet dead. He fought for survival with the passion of a beast in a trap" (1956, p. 11). Pessimistic regarding his chances of survival, Gully intones: "Gully Foyle is my name/And Terra is my nation. Deep space is my dwelling place/And death's my destination" (1956, p. 11). Before long, his desire to strive for self-overcoming is rekindled following his encounter with the ship Vorga–T:1339. Gully signals the ship but is ignored and thus left to his inevitable death. Infuriated, however, he finds his purpose, to take revenge on *Vorga*:

> "You pass me by," he said with slow mounting fury. "You leave me rot like a dog. You leave me die … I get out of here, me. I follow you … I find you … I pay you back … I rot you … I kill you … I kill you filthy." The acid of fury ran through him, eating away the brute patience and sluggishness that had made a cipher of Gully Foyle, precipitating a chain of reactions that would [make] an infernal machine of Gully Foyle. He was dedicated [1956, p. 18].

The second and most aesthetic stage in Gully's transformation takes place following his escape from the doomed *Nomad*, when he is discovered by the *Scientific People*, a group described as "savages, the only savages of the twenty-fifth century" (1956, p. 21), who decorate Gully with a full-facial tattoo, bearing the name Nomad across his forehead in acknowledgment of the crude ship in which he was found (1956, p. 27).

Following his incarceration in Gouffre Martel—for attempting to destroy the ship *Vorga* with a crudely made explosive device and for refusing to reveal the location of *Nomad*'s remains—Gully travels to space and obtains *Nomad*'s cargo—a fortune in platinum and several slugs of PyrE— for himself before returning to earth, disguised as Fourmyle of Ceres, an extremely rich and highly eccentric circus owner. In what can be seen as an allusion to Edmond Dantès, the protagonist of Alexandre Dumas's *The Count of Monte Cristo* (1844), Gully uses his newly acquired wealth and position to charm and entertain members of high society in order to gather information about the captain and crew of *Vorga*, who have become the new targets of his revenge. Gully's wealth can also be seen as the catalyst for the third stage of his transformation, for it pays for his transition from everyday individual to transhuman. Through paying a bribe of "Cr 200,000" to the "chief surgeon of the Mars Commando Brigade," Gully is physically augmented with every "nerve plexus" being rewired and having "microscopic transistors and transformers ... buried in muscle and bone," effectively turning him into an "extraordinary fighting machine" (1956, p. 115). Much like the tribal tattooing, which signaled the start of Gully's transformation, the augmentation is also indicated through physical marking of the body[8]:

> He was in magnificent condition, but his skin still showed delicate silver seams in a network from neck to ankle. It looked as though someone had carved an outline of the nervous system into Foyle's flesh. The silver seams were the scars of an operation that had not yet faded.... "More machine than man," he thought [1956, p. 115].

This augmentation gives Gully the capacity to transcend the physical limitations imposed upon ordinary individuals. As well as improved strength and stamina, Gully is also able to increase his movement and reflex speed by "a factor of five" (1956, p. 117), an ability that he puts to use primarily during physical confrontations. The capacity of Gully's augmentation, however, is best demonstrated during his interrogation of Kempsey. Gully confronts him, throws a sedative-filled dart into the man's neck, accelerates, and catches the body before it hits the ground:

> Foyle strapped the body on the operating table, opened a case of surgical instruments, and began the delicate operation.... He cut through skin and fascia, sawed through the rib cage, exposed the heart, dissected it out and connected veins and arteries to the intricate blood pump alongside the table. He started the pump. Twenty seconds, objective time, had elapsed. He placed an oxygen mask over Kempsey's face and switched on the alternating suction and ructation of the oxygen pump. Foyle decelerated, checked Kempsey's temperature, shot an anti-shock series into his veins and waited. Blood gurgled

through the pump and Kempsey's body. After five minutes, Foyle removed the oxygen mask. The respiration reflex continued. Kempsey was without a heart, yet alive. Foyle sat down alongside the operating table and waited [1956, pp. 175–176].

Similar to the monster of Mary Shelley's *Frankenstein* (1818), which embodied the potential dangers of technoscientific development, Gully, following his augmentation, represents a human made monstrous through the scientific method. In this, Gully—more accurately than other protagonists examined until this point—engenders both the fears and hopes[9] affiliated with the transhuman movement. The capabilities granted by Gully's augmentation are monstrous, as is his capacity for violence, manipulation, betrayal, and rape; subsequent chapters will explore the question of whether or not the augmentations themselves—in reference to base cybernetic components—are monstrous, once devoid of the will which drives them.

Gully's transformation, however, like the *Homo gestalt* of Sturgeon's *More Than Human*, is not complete until the novel's conclusion. After his escape from St. Patrick's Cathedral—destroyed during the accidental activation of PyrE—Gully is pressured by Presteign and two assistants to surrender what remains of the dangerous and highly volatile substance which they intended to use to their advantage in the war between the Inner Planets and the Outer Satellites. Reluctantly agreeing, Gully escorts them to the chamber where the material is being kept, but before they have time to react, he steals the remaining PyrE and travels to various locations across the world, handing out slug after slug of the rare alloy to those he comes across, arguing that if damnation or salvation is to be inevitable and achieved through the use of something such as PyrE, then it should be for the people to decide. Gully argues that the everyday individual has been "whipped and led long enough by driven men ... who can't help lashing the world before them" (1956, p. 235). Prior to his final departure—where he jaunts through space and time, gaining knowledge and power—Gully appears before a large crowd and, in a Zarathustra-like address, accuses them of being pigs and of having "the most" in them but using "the least" before issuing his challenge: "All right! God damn you ... die or live and be great. Blow yourselves to Christ gone or come and find me, Gully Foyle, and I make you men. I make you great. I give you the stars" [1956, p. 236].

Gully's address is significant for several reasons. Not only does he replicate Zarathustra's mocking, yet motivational tone, but like the Homo Superior protagonist of Stapledon's *Odd John* (who explains to the narrator that ordinary individuals were "unfaithful to the best" in themselves [1935, p. 83]), Gully too acknowledges their reluctance to engage in their full potential. Following his journey through space and time—in which secrets are revealed to him—Gully returns to the asteroid inhabited by the Scientific People. Although the extent of Gully's newly acquired power and knowledge or the potential ramifications resultant of space jaunting are never discussed within the novel, the possibility of development and the anticipation of change and transcendence are clearly expressed during the narrative's final paragraphs when Gully is discovered by Joseph, the head of the Scientific People, and Moira, a member of the Scientific People and Gully's accidental wife:

> "My husband has returned to us," Moira said ... "the god-man who almost destroyed us." Joseph's face darkened with anger. "Where is he, show me"....
> Joseph followed her to the locker aboard Nomad.... The anger in his face was replaced by wonder.... Joseph answered quietly. "He is dreaming. I, a priest, know these dreams. Presently he will awaken and read to us, his people, his thoughts...." Moira ran up the twisted corridors and returned a few moments later with a silver basin of warm water and a ... tray of food. She bathed Foyle gently and then set the tray before him as an offering. Then she settled down alongside Joseph ... alongside the world ... prepared to await the awakening [1956, p. 240].

While the impact of the posthuman is never discussed, Gully, unlike the protagonists discussed previously, transcends what Nietzsche's Zarathustra claims to be the individual's ultimate goal—achieving self-perfection (becoming the Übermensch) through the process of self-overcoming—in becoming something that is incomprehensible to ordinary individuals. Further, it might also seem ironic that Gully, unlike Zarathustra who failed to gain the attention of the people, not only obtains near God-like power but, as reflected by Joseph and Moira who wait "alongside the world," comes to be revered as a deity. The initiative or central motivation to Gully's transformation, however, can be interpreted through Nietzsche's theory of the will to power.

The Will to Power

Nietzsche's concept of the will to power—the central force driving the action of all living things—can be identified as an integral motivation which informs and determines the actions and perspectives held by the protagonists presented in the works of Stapledon, Sturgeon, and Bester.

The will to power is possibly the most important contribution Nietzsche made to philosophical theory, as Deleuze points out in *Nietzsche and Philosophy* (1983, pp. 61–64). However, Nietzsche's theory of the will to power as the central force driving all living things, is largely linked with his theories pertaining to morality, or more specifically the rejection of standard moral convention. Nietzsche introduces this idea in *The Gay Science* (1882), where he links acts of violence and cruelty, or more specifically, the individual's desire for cruelty, to the sensation of power; that is, the individual's capacity to obtain and preserve power over another (Kaufmann, 1974, pp. 86–87). Here he elaborates that even the strongest human relations and most symbolic actions are fundamentally linked to the individual's desire to obtain power: "even if we offer our lives, as martyrs do for the church, this is a sacrifice that is offered for *our* desire for power or for the purpose of preserving our feeling of power" (1974, p. 87).

In *Beyond Good and Evil* (1886), Nietzsche expanded his theory so as to present and propose a reality—both social, and, later, natural—in which all things were governed by their will, specifically their will to power. He argued that the entirety of any individual's "instinctive life" can be understood "as the development and ramification of one basic form of the will" specifically, "the will to power" (Zimmern, 2009, p. 36). At its simplest, the will to power can be interpreted as the central force driving all living things—but only insofar as the individual adheres to his will to live, which, as will be explained, is only a secondary concern—informing and determining both their actions and perspectives. This, paradoxically, is especially manifest (perhaps as a matter of consequence) in one's will to destroy or to deprive others of their own will to power.

As Pierre Klossowski explains, each individual might be perceived as "a quantum of power," which is essentially defined in terms of both the "action it exerts" and the external forces "which it resists" (1997, p. 101). Each "quantum of power" is thus indicative of "a will to do violence and to defend itself against all violence," whose primary motivation cannot be allied with "self-preservation" seeing as each atom can be identified as affecting the whole (1997, p. 101). In the posthumously published *Will to Power*, Nietzsche explains,

> Every specific body strives to become master over all space and to extend its force ... and to thrust back all that resists its extension. But it continually encounters similar efforts on the part of other bodies and ends by coming to an arrangement ... with those of them that are sufficiently related to it: thus they then conspire together for power [1967, p. 636].

Nietzsche's theory of the will to power thus extends to include all biological life, which, as will be illustrated during the examination of the protagonists presented in the works of Stapledon, Sturgeon, and Bester, is significant in the development of the paradoxical protagonist's identity as an antihero. Where Darwin saw evolution and natural selection as the process in which an organism would adapt in order to most effectively meet its basic needs—food, safety, shelter (if applicable), and reproduction (to ensure the continuity of its genetic heritage)—Nietzsche saw evolution, specifically adaptation, as the process through which individuals, or entire species, are transformed so as to maximize their capacity to obtain and preserve power.[10] In *Beyond Good and Evil*, Nietzsche explains that any organism with a living and not a dying body

> will have to be an incarnate will to power, it will strive to grow, spread, seize, become predominant—not from any morality or immorality but because it is living and because life simply is will to power.... "Exploitation" ... belongs to the essence of what lives, as a basic organic function; it is a consequence of the will to power, which is after all the will to life [1886, p. 259].

In Stapledon's *Odd John*, the protagonist exhibits much of Nietzsche's notion of the will to power, explaining to the narrator that it is because individuals—here depicted as being on the road to becoming the letzte mensch—are unable to comprehend their own will to power that, in frustration, they turn to belief (especially religious belief) to fulfill a sense of purpose (1935, p. 63). However, those unable to "swallow the Christian dope" continue to search for purpose, yet inevitably their frustration "gets mixed up with their hate need" (or will to violence, as explained previously) and is further compounded by their "fear of social revolution" (1935, p. 63). Through John, Stapledon reflects Nietzsche's ideas by suggesting that it is perhaps the rejection or failure to acknowledge one's own commitment to the will to power that increases chances of the development of the letzte mensch and decreases those of the Übermensch.

The initiation of John's will to power can be identified in his early acquisition of knowledge, yet is perhaps most prominent in his resolution to become "an invincible fighter," which is influenced by a confrontation with Stephen, "the big schoolboy neighbor," in which John is knocked down before being picked up and "pitched ... over the fence" (1935, p. 15). John maximizes his capacity to gain and preserve his power by spending an entire autumn reading "nothing but adventure stories and ... works on jiu-jitsu" and then by spending all his time "practicing this art" or in "gymnastic exercises of his own invention" (1935, p. 17). It is also here that John, having identified one of his own limitations (manifest in his troublesome digestive system) begins dieting himself "extremely carefully upon principles of his own" (1935, p. 17). In order to ensure his supremacy or dominance over the other children, John draws them into conflict, defeating one after the other. John's efforts culminate in his rematch with and subsequent victory over Stephen. During the incident, the narrator reflects that "never have I seen so arrogant, so hideous an expression of the lust of power as on that childish face" (1935, p. 18).

Later, when John begins to conceive of his capacity for development and the impact he might leave upon the world, his will to power shifts focus. He explains to the narrator that first he must make himself independent and second he must acquire power, which, in consideration of the "crazy world" in which he finds himself, "meant getting hold of much money" (1935, p. 30). Thus Stapledon acknowledges the dynamic nature of power, especially in a western capitalist society. John's attempt at contacting members of his own kind—other Homo Superior beings—can be identified as another example of his will to power, in acknowledging that he would be unable to achieve his goal without the support of other individuals, believing that, united, they might better withstand the assault of a lesser yet no less dangerous species (1935, pp. 87–95). In *The Gay Science*, Nietzsche affirms the use of other individuals as being in accordance with the will to power, explaining that it is advantageous to have others in one's power; "that way they will become more satisfied with their condition and more hostile to and willing to fight against the enemies of *our* power" (1882, p. 86).

The most important example of John's will to power, however, can be seen in the colonization of the island located somewhere in the South Pacific Ocean (1935, p. 1). Along with a number of other Homo Superiors—whom he had contacted and invited to join his settlement of the island—John plans to live in peace and provide a haven where he and his fellows might focus on improving their individual talents and the development of their species as a whole. When the band of Homo Superior colonists locates the island, however, it is to discover it already inhabited by a tribal community whom the protagonist describes as being "simple and attractive creatures" (1935, p. 124). Nevertheless, as John later explains to the narrator, they were unable to allow the island's inhabitants to interfere with their plans and "so decided to destroy them" (1935, p. 124). When the colonists land, they engage with the islanders and, implementing their ability to manipulate the thoughts of others, trick them into believing that they are gods who require their island. John addresses the tribes-people, telling them that to appease the gods they must construct a "great funeral pyre for themselves, mount it together, lie down together, and gladly die" (1935, p. 124). While this act can be identified as an example of the protagonists' will to power (and subsequently, the will to violence), it might also be considered in relation to Zarathustra's notion that, in support of the Übermensch, the individual must willingly accept his own downgoing (1961, pp. 44–45).

Once settled onto the island, the colonists use it as a means of maximizing their capacity to obtain power, primarily through the implementation of science and technology, which they use to create tools so that each individual might be more effective in his own will to power (1935, pp. 130–142). However, in support of Nietzsche's perception of the will to power being the force driving evolution and adaptation, the narrator is surprised to discover that the colonists have been conducting genetic experiments in which they impregnated the female members of neighboring islands in order to ensure their genetic continuity (1935, p. 139).

The final example of the colonists' will to power can be seen in the novel's conclusion. After John and his fellow islanders are investigated and identified as a threat by the World Powers, a group of assassins are sent in to neutralize the situation (1935, p. 154). Aware that their demise is inevitable, the islanders, rather than allow their inventions, research, and other works to fall into the hands of what they perceived as a barbaric species, choose self-destruction. By overloading the nuclear reactor that provides much of their power, the colonists sink the island, effectively leaving behind no trace of their existence save for a biography of John (promised by the narrator who sees the islanders' final moments via telepathic communication with John). Again, this correlates with Nietzsche's notion of the will to power, which rejects suicide as a symbolic act or as the foregoing or relinquishing of acquired power, arguing that "even if we offer our lives ... this is a sacrifice that is offered for *our* desire for power or for the purpose of preserving our feeling of power" (1882, p. 87).

Although Nietzsche's notion of the will to power can be observed as the motivating force driving the characters in Sturgeon's *More Than Human* (1953), particularly in relation to their formation of the gestalt, it is perhaps most apparent in Bester's *The Stars My Destination*, where it can be seen not only as a force of influence, but also as a catalyst for transformation. While Gully's initial motivation can be seen in his campaign to take revenge on *Vorga*, the craft that ignored his distress signal and left him for dead, he soon comes to realize that in order to achieve his goals he must first adapt and maximize his own capacity to acquire and preserve power.

After his return to earth, Gully feigns having lost his ability to jaunte (teleport) and is thus placed under the care of Miss Robinson, a one-way telepath. When Miss Robinson begins to suspect Gully's motives, he requests that she meet him at her house where he confronts her with information he had obtained regarding her family still living in the Outer Satellites, information that could have her arrested for treason. Embracing the acquisition of this new form of power, Gully claims "I cover myself.... I cover every weak spot down the line. I got something on everybody who could stop me before I kill *Vorga*" (1956, p. 34). As if to punctuate his point and validate the power he now holds over Miss Robinson, he coerces her into aiding in his plot to destroy *Vorga* before raping her: "Suddenly he picked her up and carried her to a deep couch. He threw her down" (1956, p. 35).

While incarcerated in Gouffre Martel, and realizing that he is required to change in order to infiltrate the aristocratic circles that hold information regarding the crew members of *Vorga*, Gully furthers his power through education, which he receives from Jisbella McQueen, another inmate[11] (1956, p. 67). Following his escape from Gouffre Martel, Gully, like John, realizes that in order to achieve his ultimate goal and extend his will to power, he will require an economic foundation. This he obtains by plundering the wreckage of *Nomad* and retrieving a fortune in platinum bullion along with several slugs of PyrE. The money represents only a means to an end for Gully: his will to power and the ability to take revenge on *Vorga*. This is reflected through his conversation with Jisbella, when he tells her that soon he will be very rich. In retort, Jisbella claims, "Yes, rich and empty. You've got nothing inside of you, Gully dear ... nothing but hatred and revenge" (1956, p. 97). Nevertheless, as the protagonist claims, for now, it's enough (1956, p. 97).

The most prominent example of Gully's will to power is seen in the last few chapters when, having discovered the captain of *Vorga* to be Olivia, Presteign's blind daughter with whom he has fallen in love, Gully seeks to strip Presteign of his power by placing slugs of PyrE into the hands of the people. It is also here that Gully comes to realize his true purpose, or will to power, which is his possession of the ability to jaunte through space and time.

Nietzsche and Morality

Nietzsche's theories of morality can be identified as providing a significant contribution in the development of the antiheroic identity within speculative fiction. Often it is the rejection of moral and social convention, as advocated by Nietzsche's moral theory, that also informs the paradoxical protagonist's adoption of the antiheroic identity.

In the preface to *The Dawn of Day*[12] (1881), Nietzsche describes himself as being an immoralist (1911, pp. 2–9). Morality for Nietzsche was something inexplicably bound by religion, specifically Christianity. In *The Gay Science*, for example, Nietzsche links morality with religion, stating that if "we simply called ourselves, using the old expression, godless, or unbelievers, or perhaps immoralists... this would [not] even come close to designating us" (1882, p. 286). Further, he goes on to explain that those who have the capacity to see beyond the morality dictated by religion no longer feel the need to turn their faithlessness into a new faith, but rather "have become cold, hard and tough in the realization that the way of the world is anything but divine; even by human standards it is not rational, merciful or just"[13] (1882, p. 286). Clearly, then, it might be said that Nietzsche's approach to morality was critical, if not openly hostile, seeing conventional morality as derived from outdated, untenable otherworldly doctrines.[14] For Nietzsche, moral and social convention was not only reductive and contrary to the human condition, but also forced limitations upon the development of extraordinary individuals, thereby constraining the progress of society as a whole. Nietzsche expands upon this notion, arguing that in its social sense, morality can be perceived as a system of customs, manifest and reinforced through ontological discourse whereby individuals and society are stifled and forced into stagnation:

> Custom represents the experiences of men of earlier times as to what they supposed useful and harmful—but the sense for custom (morality) applies, not to these experiences as such, but to the age, the sanctity, the indiscussability of the custom. And so this feeling is a hindrance to the acquisition of new experiences and the correction of customs: that is to say, morality is a hindrance to the development of new and better customs [1982, p. 19].

According to Nietzsche, it is this stagnation that leads individuals to become members of the herd mentality or to adopt what Stapledon's John describes as "a sameness of intellect and moral taste" (1935, p. 65). Such a mentality, Nietzsche claims, represents a process of sublimation whereby individuality and those unique qualities required in order transcend the human condition (or perhaps more specifically to achieve what he saw as the individual's ultimate goal, the realization of the Übermensch), collapse under the weight of conformity and social and moral convention. To this end Nietzsche argued that customs, as the continuation of moral and social convention, represent an archaic expression that denotes not so much lived experience, but rather experience of a specific time or place within history, and thus exists as a "a hindrance to the acquisition of new experiences and the correction of customs: that is to say, morality is a hindrance to the development of new and better customs" (1881, p. 19).

Through his rejection of moral and social convention, which he sees as being contrary to the human condition, Nietzsche invariably argues that violence and cruelty are inextricably linked to the natural, biological world and thus cannot be regarded as either good or evil, only neutral. Nietzsche affirms this in *On the Genealogy of Morals* (1889), where he controversially argues that "no act of violence, rape, exploitation, destruction, is intrinsically 'unjust,' since life itself is violent, rapacious, exploitative, and destructive and cannot be conceived otherwise" (1889, p. 208). Further, he goes on to argue that social, political, and legal customs—as the continuation of moral and social conventions—from a "biological point of view" are also reductive to the individual's "life-will bent on power" whose ultimate purpose is to "create greater power constellations" (1889, p. 208). The acceptance of any such custom as "sovereign and universal" is not only detrimental to the individual's ultimate goal and nature but will inevitably lead to "demoralization and, indirectly, a reign of nothingness" (1889, p. 208).

Nietzsche's perspective on and subsequent rejection of morality—manifest in convention and customs as the means by which social progress is restricted and limitations imposed upon extraordinary individuals—is clearly attributable to his advocacy of self-overcoming and the rise of the Übermensch as the individual's ultimate goal. In this view, morality becomes subjective, and apocryphal concepts such as good and evil become insubstantial, or, more simply, a matter of perspective.[15] As will be illustrated in the following section, more often than not it is the paradoxical protagonist's rejection of moral and social convention or their adoption of Nietzschean moral perspective[16] that informs his identity as antiheroes.

Nietzschean Morality in Speculative Fiction

The most obvious adoption of Nietzschean morality can be identified in Stapledon's John, who, like Nietzsche, runs his own campaign against moral and social conventions. As the narrator explains fairly early in the novel, John is indeed "as contemptuous of the morality as of the intelligence of Homo sapiens" (1935, p. 41). John perceives himself as both intellectually and morally superior to existing individuals, believing that his survival and will to power should take precedence over other individuals, even at the cost of their own lives. This is first reflected during his encounter with the local policeman. Attempting to gain some economic collateral and simply indulging in the rebellion afforded by youth, John is caught hanging from the window of a house he had just burgled. The protagonist berates himself for having been so stupid and naïve as to believe the petty gain of thievery could possibly outweigh the potential consequences of his being caught. Though for some time John has deduced that he is biologically different from *Homo sapiens*, it is at this point that he discovers this difference "carried with it what I should now describe as a far-reaching spiritual difference" and that his life was going to be "different from anything which the normal species could conceive ... far beyond the reach of those sixteen hundred million crude animals that at present rule the planet" (1935, p. 32). In accounting for his superiority, John explains that he simply couldn't allow himself to be caught, as it would interfere with his plans and thus decided that he would be forced to murder the officer, a murder which "just had to be" (1935, p. 32). Surprised by the protagonist's admission, the narrator suggests that surely he must have felt some degree of guilt or remorse for having taken the life of another living creature. In response, however, John explains, "As a matter of fact ... I didn't. The bad feeling ended when I made my decision" (1935, p. 33). Further, intoning a fatalistic approach to the event, he explains that it was necessary and what he came to realize was that "what must be, must be" (1935, p. 33). Undeniably, the willful murder of another individual, let alone the flippant acceptance of the act as "a matter of fact" (1935, p. 33) clearly places John in opposition to recognized or commonly accepted modes of heroic action, as defined within the introduction. The latter, however, is not the only murder John or his fellow Homo Superiors commit, citing their superiority as justification. During the maiden voyage of the *Skid*,[17] for example, the group happens across a damaged British steamer, *The Frome*, which sends a distress signal. The passengers manage to pile themselves into two small life-rafts as the steamer sinks. A member of John's group, Ng-Gunko, attaches a tow-line to the rafts, so they might use the *Skid* to pull them to safety. The two surviving crew members are taken aboard, where they proceed to tell John that they will sing their praise and tell everyone they meet of their rescue. Aware that this would interfere with his plans for the colonization of the island, John produces an automatic pistol and shoots the two guests before slipping the tow rope from the other craft (1935, p. 120). So as to ensure rumor of their existence never reaches land, "Ng-Gunko and Lo, lying on the deck with rifles, disposed of all the *Frome*'s survivors. When this grim task was finished, the corpses were thrown to the sharks. The boat was scrubbed of blood stains, and then scuttled" (1935, p. 120).

In recounting these events to the narrator, John further illustrates the apparent moral disparity between superior and lesser beings by explaining that had they been members of the same species, their actions "would have been a crime" (1982, p. 121). Just as *Homo sapiens* might be required to kill dangerous creatures so as to reduce the risk posed to their greatest minds, so too had they needed to destroy "those unfortunate creatures we had rescued" because, unknowingly, the crew and passengers had "threatened the noblest practical venture that has yet occurred on this planet" (1982, p. 121). Other murders are also instigated when the colonists discover the island to be already inhabited. Here they implement their powers of influence so as to trick the inhabitants to believing that they are gods before ordering them to participate in a mass suicide (1982, p. 124). Although John and his fellow Homo Superiors' killings and atrocities are "monstrous" according to Swanson, their progression toward "higher states of existence may be seen as prophetic of human progression" (1982, p. 285). Nevertheless, the readers, Swanson suggests, will "sympathize with Odd John as they wishfully contemplate the elevation that will transmute *Homo sapiens* into Homo superior" (1935, p. 287). Of course, acceptance of the monstrous other can be taken only so far, and the readers will no doubt "withhold their sympathy if they qualify their wish with an unwillingness to be what John actually is, that is, to be something other than human" (1982, p. 287).

A similar act of violence takes place in Sturgeon's *More Than Human*, thus effectively raising the issue of moral disparity between superior and lesser species. After Lone's death, Gerry and the other children, following the late Idiot's orders, seek out Alicia Kew, who reluctantly agrees to take them in. The children are separated and cared for individually and soon find themselves engaged in a daily routine not dissimilar from that experienced by everyday children, including three square meals, schooling, and various other activities. Becoming aware of the detrimental effect this is having on the formation of the gestalt, Gerry takes drastic action, which he later recounts to a psychologist, explaining that he "had to go and kill her. And that's all" (1953, p. 96). Like John, who cites superiority to every-day individuals as his justification for committing murder, Gerry explains that the dynamics of the group were incomprehensible to ordinary humans and that while under Miss Kew's influence they "lived ... someone else's way" and that the murder was necessary as the group "didn't blesh"[18] (1953, p. 97). Again, this violence perpetrated toward Alicia Kew in exchange for her benevolence identifies Gerry—as the central protagonist and head of the *Homo gestalt*—as an antihero, in that his actions are contrary to those associated with heroism.

John's antiheroic identity, on the other hand, also comes to be expressed through other means, most notably his rejection of accepted social and moral convention. John seeks to distance, if not completely detach, himself from the morality held by everyday individuals through his incestuous relationship with his mother, Pax. Following his failed sexual encounter with Europa, a young local girl whom John had seduced, he returns home traumatized by the experience. Recounting what he had been told by the protagonist, the narrator explains that, to his mind, John's motive for engaging in such an act was twofold: following his disastrous encounter with Europa, he required soothing and thus sought delicate and intimate contact with a being "whose sensibility and insight were not wholly incomparable with his own" (1935, p. 53). Further, in order to assert his "moral independence of Homo sapiens" and to "free himself of all deep unconscious acquiescence in the conventions of the species that had nurtured him" John needed "to break what was one of the most cherished of all the taboos of that species" (1935, p. 53).

Undeniably, *Odd John* presents Stapledon's cynical perspective on *Homo sapiens'* capacity to allow for the existence of a superior species. However, as Swanson points out, to sympathize with John—who kills without "moral compunction" and is depicted (irrespective of his identity as Homo Superior) as "a thief and a murderer" and later dies the victim "of the 'normal' world" (1982, p. 285)—is to entertain the "nonhuman" and to accept monstrosity as a human attribute. It is John's identity as a paradoxical protagonist that evokes the sympathy of the readers, who, perhaps unknowingly, accept the inevitability of their down-going and celebrate the destruction of the species as a whole. Swanson draws a similar conclusion, arguing that while Stapledon "directs our concern to the dangers of transcendence" he also shows "us how easy it is to applaud our own imminent destruction as a species" (1982, p. 284). In consideration of John's more monstrous attributes and Swanson's comment regarding the acceptance of the monster, the nonhumans presented in Stapledon's (and perhaps Sturgeon's) work might therefore be thought of as a celebration of diversity, or the sense of difference evoked by the nonhuman, rather than a direct confrontation to the crisis of identity derived from representations of the monster or nonhuman other, as discussed in the previous chapter.

Unlike John, whose motivation stems from his desire to contribute toward the progression of the species as a whole, Bester's Gully Foyle is, for the most part, driven by purely selfish desires. Following his escape from the doomed wreckage of *Nomad*, after he is discovered and nursed back to health by the Scientific People, Gully, unconcerned with their safety and focused only on his own revenge, constructs a crude rocket to launch from inside the asteroid inhabited by the Scientific People. When Moira, his accidental wife assigned by the Scientific People, asks what he is doing, Gully replies "Got to get out of here, girl.... Got business with a ship.... Going to ram out in this boat" (1956, p. 25). Moira panics, but is quickly subdued by Gully, who rips her nightgown off and "bound and gagged her with it" (1956, p. 25). Once his rocket is prepared, Gully puts Moira in the main hatch, telling her that he is going to "blast right out of asteroid. Hell of a smash, girl. Maybe all die, you. Everything busted wide open" (1956, pp. 25–26).

Another example of Gully's immorality can be seen in a similar act of sheer selfishness. Following their escape from Gouffre Martel, Gully and Jisbella return to the wreckage of *Nomad* so as to reclaim its cargo in platinum bullion. However, when they are discovered by Dagenham (who has been charged by Presteign with the task of following them), Gully, once in possession of the platinum, abandons Jisbella (1956, p. 108). The most accurate account of Gully's actions is provided by the character himself during his conversation with the lawyer, Sheffield. Debating whether to take the protagonist as a client, Sheffield asks Gully to briefly describe his crime. "Crimes," Gully corrects in response, going on to claim they include "robbery and rape.... Blackmail and murder ... treason and genocide" and that "we may be able to unveil a few more when we get specific" (1956, p. 203).

Although violence might be identified as the unifying factor, contributing to the antiheroic identities of the protagonists examined throughout this chapter, often, as illustrated above, it is rejection of moral and social convention—such as John's incestuous relationship with his mother, Jerry's pragmatic view on his murder of Miss Kew, or Gully Foyle's manipulation of those around him—that solidifies their identity as anti-heroes.

Nietzsche's conception of the Übermensch, as this chapter has demonstrated, can be identified in a number of antiheroic speculative fiction narratives. While authors' interpretations of the Übermensch—as an intellectually, philosophically, or morally superior being—might vary, what remains consistent is their focus on the superiority of the Übermensch, the transcendence of the human condition through self-perfection, the disparity between such beings and everyday individuals, and the potential impact their existence might have on existing social reality. Described by the author as his most personal work and significant contribution to philosophical theory (1999, pp. 7–8), Nietzsche's vision of the Übermensch, as well as those ideologies advocated by the prophetic protagonist of *Thus Spoke Zarathustra*, are, as discussed in the second part of this chapter, clearly linked with his broader philosophical concerns relating to self-overcoming, sublimation, the will to power, and advocacy for the rejection of standard moral and social convention. Through the examination of the protagonists in the works of Stapledon, Sturgeon, and Bester, what becomes evident is that, though their identities as Übermenschen undeniably contribute to their alienation/isolation from social reality, often it is their rejection of moral and social convention—and in turn their acceptance of superiority and dismissal of their human identities—that informs and determines their antiheroic identity, thus affirming the significance of both Nietzsche's Übermensch and broader philosophical concepts in the development of the paradoxical protagonist.

THREE

V for Vendetta

This chapter will examine narratives in which the depicted social reality prompts the antihero into acts of violence that challenge the reader's perception of right and wrong, good and evil, and which ultimately position the reader to accept (if not condone) actions or ideologies they would otherwise condemn—such as terrorism. As a result, the social reality in which the antihero is depicted becomes indispensable in gaining an understanding of his actions and the ideologies underpinning his perspectives and motivations. The chapter will focus on Alan Moore and David Lloyd's *V for Vendetta* (1982–1989). As with all the protagonists examined throughout this study, Moore's protagonist, V, is a paradoxical antihero: he is a scientifically-created monster, similar to the being created by Victor Frankenstein in Mary Shelley's *Frankenstein*; and although he is a heroic fighter for freedom against oppression (strongly advocating an anti-establishment and anarchic ideology), his actions can also be seen as those of a terrorist driven by a petty desire for revenge.

Dystopian Realities

Alan Moore claims it is often the case that, with the worlds or societies presented in science fiction, "you're not actually talking about the future; you're talking about the present" (Vylenz, 2008), and the issues involved are reflections of existing, real-world concerns. In *V for Vendetta*, Moore and Lloyd confront the reader with a dystopian future in which the United Nations has been dismantled, the global economy is in a perpetual state of turmoil, and the alliance between the U.S. and the U.K. has disintegrated. As one of the few remaining stable economies, England has closed its doors to the rest of the world and withdrawn from the international political stage. Though still aesthetically iconic, the England presented in the narrative is one much changed from that of today: the monarchy has fallen and the former democratic political system has been replaced by a fascist, deeply religious, ultra-conservative political body known as the Norsefire Party. Fiercely strict in its moral beliefs, the Norsefire Party demands the complete and utter obedience of its citizens, claiming to offer safety and security in exchange for this forced allegiance. In order to ensure compliance, citizens are kept under 24-hour surveillance through the implementation of a mass network of video cameras (called the Eye) and random audio scanning (called the Ear). Law is enforced through a special branch of police (the Finger) and crimes against the political agenda of the government are investigated by a detective unit (the Nose). Those who deviate outside the strict social and moral conventions or speak out against the party quickly disappear: they are arrested (black-bagged), detained for interrogation, and then executed without judicial process.

Both the similarity to and difference from contemporary England, Moore claims, was a deliberate strategy used to encourage readers to consider the disturbing similarities between the social reality depicted in the narrative and their own:

> Thatcher is entering her third term of office … talking confidently of an unbroken Conservative leadership well into the next century. My youngest daughter is seven and the tabloid press are circulating the idea of concentration camps for people with AIDS. The new riot police wear black visors, as do their horses, and their vans have rotating video cameras mounted on top. The government has expressed a desire to eradicate homosexuality, even as an abstract concept, and one can only speculate as to which minority will be next legislated against [1982–1989, p. VI].

The social realities depicted in *V for Vendetta* serve as vehicles through which existing social, political, or moral issues and concerns might be explored. As Moore says, "there were probably quite a few things about [*V for Vendetta*] which chimed well with the times" (Vylenz, 2008). Moore goes on to explain that what is most significant about the narrative is its depiction of a social reality that "didn't quiet hang together in terms of linear cause and effect but was instead seen as some massively complex simultaneous event with connections made of coincidence" (Vylenz, 2008). According to Moore, the bleak, largely cynical worldview encompassed by *V for Vendetta* resonated, largely, with individuals who had suddenly come to realize that their previous conception of social reality was no longer "adequate for the complexities of this scary, shadowy new world that we were entering into" (Vylenz , 2008). Moore explains that the narrative emerged during what was, at least politically speaking, a rather depressing era (2008). *V for Vendetta* was released during a time when "most of the liberal world was watching in horror at the … rise of the Reagan, Thatcher, right-wing fuck-buddy coalition" while at the same time there were "elements of fascism starting to make themselves present on the streets of Britain" and "all in all, things were looking fairly bleak" (Vylenz, 2008).

V as Transhuman

This section examines V's transhuman characteristics and also draws comparisons between V and the scientifically created monster of Mary Shelley's *Frankenstein* (1818) so as to illustrate the development of the literary transhuman and to acknowledge its affinity with the concept of the monster. However, unlike the monstrous transhumans examined previously, which, more often than not, posed a threat to axiomatic boundaries and the liminal space separating human from nonhuman, V can be interpreted as a force of nature or a natural response to the social reality in which he exists and the experiences by which he was created.

V is a complex, multifaceted protagonist who, on the one hand, is inarguably human, yet on the other, has also transcended many of the limitations imposed upon the human condition. V's status as a transhuman, as will be shown, is most clearly validated by his superior strength, agility, and intelligence. Unlike the natural transhumans such as those depicted in Stapledon's *Odd John* (1936) or Bester's *The Stars My Destination* (1956) examined in the previous chapter, whose transcendence of the human condition was the result of natural selection or other biological factors, V has an affinity with the monster of Shelley's *Frankenstein* (1818). Like Victor's monster, V's transhuman status was the result of direct human intervention and scientific experimentation. As the narrative reveals, V's transition from everyday individual to transhuman is the result of secret medical experiments conducted by the Norsefire Party in which unwilling participants were injected with the hormone "Batch 5" (1982–1989, p. 80). Although V's physical capabilities are fairly superficial, allowing him to excel, for example, in hand-to-hand combat, the superior cognitive function resulting from the Norsefire Party's experimentation lends the protagonist certain psychopathic qualities, leading others to believe him insane. As Delia Surridge, the medical researcher heading the hormone experiment at the Larkhill facility, explains in her diary, although there doesn't seem to be anything physically abnormal about the patient in room five (V), he seems "quite insane," the hormone experiments having brought on "some kind of psychotic break-down" (p. 81). In spite this observed insanity, subject V is described as largely charismatic, having "developed one of those curious side effects which seem to afflict certain categories of schizophrenic: his personality has become totally magnetic" (1982–1989, p. 81). V's charisma, however, was simply a means of hiding his manipulation and deceit of those around him. This is revealed in Delia's final entry, which describes V's destruction of and subsequent escape from the Larkhill facility where he was being held captive:

> In the centre of the camp everything was on fire.... It was the man from room five who had got out, who had got away, he blew it up, he killed.... I couldn't have known ... the ammonia. The grease solvent and all the other stuff. He'd been making things with them. Mustard gas and napalm. And in the yard I saw him. He looked at me. As if I were an insect ... as if I were something mounted on a slide [1982–1989, p. 83].

The latter might also be seen as an allusion to metamorphosis, or the frequently cited image of the phoenix rising from the ashes, a sentiment mirrored in V's dying words to Evey, the narrative's female protagonist, regarding the resurrection of society (1982–1989, p. 245). More specifically, however, it reflects V's metamorphosis, not only from human to transhuman, but paradoxically, from human to nonhuman or monster. The former facet of V's transformation, from human to transhuman, is reflected in Delia's description of V as perceiving her as "an insect" (1982–1989, p. 83) or a lower class of species, something to be studied and examined, rather than recognized as an equal. The second, infinitely more complex facet of V's transformation—from human to nonhuman—is marked by a loss of human identity and distinguishing characteristics. Through the hormone experiments conducted under the order of the Norsefire Party, V, as an individual, lost both his past and future. During his escape, he was badly burned by the incendiary explosives he had built and subsequently deformed beyond recognition—forced to relinquish all previous physical markers pertaining to his physical identity. Unable to take part in the social reality he once knew, V is essentially alienated and forced into hiding. To compensate for his loss of identity, V adopts the Fawkesian mask which acts, ironically, to foreshadow the events which he is to set in motion. Further, as will be shown, V's use of the Fawkesian mask also serves as an allusion, drawing a link between the protagonist and the figure of Guy Fawkes, or more specifically the rebellion that he sought to instigate.

V's fragmented, nonhuman nature is also significant in context to understanding the protagonist, not only as a transhuman, but also as an antihero. During their first encounter, for example, Evey inevitably asks "Who are you?" (1982–1989, p. 13). V, in response, tells her that he is "the king of the twentieth century ... the bogeyman. The villain ... the black sheep of the family" (1982–1989, p. 13). Clearly, V's reference to himself as "the bogeyman" and the "villain" (p. 13) serves to acknowledge the amorality of his actions. In describing himself as "the black sheep of the family" (1982–1989, p. 13), V also shows his rejection of the normative justice implemented under the Norsefire Pary and his subsequent rejection of social and moral obligations.

Irrespective of his physical form or even his symbolic value, it is hard to identify V as a human individual at all. Although protagonists discussed previously have acted in response to the social reality in which they exist, V is the direct product of Moore's envisioned dystopian England. Even to V, his presence and the unique abilities he gained as a result of the hormone experiments are no mere coincidence, but rather a chain of causality whereby each event is linked to another. In its cinematic adaptation, produced by Joel Silver and the Wachowski brothers, V's belief in causality as an underpinning force in individual development is highlighted in his quoting Isaac Newton's law of motion: "To every action there is always an equal and opposite reaction" (Silver, Wachowski, and Wachowski, 2005). Further, when Evey confronts the protagonist about his violent, often brutal methods, he explains that it is simply a matter of action and reaction; his methods are monstrous because what the Norsefire Party did to him "was monstrous" (2005). In response, however, Evey thus concludes that the party had indeed, "created a monster" (2005). While the latter interaction between V and Evey does not take place within the narrative itself, the notion of causality still can be identified as a fundamental attribute of V's ideological perspective. Causality is alluded to on several occasions throughout the narrative. During V's interaction with Delia Surridge, for example, years after the events at Larkhill, Delia, aware that V had come to take her life for the part she played in the Norsefire Party's hormone experiments, tells V that earlier she had been given one of his roses[1]: "I wasn't sure that you were the terrorist, not until I saw the rose. What a strange coincidence that I should be given it today" (1982–1989, p. 74). In response, V states, "There is no coincidence, Delia. Only the illusion of coincidence. I have another rose for you" (1982–1989, p. 74). Later, prior to his bombing of the Tower of London, V again alludes to the concept of causality and the predetermination of events, telling Evey that "the ending is nearer than you think, and it's already written. All that we have left to choose is the correct moment" (1982–1989, p. 183). Further, towards the end of the novel, as V's machinations to topple the Norsefire Party are coming to fruition, he tells Evey that the end is within sight, that all "the pieces are set out ... perfectly aligned" but only when they are complete is one capable of perceiving their "design; their grand significance" (1982–1989, p. 207). He goes on to tell her that "everything is connected" (1982–1989, p. 219). Indeed, all of V's plans were but the foundation of a broader, far more complex pattern, ultimately shaped not only to emancipate the citizens suppressed under the Norsefire Party but also to return autonomy to the people. This is aptly reflected when V leaves the final decision to Evey.

As both creator and destroyer, V is a character difficult to define or even to perceive as a human individual, rather than a force of nature. This is especially evident in V's rejection of his own human or individual identity. In planning for his own death, V effectively withdraws himself from the social reality that is to exist following the fall of the Norsefire Party. Indeed, even V, aware of his imminent demise and the completion of his plan to emancipate those individuals oppressed under the Norsefire group's tyrannical rule, no longer recognizes or wishes to identify himself as a human individual. With his personal vendetta against the Norsefire Party settled—as will be discussed later in the chapter—and those accountable for the hormone research project that initiated his transformation dead, V is able to, at last, fully transcend the human condition, as is evident towards the end of the narrative. Here, V is perhaps best interpreted as the embodiment of the anarchic ideology for which he stood. When shot by Fitch, for example, despite knowing that he has received a mortal injury, he leans forward and asks, "Did you think to kill me?" before going on to explain that "there is no flesh or blood within this cloak to kill. There's only an idea and ideas are bullet-proof" (1982–1989, p. 236).

Paradoxically, in spite being aware of his imminent death, V, having fully transcended the human condition, also attains a state of immortality, living on through the anarchic ideology which he embodied. This is most evident in the events following V's death when Evey discovers V's body and removes "the maddening smile" (1982–1989, p. 250) only to find a reflection of herself as a child staring back at her. Metaphorically, then, this is to suggest, as Fitch discovers in retracing V's steps back through the Larkhill facility while under the influence of psychedelic drugs (1982–1989, pp. 210–215) that V, as an individual, represented not only an anarchic ideology, but also the freedom for which the oppressed citizens yearn. In recognizing the reflective and self-fulfilling nature of V's anarchic ideology, Evey makes the decision to take up his mask and continue with his work, guiding individuals in the development of an anarchic society. Disguised as V, Evey addresses the rioting crowds:

> Since mankind's dawn, a handful of oppressors have accepted the responsibility over our lives that we should have accepted ourselves. By doing so, they took our power. By doing nothing, we gave it away. We've seen where their way leads, through camps and wars, towards the slaughter house. In anarchy there is another way ... from rubble comes new life.... Tomorrow Downing Street will be destroyed.... Tonight, you must choose what comes next. Lives of our own, or a return to chains [1982–1989, p. 258].

Again, the latter can be interpreted as an allusion toward the prophetic protagonist of Nietzsche's *Thus Spake Zarathustra* (1885), discussed in the previous chapter, who similarly addresses the masses, giving them the choice between evolution and development or a return to animalistic degradation: "and do you want to be the ebb of this great tide, and return to the animals rather than overcome man?" (1961, p. 41). In spite of transcending the human condition and attaining not only a state of transhumanism, but in the end, ideological immortality, V, unlike a majority of the protagonists discussed in previous chapters—whose actions were primarily selfish—uses his transhuman capabilities to benevolent ends.

The Antihero as Freedom Fighter

As previously mentioned, V is a complex, multifaceted, and largely paradoxical protagonist. The paradox manifest in V is compounded by the seemingly contradictory nature of his actions and ideology. Many of the actions undertaken by the protagonist throughout the narrative such as mass murder, the assassination of political figures, and acts of terrorism targeting symbolic structures—which will be examined more closely in the following section—are unequivocally amoral. V's actions represent a rejection of the moral, social, and political conventions imposed by the social reality and socio-political climate in which he is forced to exist. However, as V's actions—though largely motivated by revenge—are directed toward the totalitarian police state established under the Norsefire Party, which suppresses core elements of democratic ideology, specifically freedom of choice and free speech, even his more detestable actions such as his attack on the Old Bailey or the kidnapping and torture of female protagonist Evey Hammond can be interpreted as necessary, or justified.

V's actions thus reflect an idealized, almost romanticized notion of rebellion. In this sense, V implements rebellion as a mode of action that while morally reprehensible is nonetheless necessary for achieving his desired goal. The significance of rebellion in relation to the protagonist is outlined by Moore, who claims rebellion is what "drives British comic writing"[2] (Mapstone, 2012). Further, Moore also explains that there is a tradition, especially in Britain, of making "heroes out of criminals or people who in other centuries might have been regarded as terrorists" (BBC HARDtalk, 2012).

In Albert Camus's *The Rebel* (1956), the rebel, as an individual, is described as a paradoxical figure that both rejects and advocates simultaneously, thus providing the foundation for rebellion and, subsequently, revolution. On the one hand, the rebel rejects some facet of the social reality in which he exists, stipulating that the current environment is unacceptable, while at the same time advocating his belief in a system in which experiences, conditions, and actions can be deemed either right or wrong, good or bad, in accordance with a universal sense of morality of conduct (1956, pp. 7–11). In this, the rebel can be seen as rejecting the normative social justice to which he is subject, yet maintaining the belief that somewhere or somehow "one is right" (1956, p. 10). Abstract though it might be, in this sense rebellion refers to an intrinsic social, cultural, political, philosophical, or in some cases individual value. In relation to the narrative, this can be seen through the protagonist's rejection of the Norsefire Party's political ideology and V's desire to emancipate the citizens from its oppressive rule.

For Camus, rebellion was largely a symbolic act that sought to reveal deeper, symptomatic causes, arguing that "every act of rebellion tacitly evokes a value" (1956, p. 11). In spite of the logic in which acts of rebellion might be undertaken and subsequently justified, rebellion, as both an ideal and mode of action, is inevitably doomed to failure. Camus recognizes the absurdity of rebellion, suggesting that even the rebel is all too aware that, as a course of action, rebellion "is not realistic" (1956, p. 13). Often individualistic in nature, the desire for rebellion is, more often than not, derived from the individual rebel "wanting to be something other than what they are" (1956, p. 13). Rebellion, however, might also be seen, if only symbolically, as an act of desperation. Richard Billow argues that rebellion reflects social, or collective, resistance rather than individual desire, which "denotes a strategy adopted by a faction, when other avenues of influence seem unappealing, or even futile … that depends on the group's *authenticity*" (2010, p. 191).

Although many of the protagonists already discussed rebellion in response to their environments, their rebellion is not a direct product of the social realities in which they exist, but rather a response to their individual situations. Nor are their acts of rebellion motivated by an inherent socio-political ideology.

It is clear that V's rebellion stems from his personal desire to take revenge. Aside from his vendetta against the Norsefire Party, V's contempt for the reigning political body stems from its suppression of individuality and cultural expression, specifically in context to art, literature, and music. For V, the Norsefire Party set about the systematic eradication of culture, which it "tossed … away like a fistful of dead roses" (1982–1989, p. 19). As V explains, however, the Norsefire Party "eradicated some cultures more thoroughly than they did others" leaving citizens with "No Tamla and no Trojan. No Billie Holiday or Black Uhuru. Just his master's voice every hour, on the hour. We'll have to see what we can do about that" (1982–1989, p. 19). V sees this eradication of culture and the suppression of individuality perpetrated by the Norsefire Party as an intolerable transgression. V's rebellion is thus a rejection of the normative social values set in place by the Norsefire Party, but also an avocation of a core, anarchic ideology.

Another facet of rebellion, perhaps its most controversial, is the use of violence. For Camus, when used in context to rebellion, violence against others—whether symbolic or as a mode of action—is equivalent to violence against the self. That is to say, murder and suicide are two facets of a single system that, according to Camus, the "misguided intelligence" of the individual prefers to the "suffering imposed by a limited situation, the dark victory in which heaven and earth are annihilated" (1956, p. 8). This is to suggest violence, as an absolute, is always immoral, irrespective of course, motivation, or personal justification. It is impossible for the rebel, in utilizing violence, to defend his actions. For Camus, once the rebel recognizes the "impossibility of absolute negation," he must acknowledge that "the very first thing that cannot be denied is the right of others to live" (1956,

p. 8). The simultaneous recognition of "absolute negation" and the "right of others to live" (1956, p. 8) is again representative of the rebel's paradoxical nature. As an individual, the rebel—as the instigators of revolution—if he is to recognize "absolute negation" must also acknowledge that he is unable to prevent or justify violence of any kind (1956, p. 8). Resulting from such paradoxical ideologies, rebellion, if it is to exist at all, must do so through absurdity. Rebellion is largely a rejection of reason, whether moral or philosophical, and can only exist in acknowledgment of its contrary nature.

In *V for Vendetta*, the link between absurdity and rebellion is clearly present in the protagonist's ideological perception. For the protagonist, however, violence and rebellion—especially due to the social reality in which V's rebellion and subsequent revolution takes place—go hand in hand. Further, violence, as discussed in the introduction, is one of several facets contributing to the protagonist's antiheroic identity. During his rescue of female protagonist Evey Hammond, for example, V quickly dispatches two members of the special security force (stabbing one and burning the other using an incendiary device concealed in a fake hand) (1982–1989, p. 12). Shortly after, V kills a bodyguard and kidnaps Lewis Prothero (1982–1989, p. 21), whom he tortures to the point of madness before dressing him up as a doll and leaving him outside Scotland Yard (1982–1989, p. 36). Later, V lures Bishop Anthony Lilliman, a pedophile, into a trap by using Evey as bait and kills him using an arsenic-laced communion wafer. Following this, however, Evey confronts V regarding his methods, telling him that "killing's wrong" before asking, "Isn't it?" (1982–1989, p. 64). Acknowledging the contradictory nature of rebellion, V remains neutral in his response, simply shrugging and querying "Why are you asking me?" (1982–1989, p. 64).

Rebellion is a significant facet of V's personal ideology. The relationship between V and rebellion is reinforced upon an aesthetic level. Most implicit is the Fawkesian mask worn by the protagonist, which serves to directly link the protagonist's ideology with that of historical figure Guy Fawkes. Further aesthetic allusions can be seen upon V's bookcase in the Shadow Gallery, with titles including *Don Quixote*, *French Revolution*, Thomas More's *Utopia*, Harriet Beecher Stowe's *Uncle Tom's Cabin*, and Karl Marx and Friedrich Engles' *Capital*, which is here depicted alongside Adolf Hitler's *Mein Kampf* (1982–1989, p. 18).

Although V can be interpreted as a rebel, many of the protagonist's actions, such as the destruction of iconic landmarks and the assassination of key political figures, transcended simple rebellion and share closer affinity with the concept of terrorism. In context with rebellion, however, terrorism likewise reflects a rejection of factors deemed unfavorable by the individual and exists in direct contradiction to accepted social and moral convention. Even terrorism, however, can be interpreted as acceptable, though perhaps not condonable, in response to the hostile social reality in which the narrative is set.

Sympathy for the Devil

As will be shown, V's use of terrorism is perhaps the largest contributor to his identity as an antihero. Through considering a number of V's actions, which include the bombing of several iconic landmarks, the assassination of key political Norsefire Party members, theft of government property, conspiracy, kidnapping, torture, and the distribution of propaganda, one thing becomes evidently clear: the protagonist is a terrorist. Paradoxically, however, V is a terrorist whose actions, though perhaps unsavory, seek to reinforce the very moral and social conventions terrorism seeks to destabilize. The term terrorism itself, however, is of course ambiguous and highly contested. In *Terrorism and the Ethics of War*, Stephen Nathanson defines terrorism as:

1. Acts of a serious, deliberate violence or credible threats of such acts;
2. Are committed in order to promote a political or social agenda;
3. Generally target a limited number of people but aim to influence a larger group and/or the leaders who make decisions for a group;
4. Intentionally kill or injure innocent people or pose a threat of serious harm to them [2011, p. 24].

Even identifying an individual as a terrorist is largely ambiguous, specifically in considering the frequently cited aphorism "one man's terrorist is another man's revolutionary."[3] Nevertheless, V's actions and the reader's ability to identify, or even sympathize, with either him as a character or the philosophical logic underpinning his actions—actions, it should be pointed out, that lead to large-scale destruction and the murder of many individuals, many of whose only crime was that of compliancy—raise a number of questions regarding the depiction of V as a terrorist and, consequently, the reader's understanding of his agenda and underpinning motivation. This is especially true in a social reality still bearing witness to the ramifications of the World Trade Center attacks of September 11, 2001.

When Time Warner announced the release of its cinematic adaptation of Moore's and Lloyd's narrative, some critics were baffled, others outraged. Ted Baehr, founder and publisher of *Movieguide*, for example, attacked the movie, describing it as a "vile, pro-terrorist piece of neo-Marxist, left-wing propaganda filled with radical sexual politics and nasty attacks on religion and Christianity" (2006). In acknowledging the source material used for the movie's production, Baehr goes on to criticize Moore's original narrative, arguing it to have been a thinly veiled attack on the "conservative administration" of "Prime Minister Margaret Thatcher, one of the greatest political leaders of the 20th century" (2006). The graphic novel's adaptation also prompted Lev Grossman to raise the question "Is it possible for a major Hollywood studio to make a $50 million movie in which the hero is a terrorist? A terrorist who appears wearing the dynamite waistcoat of a suicide bomber" (Grossman, 2006). As Nathanson points out, however, if the individual is to condemn terrorist actions while failing to provide a definition of the term itself, he must at the same time acknowledge that his "condemnations have no moral validity" and only express a "personal distaste" (2010, p. 11). Nevertheless, what should be queried is whether V's implementation of terrorist-based action makes the moral, political, and social criticisms underpinning the narrative, as a whole, any less cogent?

It would seem what both Baehr and Grossman have failed to address is the fundamental question: Can V's actions be justified? What is of primary concern in this chapter is not whether V is a terrorist—though his ideological stance and actions clearly indicate that he is, perhaps rendering the question moot—but whether his actions, no matter how contrary to existing moral and social convention, can be deemed acceptable or necessary, if not condonable, to the reader's mind. As Margarita Carretero-Gonzalez points out, *V for Vendetta* "problematizes" the "sensitive issue" of terrorism through its depiction of "a dystopian setting that, however exaggerated, bears striking similarities with our world at the beginning of the 21st century, where fear of terror is impelling governments to take drastic measures to increase safety, while jeopardizing freedom and, on some occasions, even trespassing basic human rights" (2011, p. 191). At this point, it is perhaps important to point out that the contradiction between social and moral convention and those actions undertaken by V is in no way coincidental or even unintentional. According to Moore, his primary goal, in presenting readers with the contrast between V and the social reality in which he exists, was to encourage them to ask, "Is this guy right? Or is he just mad?" (MacDonald, 2005). Undeniably, revolution is at the heart of the narrative, explains Moore: "I didn't want to tell people what to think, I just wanted to tell people to think and consider some of these admittedly extreme little elements, which nevertheless do recur fairly regularly throughout human history" (MacDonald, 2005).

This relationship between V's terrorist ideology and the concept of revolution is also noted by James Keller, who rightly observes that *V for Vendetta* is a narrative laden with inter- and hypertextuality that make effective use of both aesthetic and textual signifiers to draw attention to the juxtaposition of V, as a terrorist, and the social reality in which he exists (2008 pp. 4–8).

Perhaps the most recognizable, if not significant, of these signifiers can be identified in the protagonist's use of the modern mythology surrounding Guy Fawkes, which is manifest on a number of levels. At its most superficial, it can be seen in the Fawkesian mask V uses to conceal his identity and his evocation of the Gunpowder Plot[4] (1605): "Remember, remember, the Fifth of November: the gunpowder, treason, and plot. I know of no reason why the gunpowder treason should ever be forgot" (1982–1989, p. 14). In spite of claiming to have conducted a critical analysis of both film and narrative, much of Keller's focus remains directed toward the cinematic adaptation; his conclusion, with the exception of a brief footnote, fails to acknowledge Moore's original narrative. As a result, Keller, though able to comment more broadly on the inherent intertextuality generated though the narrative's film adaptation, fails to acknowledge or even recognize the foundation of V's political ideology and the primary influence underpinning the narrative as a whole: anarchy.[5] Whether V's avocation of anarchist ideology makes his terrorist actions more commendable, or justifiable, however, is perhaps simply a matter of perspective. Nevertheless, anarchy, as will be shown, is fundamental in understanding both the narrative and the protagonist's moral and political ideology.

While the notion of rebellion and the ambiguity surrounding the possible justification of terrorist actions are clearly integral to the construction of V—and a clear indication of his antiheroic identity—both evoke a sense of determinism that exists contrary to the anarchic philosophical, or at least moral and political, ideology advocated by the protagonist. V's own perception of anarchy as an ideal is clearly reflected several times throughout the narrative. The first and perhaps most significant of such depictions is reflected through V's conversation with the statue of Lady Justice, mounted atop the Old Bailey, London's Central Criminal Court:

> I loved you as a person. As an ideal. That was a long time ago. I'm afraid there's someone else now.... It was your infidelity that drove me into her arms.... So you stand revealed at last. You are no longer my justice. You are his justice now. You have bedded another. Well, two can play at that game.... Her name is anarchy and she has taught me more as a mistress than you ever did. She has taught me that justice is meaningless without freedom. She is honest, she makes no promises and breaks none [1982–1989, pp. 40–41].

Anarchy, specifically the anarchy advocated by V, is largely the rejection of Hobbesian political and social theory. In *Leviathan*, for example, Hobbes not only argues that individuals are equal, that individual claims to nobility or superiority are devoid of merit, but also that the individual should prefer to live under the dominion of "The State" even if it should prove to be a tyrannical one, rather than in what he calls the "state of nature," which describes a state devoid of political, judicial, social, and economic governance (1651, pp. 65–66). To this end, anarchy presents a more natural state of affairs, specifically from a biological point of view. Here, anarchy as the rejection of the individual leader, or ruling class, promotes progress or, sociologically speaking, social and individual development. The natural, anarchic state, in this way, however, would demand both individuality and diversity, precisely the two social facets suppressed and removed by the Norsefire Party. The notion of an anarchic system of social development that demands individuality and diversity is expressed by V during his address to the people, following his infiltration and hijacking of a major broadcasting network. Here, V poses as a god-like, omnipresent narrator:

> You're wondering why I've called you here this evening. Well, you see, I'm not entirely satisfied with your performance lately ... your work's been slipping.... I'm afraid we've been thinking about letting you go.... I know you've been with the company a long time.... I remember the day you commenced your employment, swinging down from the trees, fresh-faced and nervous, a bone clasped in your bristling fist [1982–1989, p. 113].

The latter can also be interpreted as an allusion to the prophetic Zarathustra of Frederick Nietzsche's *Thus Spake Zarathustra*—discussed in the previous chapter—who, like V, accuses individuals of being no more than "beasts" and "apes" who have failed to create something "beyond themselves" (1883, pp. 41–44). In furthering this allusion, V goes on to explain that contemporary issues largely stem from the individual's "unwillingness to get on within the company" and that "we've offered you promotion time and time again and each time you've turned us down" (1982–1989, p. 114). According to V, in accepting the social and moral conventions forced upon them by the Norsefire Party, individuals have done away with diversity and individuality and, in doing so, have reduced their capacity to evolve or develop, not specifically in the biological sense, but socially, culturally, politically, and morally.

As responses to the reality in which he exists and the social and cultural issues by which he is confronted, V's implementation of rebellion and terrorism and his advocation of anarchic ideology are inextricably linked. Rebellion, terrorism, and anarchy, to V, are simply tools employed to fulfill two inherent desires: at a personal level, V wants to settle his vendetta and take revenge on those individuals who contributed to his identity as both an antihero and a transhuman. On another level, however, V desires a social revolution through the destruction of the Norsefire Party and the emancipation of its citizens. Although an anarchist, in order to achieve his revolution, V implements both rebellion and terrorism, both often affiliated with violence. While this reflects a sense of reason regarding the inevitability of social decline, perhaps, left with few other alternatives, that is precisely the risk V is willing to take.

This is especially evident towards the end of the narrative. Here, V is wounded by detective Fitch, the individual charged with investigating V's terrorist activities, and returns to the shadow gallery, his home beneath the streets of London, before collapsing and later being discovered by Evey. Just prior to his death, V explains to Evey:

> This country is not saved.... But all of its old beliefs have come to rubble and from rubble may we build. That is their task: to rule themselves, their lives and loves and land. With this achieved then let them talk of salvation. Without it they are surely carrion. By turn of the century they'll know their fate: either a rose midst rubble blooms, or else has bloomed too late [1982–1989, p. 245].

Thus V not only explains what he hoped his actions of rebellion and terrorism might achieve, but also what he saw as the logical conclusion to the totalitarian Norsefire Party and the potential future of the country it had oppressed; that is, the fall of fascism, a reimplementation of individual freedom, and the reconstruction or redevelopment of social order through anarchy. That V should die for the creation of this anarchic, or more specifically, leaderless society, had been acknowledged by the protagonist from the very start of his campaign, as is illustrated just prior to the commencement of his final plan. Shown preparing a train packed with explosives that will travel underground and destroy 10 Downing Street, effectively bringing the Norsefire Party's rule to an end, V explains to Evey that "anarchy wears two faces, both creator and destroyer.... Destroyers topple empires, make a canvas of clean rubble where creators can then build a better world" (1982–1989, p. 222). In an established anarchic society, however, if it is to be effective, there can be no destroyers, rebels, or terrorists, only creators, developers, and propagators. Like violence, such individuals are tools, and though effective, their use and methods cannot be justified, and therefore, they must be disregarded when no longer required. To this end, V tells Evey:

> Away with our explosives, then! Away with our destroyers! They have no place within our better world. But let us raise a toast to all our bombers, all our bastards, most unlovely and most unforgiveable. Let's drink their health ... then meet with them no more [1982–1989, p. 222].

This acknowledges the imminence of V's success while also foreshadowing the protagonist's death, an event which had always been factored into V's plan. This is verified through two events: In the first, when Evey asks V what he is waiting for, he tells her that that he is "waiting for the man"[6] (1982–1989, p. 223); in the second, while dying in Evey's arms, he states, "The one I waited for has called, and now I have not long" (p. 245).

The social reality presented in a given narrative has the capacity to alter a reader's perception of right and wrong, good and evil, ultimately positioning them to accept, if not condone actions and ideologies they would otherwise condemn. The social reality presented in Alan Moore's and David Lloyd's *V for Vendetta* (1982–1989) depicts a future England governed by a fascist, ultra-conservative totalitarian group known as the Norsefire Party, which not only demands the compliance of its citizens but has also stripped them of their individuality and freedom of choice. The novel's protagonist, V, however, is, like many of Moore's characters, complex and multifaceted. Though motivated by revenge, V seeks to topple the totalitarian Norsefire Party and to emancipate those individuals who have been oppressed beneath its rule. However, his actions—including mass murder, the assassination of political figures, the destruction of iconic landmarks, theft, and the distribution of anti-government propaganda—are inarguably immoral, thus reinforcing his status as an antihero. He is also an advocate of anarchic ideology, like the novel's author, Alan Moore, believing that the only truly effective society is a leaderless one in which individuals are free, both socially and politically. V is also flawed, a character driven by the petty motivation of revenge.

More controversially, however, through murder, the targeted destruction of iconic structures and landmarks, the distribution of propaganda, and the assassination of key political figures, V invariably comes to be identified as a terrorist. Many of V's actions exist contrary to existing moral and social conventions. However, in their rejection of the normative law or social order established under the reign of the Norsefire Party, whose fascist, ultra-conservative, and oppressive ideologies doubly contradict existing moral and social convention, especially in the Western democratic world, V's actions, while not condonable, come to be accepted or even justified. Further, in spite of his fragmented identity, V also reflects a sense of the transhuman. As an unwilling participant in the hormone experiments conducted under the authority of the Norsefire Party, V has gained enhanced physical and cognitive function, which, as Delia Surridge points out, has made him "quite insane" (1982–1989, p. 81), yet also provided him the capacity required to topple the Norsefire Party and emancipate its citizens. For V, his existence and the abilities gained from the experiments are simply a matter of causality, a chain of events inexplicably linked. To this end, V can also be interpreted as a force of nature, a natural response to the social reality in which he exists and the social and political issues by which he is confronted.

FOUR

Watchmen and the Deconstruction of the Superhero

This chapter focuses on the deconstruction of the superhero and the role of madness in Alan Moore and Dave Gibbon's *Watchmen* (1986–1987). The chapter makes three separate, yet linked observations. First, based on Victor Brombert's comment that the "negative hero" or antihero "more keenly perhaps than the traditional hero, challenges our assumptions, raising anew the question of how we see, or wish to see ourselves" (1999, p. 2), this chapter examines how Moore's deconstruction of the superhero in *Watchmen* presents the reader with a more realistic, humanized account of the traditional, mono-mythic superhero. Second, building on Michael Woolf's argument concerning the two iconic modes of madness manifest within the antihero (in "The Madman as Hero in Contemporary American Fiction" [1976]), this chapter identifies a third manifestation in the protagonists of *Watchmen* which might be considered the madness of knowing. Third, this chapter posits that Moore's deconstruction of the superhero offers insight into the consequences of the existence of beings that have transcended the human condition, especially in relation to their obligation to observe moral and social conventions.

Superheroes and Watchmen

Since "*Watchmen* relies heavily on the readers' notion of the superhero," according to Dana Lucchine in "Beneath the Mask and Spandex" (2009, p. 4), any analysis of Moore and Dave Gibbons's *Watchmen* (1986–1987) should begin with a discussion of the superhero genre.

The comic-book superhero has been an important contributor to the development of contemporary popular culture since Jerry Siegel's and Joe Shuster's creation of the Superman character in 1939. Today, the superhero remains the most widely recognized facet of the comic-book industry, specifically in America, and the foundation for countless cross-media adaptations.[1] In *Superheroes* and *Philosophy*, Tom and Matt Morris compare the impact and literary immortality of the superhero to that of the classic philosophers, arguing that like "Plato and Aristotle," comic and cultural icons such as Superman and Batman "are here to stay" (2001, p. ix). In recent years, iconic superheroes have become increasingly prevalent, mainly due to what Paul Lopes describes as Hollywood's current addiction to the superhero genre, churning out adaptation after adaptation (2009, p. 1). Knowles and Linsner acknowledge this, stating that "Superman, Batman and the X-Men rule the box office, with the Spider Man movies alone earning almost $2.5 billion" (2007, p. 3). Even so, as Lopes rightly observes, what is most ironic in relation to the superhero genre's recent popularity is the "decidedly minor presence of actual comic books" (2009, p. ix).[2]

The exact definition of the superhero remains a frequently asked, yet highly contested topic for critics of the genre. For Morris and Morris, superheroes are "and always have been an adolescent power fantasy" (2001, p. 5). Moore agrees, stating, "If you're talking about superheroes, it's very likely to become a meditation on power" (Gravett, 2007). It is perhaps of little surprise, then, that one of the primary attributes of the superhero relates to power. According to Loeb and Morris, it is a general rule that superheroes have extraordinary powers or unique abilities "far beyond those of ordinary mortals" (2001, p. 11). Within the comic book universe, or multiverse,[3] the possession or acquisition of power often serves to justify the individual superhero's role or objective. These objectives, however, are often simplistic, perhaps even immature in nature and commonly relate to the pursuit of justice and "defending the defenseless, helping those who cannot help themselves and overcoming evil with the force of good" (2001, p. 11). Such noble integrity illustrates what might be described as the black and white moral mentality that, at least until the publication of *Watchmen*, prevailed over the social realties in which comic-book narratives were set. This concept is often linked to superhero morality: superheroes are depicted as being moral because they ought to be, or perhaps more specifically, because that is what has come to be expected. To further reinforce this moral transparency, superheroes are often juxtaposed with villainous figures that represent the darker forces that threaten the ideologies for which the superhero stands. This is not to suggest that superheroes are without controversy, for they are often depicted as being at odds with the very systems or socio-political conventions they have sworn to protect. As a result, Roz Kaveney points out that most superheroes are to "some degree vigilantes" (2008, p. 6) which often results in their having an "ambivalent relationship with the authorities" (2008, p. 8). Superheroes, nevertheless, are designed to appeal, not just morally or ideologically, but also physically or aesthetically. The physical appearance of a superhero usually conveys conventional stereotypes of masculinity and femininity and thus appeals to a mainstream, predominately male, heterosexual audience. Kaveney correctly observes that almost all "superheroes are good-looking and muscular, and wear costumes that emphasize the fact" (2008, p. 10).

Superheroes, however, are not simply the products of contemporary popular culture. According to Angela Ndalianis, superheroes can be identified as modern reinterpretations of the kind of mono-mythic hero exploits and extraordinary deeds that have been the focus of countless narratives (both oral and literary) since the beginning of civilization (2009, p. 3). She points out that the cult of heroism and the admiration evoked by such beings is a social and cultural construct that began long before "Hercules slew the Nemean lion with his bare hands or Odin killed the giant Ymir" (2009, p. 3).

Today, the position held by contemporary superheroes is similar to that maintained by the traditional mono-mythic hero. Marc DiPaolo suggests that people searching for religion in a "secular age" may come to see superheroes as "replacements for gods and angels" (2011, p. 15). Such observations reinforce the superhero's affinity with Joseph Campbell's conception of the mono-myth, defined in the introduction, which he examines throughout *The Hero with a Thousand Faces* (1949). The symbolic values from which mythology and mythological figures derive their significance, however, are diverse. It would be only too simple to apply Campbell's theory of the mono-myth to just about any superhero existing within the comic-book universe today. This is perhaps most evident through comparison: the figure of Jesus Christ, for example, might be compared with any number of superheroes, as both are of supernatural/divine origin and have the capability to perform feats and miracles far beyond the capacity of the everyday individual. Similarities between the mythological and contemporary superhero are undeniable. While it is important to acknowledge the existence of such relationships, the application of a theory so reliant on similarity and categorical imperatives would result in the simplification of the source material. Ben Saunders shares this argument, suggesting that critics who deconstruct or analyze contemporary protagonists and comic-book icons in relation to one or a number of mythologies or theological elements often fail to acknowledge that the characters presented in these narratives are "very much a product of popular modernism" (2011, p. 17). However, in consideration of the argument raised in the previous chapter, it is perhaps also reasonable to claim that the superhero is not only a product of "popular modernism" as Saunders states but one greatly informed by contemporary social reality and the social, moral, cultural, and political issues present during the time of their conception. It is this notion of tried and tested heroic value that Moore seeks to deconstruct throughout his narrative so as to reveal a more authentic, albeit largely flawed, image of the superhero.

Deconstructing Mythology

Watchmen is a deconstruction of superhero convention. Thomson suggests Moore "deconstructs the superhero [by] extending traditional hero fantasies beyond their limits" (2005, p. 101) until they are forced to collapse under their own weight. The protagonists depicted in *Watchmen* are thus able to effectively renegotiate the juxtaposition between good and evil, which provides the foundation for so many superhero conventions, blurring the boundaries between heroic and villainous. As Moore explains, "It was so easy to have an effect because none of the writers or artists who had come before us never thought of challenging these assumptions regarding the superhero genre" (Iannucci, 2007). For Annalis Di Liddo, the deconstruction of the superhero depicted in *Watchmen* allows for the manipulation and reinterpretation of traditional narrative forms whereby questions concerning "Western—and above all English—culture, politics and identity" (2009, p. 15) can be raised through an alternative medium. Indeed much of *Watchmen*'s impact can be related to its acknowledgment of real-world issues and concerns. Moore explains that in the development of superheroes, no one "had applied a political interpretation … or a sexual interpretation" (Iannucci, 2007).

Moore's deconstruction and subsequent reinterpretation of the superhero is perhaps most evident in the appearances of the superheroes themselves. This is especially true when considering Kaveney's comment that traditionally "superheroes are good-looking and muscular, and wear costumes that emphasize the fact" (2008, p. 10). Yet in spite of Kaveney's observation, the first character encountered in *Watchmen*, the Comedian, is thus described as being in "terrific shape" for a guy "his age" (1986–1987, ch I, p. 2), but he is illustrated as a somewhat scruffy fifty-something-year-old man with greying hair, a more than five-o'clock shadow, sitting around his apartment and watching television in his bathrobe (1986–1987, ch I, pp. 2–3). The second superhero introduced is Rorschach, a thin, middle-aged, disheveled-looking man with a shock of red hair. Forgoing the spandex, Rorschach's costume consist of old pinstripe pants, a crumpled brown trenchcoat, a tan fedora, an ink-blot mask that constantly changes shape, and padded "elevator shoes" (1986–1987, ch VII, p. 28) to compensate for his short stature. Nite Owl the second, or Daniel Dreiberg, is portrayed as a washed-up former academic, with a less than athletic figure and bookish looks (1986–1987, ch I, p. 9).

The second and perhaps most significant facet of Moore's deconstruction of the superhero can be seen in the narrative's depiction of the human condition. Far from the overly confident, almost arrogant superheroes of previous decades, the protagonists in *Watchmen* are revealed as essentially human, struggling with their own inner demons as well as the external forces derived from the social reality in which they exist. To this end, Moore presents the reader with superheroes who are uniquely individual, whose personalities, actions, and perhaps most importantly, motivations are influenced by their private lives, previous experiences, and personal idiosyncrasies. The imperfection manifest within each of *Watchmen*'s characters serves to strip away the sense of perfection and moral superiority so often attributed to traditional mono-mythic figures, leaving behind individuals that are fallible, uncertain, and, to some extent, fragile. Bradford Wright makes a similar observation, explaining that "Moore's superheroes immediately appeared different" if only for the fact that they spoke and "behaved like real people" (2001, p. 271).

In his development of these more humanized superheroes, Moore borrows from the traditional antihero what Michael Woolf in "The Madman as Hero in Contemporary American Literature" describes as a new, "peculiar kind of heroism, perhaps one more suitable to the social and political atmosphere of contemporary times" (1976, p. 263). Daniel Dreiberg, or the second Nite Owl, for instance, is first introduced during his interaction with Hollis Mason—the first Nite Owl, from whom Daniel

obtained his identity after the former's retirement—in which they remi-
nisce about their time as costumed adventurers or "masks." At first Daniel
appears to be a quiet, socially awkward forty-something who, according
to Geoff Klock, is visually reminiscent of an "impotent, middle-aged Clark
Kent" (2002, p. 66). He is an insecure character who sees himself as having
failed to live up to his father's expectations, which he confesses to Laurie
Juspeczyk (the second Silk Spectre):

> My dad was in banking. He left me a lot of money when he died. I was always
> kind of surprised about that ... he always seemed disappointed in me. He
> wanted me to follow him into banking but I was just interested in birds and
> airplanes and mythology [1986–1987, ch VII, p. 5].

Though identified as a superhero, Daniel nevertheless expresses frustration due to his inability to effect change when faced with the possibility
of Armageddon. Daniel confides in Laurie, explaining his fears: "It's this
war,[4] the feeling that it's unavoidable. It makes me feel so powerless ... so
impotent.... I can feel this anxiety, this terror bearing down" (1986–1987,
ch VIII, pp. 19–20). Later, Daniel is also revealed to be a fetishist, unable
to perform sexually while un-costumed. Following a particularly impas-
sioned moment aboard *Archimedes*,[5] Laurie asks, "Did the costumes make
it good?" to which Daniel replies, "I guess the costumes had something
to do with it. It just feels strange, you know? To come out and admit that
to somebody" (1986–1987, ch VII, p. 28).

Laurie is similarly flawed. Like Daniel, she gained her superhero identity second-hand, taking up the position of her mother, Sally Jupiter,[6]
following her retirement. Laurie's relationship with her mother is dysfunc-
tional. She sees her mother as having forced her into adopting her crime-
fighting alter-ego, which Laurie believes has been a waste of her time.
During a dinner engagement with Daniel, she explains: "I'm thirty-five and
what have I done? I've spent eight years in semi-retirement preceded by ten
years running round in a stupid costume because my stupid mother wanted
me to" (1986–1987, ch VII, p. 25). And later, when rebuking Daniel for what
he sees as his daydreaming, she explains, "At least you were living out your
own fantasies. I was living out my mother's" (1986–1987, ch VII, p. 7).

The Comedian, later revealed to be Edward Morgan Blake, is one of
the most violent of *Watchmen*'s protagonists. He is also highly cynical, a
facet of his personality that, like Rorschach, greatly informs both his madness and antiheroic identity, as will be discussed later in the chapter.
Despite his violent, cynical disposition, Blake is shown to be a highly vain
individual. This vanity is highlighted on two separate occasions: in the

first, he proceeds to beat Sally Jupiter, the former Silk Spectre, who is forced to defend herself after rejecting the Comedian's sexual advances; in the second incident, Blake is shown gunning down a women, who was pregnant with his child, because she had cut his face with a broken bottle. Just prior, Blake exclaims "My face ... what did you do, you bitch, you hurt my face" (1986–1987, ch II, p. 14). Much like Daniel, however, even the Comedian is depicted as feeling impotent when faced with external forces far beyond his control, as reflected through his conversation with Moloch[7]:

> When I started out, when I was a kid, cleanin' up the water-fronts, it was like, real easy. The world was tough, you just hadda' be tougher, right? Not anymore.... I thought I knew how it was, how the world was. But then I found out about this gag, this joke[8] [1986–1987, ch II, p. 23].

Essentially, the foundation of Moore's deconstruction of the superhero can be identified in his bridging the gap between the superhero and the human condition. The superheroes presented in *Watchmen* are thus revealed to be susceptible to vice, self-doubt, and frustration. What the narrative comes to suggest is that if superheroes were to exist, there would be no reason to think that, exposed to the same external pressures and social experiences, that their lives would be any less complicated or more glamorous than those of ordinary individuals. Toward the end of the narrative, even Ozymandias (Adrian Veidt), who clearly sees himself as being superior, both intellectually and morally, not only to everyday individuals, but also to his fellow superheroes, is shown during a rare moment of weakness, doubting his actions and seeking the confirmation of the only being more powerful than himself, Dr. Manhattan, whom he asks, "I did the right thing, didn't I?" (1986–1987, ch XII, p. 26).

Through his deconstruction, Moore also seeks to explore the psychology of the superhero. Unlike the confident, self-motivated superheroes of traditional comics, a number of the protagonists depicted in *Watchmen*, especially the Comedian and Rorschach, are characterized by mental instability, or more bluntly, madness. While this can be seen in conjunction with Moore's desire to present readers with a more realistic vision of the superhero, the madness by which these characters are affected inevitably informs their actions and thus contributes to their antiheroic identities.

Watchmen *and Madness*

Building on Woolf's theory of the mad antihero, this section argues that as well as the two modes of madness identified within Woolf's article, the protagonists of Moore's narrative are also afflicted by a third element, a madness derived from knowing, or having come to fully understand, the violent nature of the human condition. As will be shown, it is the madness manifest from this understanding that influences both the characters' actions and their antiheroic identity.

The relationship between madness, the antihero, and its presence within fiction is examined by Michael Woolf in "The Madman as Hero in Contemporary American Literature" (1976). Anticipating Brombert's argument regarding the appropriateness of the antihero as a symbol more in tune with modern social reality (1999, p. 2), Woolf stresses that the traditional hero is an "inappropriate concept in the context of contemporary culture" (1976, p. 257). Like Brombert, who argues that the "negative hero, perhaps more keenly than the traditional hero, challenges our assumptions" and raises the question "of how we see, or wish to see ourselves" (1999, p. 2), Woolf suggests that the antihero far more accurately embodies the problems, issues, and concerns present within contemporary society (1976, p. 257). According to Woolf, the traditional antihero (regarded as the *human* antihero in this study), depicts a more accurate representation of the human condition through its portrayal of individuals with "no special powers that distinguish [them] from others" and who remain unable "to act as a dynamic factor in the evolution of a given fictional system" (1976, p. 258). Woolf's statement is perhaps most appropriate in consideration of the protagonists depicted in *Watchmen*, none of whom (except for Dr. Manhattan and Ozymandias) have any special powers or have the capacity to radically change the situation by which they are confronted.

According to Woolf, both contemporary society and those depicted within fiction represent social realities no longer "hospitable" to the individual, having become devoid of all possible logic (1976, p. 257). As a result, the individual's capacity to effect change is reduced, if not removed completely, at both a personal and social level. The individual is inevitably revealed as powerless, "buffeted by forces too massive, too nightmarish" (1976, p. 257). This latter observation by Woolf is especially relevant in the case of Rorschach, a character all too aware of social reality's growing hostility, stating in his journal, "This city is dying of rabies" (1986–1987, p. 16). Rorschach is a character driven by his own internal motivation and a personal sense of justice. For Rorschach, there is no giving up, no compromise, "even in the face of Armageddon" (1986–1987, ch XII, p. 24). Nevertheless, even he, perhaps the most active of the superheroes depicted in the narrative, acknowledges the inevitable limitations of his actions when he questions, "Is the best I can do to wipe random flecks of foam from its lips?" (1986–1987, ch I, p. 16).

Rorschach's question is justified. Even Dr. Manhattan, whose ability to shape and destroy physical matter at will clearly identifies him as the most powerful protagonist depicted in *Watchmen*, is likewise pessimistic due to his inability to effect change in either his own reality or that which is shared with other individuals. This is expressed when he explains to Laurie that life and reality are predetermined, following a set of infinitely complex patterns, and that despite the existence of multiple, parallel realities, the future has already happened and thus will have always happened.[9] To Dr. Manhattan's mind, the future is unavoidable: "We're all puppets, Laurie. I'm just a puppet who can see the strings"[10] (1986–1987, ch X, p. 4).

Woolf identifies two distinct modes in which the mad antihero appears. The first is as the comical figure who jerks "powerlessly through a set of circumstances framed by pressures quite external to [them], beyond [their] control and perhaps, [their] understanding" (1976, p. 258). The second is the anguished figure. Often introverted in nature, these are representative of individuals crushed and rendered impotent when confronted with a consistently hostile reality or set of circumstances (1976, p. 258). More often than not, however, the antiheroes described by Woolf appear as a synthesis of the two, a figure moved and manipulated by forces beyond their comprehension whose experience within an inhospitable social reality evokes in the reader a sense of anguish that is indicative of their own experience and frustration.

Woolf's depiction of the comic figure is one that could easily be applied to each protagonist of Moore's narrative. Undeniably, the frustration derived from their positions and inability to effect change can be identified not only as a primary motivation governing their actions, but also how they are interpreted and understood by the reader. Rorschach, Nite Owl, and the Silk Spectre, for example, are all shown to navigate the complexity of the narrative's plot, oblivious to the fact that they are all mere pawns in Ozymandias's plan to destroy the city of New York, killing millions in the process, in an attempt to unite humanity under a single banner. Even Dr. Manhattan, in spite of his ability to see the events of his past and future, simultaneously, is blind to Ozymandias's plan.[11] Later, however, the limitations of Ozymandias's own perception are revealed when Dr. Manhattan tells him, "Nothing ever ends, Adrian. Nothing ever ends" (1986–1987, ch XII, p. 27). Dr. Manattan's final statement refers to his awareness that any unity or peace achieved by Ozymandias' plans will inevitably be undermined, either by the human condition's violent nature or by the public gaining knowledge of Adrian's involvement in the events surrounding the destruction of New York City. The latter is confirmed during the narrative's final panels, in which a journalist at "Pioneering Publishing" is shown receiving Rorschach's journal, containing a full account of his investigation into the murder of the Comedian (1986–1987, ch XII, p. 31). Further, the inevitability of Ozymandias's failure and the irony of his efforts are reflected through *Tales of the Black Freighter*, a graphic novel that is being read throughout the narrative by a young man, Bernie, who is shown sitting outside a newsstand. *Tales of the Black Freighter* focuses on a sailor who becomes marooned on a deserted island following the destruction of his ship by the Black Freighter, a phantom vessel which plays host to the souls of the damned. In a desperate effort to return home and warn his family of the Black Freighter's imminent arrival, the sailor uses the bloated, gas-filled bodies of his fellow crew to construct a craft. Upon his return, the sailor, believing his hometown to be under siege, kills a couple and disguises himself in the man's clothes. When he reaches his house, he kills a night watchman, but soon realizes he has just killed his own wife and that there had been no attack. He returns to the shore where he finds the Black Freighter waiting. He boards the ship, presumably to take his place among the damned.[12]

In spite of their intentions, both the sailor depicted in *Tales of the Black Freighter* and Ozymandias are ultimately damned as a result of their actions. The link between the sailor and Ozymandias is illustrated toward the end of the narrative. Here, following the destruction of New York and the completion of his plan, Ozymandias explains to Dr. Manhattan that he has made himself feel every death and at night he dreams about "swimming towards a hideous..." (ch. 12, ch XII, p. 27).

It is their limited perception and realization that, in spite of their best intentions, they are unable to effect change within their immediate environment that lend to the characters a sense of anguish or grief. As Moore states, this was perhaps one of the most significant facets of deconstruction employed in *Watchmen*, allowing much of the bravado and self-confidence often affiliated with the traditional superhero to be stripped away, revealing characters that were "sad and touching" (Iannucci, 2007).

For Woolf, much of the antihero's development is marked by a "theory of reality" wherein the terrors to which he is exposed and the events he suffers become indistinguishable from the tournament of his subconscious

(1976, p. 258). As a result, Woolf claims, actions, whether heroic, antiheroic, or otherwise, become devoid of meaning and the status of the individual "radically undermined" (1976, p. 259). Logic, too, becomes meaningless in the inhospitable social reality in which the antihero is manifest. It is precisely this environment, however, one of both inner and outer "horror" and pressure, in which antiheroic action and madness become united. If the individual is "radically undermined" and all action rendered meaningless or ineffectual due to the hostility of the social reality perceived, the individual has little choice but to conclude this to be a normal, if not entirely acceptable, state of affairs. As Woolf points out, however, it is only the "lunatics who defy the prevailing norms" (1976, p. 259). Through defiance, these characters come to represent "deranged activists" who ultimately refuse to accept the "inevitability of their powerlessness" (1976, p. 259).

Although Woolf's description of the cosmic and anguished figure can clearly be identified in many of the characters presented throughout the narrative, *Watchmen* also depicts a further manifestation of the mad antihero whose instability is not only derived from powerlessness, or anguish, but from having come to understand, or at least acknowledge, the savage, violent nature of the human condition. The antiheroic actions undertaken by the narrative's protagonists stem from their having gained a deeper insight into the human condition and their own individual inability to effect change. This form of madness is especially significant when examining the narrative's three primary protagonists, Rorschach, The Comedian, and Ozymandias.

Unlike a number of the superheroes depicted in *Watchmen*, who took to crime-fighting so as to further their own means and serve personal interests, Rorschach took up his mask in an attempt to make a difference and so that he might dish out his own brand of harsh, street-based justice. Rorschach's perception of the world is relatively simple: "There is good and there is evil, and evil must be punished" (1986–1987, ch IV, p. 24), a task which he takes upon himself. Rorschach, perhaps more so than other characters in the narrative, is representative of the traditional black-and-white moral mentality reflected by more conventional comic book superheroes such as Superman or Batman. Moore affirms this, explaining that Rorschach was primarily developed so as to explore the psychology of such characters and to see what a "Batman-type, driven, vengeance-fueled vigilante" would be like in the real world (2007). Ultimately, it is this alignment of vigilantism, violence, the superhero, and reality that determines and provides Rorschach his identity as an antihero.

As previously mentioned, Rorschach is fully aware of his limited ability to effect change, yet continues to hunt down criminals and punish them, often violently, as he sees fit. The task, as Rorschach acknowledges, is a large one as there are so many "deserving of retribution ... and there is so little time" (1986–1987, ch I, p. 24). As Jacob Held correctly observes, Rorschach is indicative of retributive justice taken to the extreme (Irwin and White, 2009, p. 20); according to Held, despite his overly violent approach, the reader identifies with Rorschach because all individuals believe to some extent in retributive justice and want to see "wrongs righted and wicked people suffering" (2009, p. 20). Drawing from Kant's *Groundwork for the Metaphysics of Morals* (1797), Held goes on to point out that retributive justice is philosophically flawed, not due simply to morality and ethics, but also to application (2009, p. 20). What this suggests is that Rorschach's perception of good and evil looks only beyond the self, blinding him to the immorality of his own actions. For Held, Rorschach's inability to judge his actions is reflected in the narrative, both philosophically and aesthetically: "If Rorschach had just a little humility, had recognized he might be wrong and others might be right, he might not be so fascinatingly ugly" (2009, p. 30). Alex Nuttall also sees Rorschach's actions as stemming from his own internal ignorance and his unwavering focus on justice[13] "or his sense of it, at least" (2009, p. 92).

Though Rorschach is an advocate for retributive justice and undeniably blind to his own wrongdoing, what both Held and Nuttall fail to acknowledge is the character's development, or more specifically, they fail to distinguish precisely where the individual Walter Joseph Kovacs ends and the vigilante Rorschach begins. The significance of this distinction is outlined during Kovacs's conversation with psychiatrist Dr. Malcolm Long, following his arrest for the suspected murder of Moloch.[14] Essentially, he explains that he had not always been Rorschach, just "Kovacs pretending to be Rorschach" (1986–1987, ch VI, p. 14). Like so many of his peers, whom he perceives as "soft," all Kovacs could have been was "a man in a costume" which is "not Rorschach. Not Rorschach at all" (1986–1987, p. 15).

Kovacs's transformation into Rorschach had been a gradual one, driven by perspective and experience. As he goes on to explain, his treatment of criminals had not always been so extreme, so violent: he had been "very naïve, very young. Very soft ... soft on scum. Too young to know any better. Molly-coddled them. Let them live" (1986–1987, ch VI, p. 14). Kovacs' transformation is ultimately instigated by the simultaneous acquisition of madness and knowledge, or perhaps more accurately, the gaining of knowledge so overbearing as to send him insane. The culmination of his transformation, as he explains to Dr. Long, occurred during his investigation into the disappearance and suspected kidnapping of "Blair Roche. Six years old" (1986–1987, ch VI, p. 18). Following leads to an abandoned dressmaker's facility in Brooklyn, Kovacs finds two dogs fighting over a "knob of bone" (1986–1987, ch VI, p. 18) which he later identifies as the remains of Blair Roche. Kovacs enters the disused facility and finds a meat-cleaver, which he uses to slaughter the dogs. He explains that with the first strike, "a jet of warmth spattered on chest ... it was Kovacs who said 'mother' then, muffled under latex. It was Kovacs who closed his eyes. It was Rorschach who opened them again" (1986–1987, ch VI, p. 21). When the kidnapper returns, Rorschach beats him, handcuffs him to a boiler pipe and spreads kerosene through the facility. He indicates a hacksaw which he has left within easy reach of the kidnapper before striking a match and igniting the kerosene on his way out (1986–1987, ch VI, pp. 22–25).

During his investigation into the disappearance of Blair Roche and the discovery of her fate, Rorschach recognizes that "we are alone. Live our lives, lacking anything better to do ... born from oblivion; bear children, hell-bound as ourselves; go into oblivion. There is nothing else" (1986–1987, p. 27). This acquisition of knowledge, for Rorschach, obliterates any possibility of the divine. What Rorschach thus discovers is that social reality is ultimately devoid of any significance, other than what the individual chooses to impose. There can be no grand scheme, nor any possibility of abstract concepts such as fate; both action and reaction are products of the human condition, individuals and the choices they make. In conclusion, he tells Dr. Long: "This rudderless world is not shaped by vague metaphysical forces. It is not God who kills children. Not fate that butchers them or destiny that feeds them to the dogs. It's us. Only us" (1986–1987, p. 26). This realization, Rorschach concludes, simply turned his previous "illusions to ice, shattering them" but in the process, he was reborn, "free to scrawl design on ... [a] morally blank world" (1986–1987, ch VI, p. 26). For Rorschach, violence is the only logical response to the immorality by which he is confronted. His actions are not a choice, but a necessity. When Dr. Long points out that his actions are illegal, Rorschach explains, "We do not do this thing because it is permitted. We do it because we have to. We do it because we are compelled" (1986–1987, ch VI, p. 15). Rorschach's antiheroic identity thus stems, not only from the immorality of his actions, but largely from the reader's ability to identify—perhaps as a result of his enforcement of retributive justice—with him as a character.

Walter Kovacs and Rorschach are two entirely different entities. The gulf by which the two are separated is illustrated through Dr. Long's notes, which contain an essay written by Kovacs, age eleven. In the essay, titled "My Parents," Kovacs expresses his admiration for President Truman for having made the decision to bomb Hiroshima and Nagasaki:

> I like President Truman, the way my dad would have wanted me to. He dropped the atom bomb on Japan and saved millions of lives because if he hadn't of, then there would have been a lot more war than there was and more people would have been killed. I think it was a good thing to drop the atomic bomb on Japan [1986–1987, p. III].

In this, Kovacs sees the death of the few in order to save the many as a positive strategy and worthy of admiration. Toward the end of the narrative, following the discovery and accomplishment of Ozymandias' plot to destroy a large portion of New York city in order to unite the world's nations and prevent nuclear holocaust, the present superheroes (Nite Owl, Silk Spectre, Rorschach, and Dr. Manhattan) are requested to keep Ozymandias' secret, knowing that if the truth were to be revealed, the possibility of peace would vanish. Unsurprisingly, Rorschach is the only one to reject Ozymandias' offer, steadfast in his belief that murder cannot be justified: "Not even in the face of Armageddon. Never compromise" (1986–1987, ch XII, p. 20). Determined to reveal the truth, believing that "people must be told" (1986–1987, ch XII, p. 23), irrespective of the consequences, Rorschach leaves Ozymandias's base of operation, but is soon confronted and killed by Dr. Manhattan. Rorschach dies for his belief, unwilling to acknowledge that the murder of innocent people might be acceptable or justified. This reveals the separation between Walter Kovacs and the masked hero known as Rorschach and illustrates the impact of his madness; madness, it should be pointed out, that he acquired from having come to understand the true nature of the human condition and the limitations imposed upon his actions as an individual. In sum, Rorschach dies as the result of his condemnation of Ozymandias' actions, which, by comparison, can be interpreted as being the same as those of President Truman which Kovacs condoned.

The Comedian, or Eddie Blake, much like Rorschach, is another violent, immoral superhero whose madness is derived from his unique understanding of both the world and other individuals. The atrocities committed by the Comedian throughout the narrative are numerous. After his sexual advances are rejected, he beats and attempts to rape Sally Juspeczyk (1986–1987, ch II, pp. 6–7); he guns down a young Vietnamese woman who is pregnant with his child (1986–1987, ch II, p. 15); during a riot, he takes his shotgun to the crowd, killing one man for defacing a wall (1986–1987, p. 16).

As the narrative begins with the character's death, the Comedian is described and discussed through *Watchmen's* other characters, who provide a vivid testament to his madness. In *Under the Hood,*[15] Hollis Mason (the first Nite Owl) describes the Comedian as a "disgrace to our profession," explaining that while he acknowledges the Comedian's effort in the war and his attempt to make a name for himself, all he can think about "is the bruises along Sally Jupiter's ribcage and hope to God that America can find itself a better class of hero than *that*" (1986–1987, p. 10). Following Blake's funeral, Rorschach contemplates the ideology expressed by the Comedian during his life:

> The future is bearing down like an express train. Blake understood. Treated it like a joke ... he saw the cracks in society and saw the little men in masks trying to hold it together. He saw the true face of the twentieth century and chose to become a reflection, a parody of it. No one else saw the joke. That's why he was lonely [1986–1987, ch II, pp. 26–27].

Dr. Manhattan gives a similar though more poignant description of the Comedian, whom he met in Vietnam:

> I'm in Saigon, being reintroduced to Edward Blake.... Blake is interesting. I have never met anyone so deliberately amoral. He suits the climate here; the madness, the pointless butchery. As I come to understand Vietnam and what it implies about the human condition, I also realize that few humans will permit themselves such an understanding. Blake's different. He understands perfectly ... and he doesn't care [1986–1987, ch II, p. 19].

Much like Rorschach, the Comedian's madness is largely derived from his understanding of the violent nature of the human condition and in acknowledgment of his own limited capacity to effect change at either an individual or social level. Where the madness possessed by Rorschach lead to the creation of an unkempt, violent sociopath of few words, the Comedian's madness comes to be expressed through his often patronizing, world-weary cynicism.

The Comedian's perspective, however, affects everyone around him, even Ozymandias. This is revealed during a meeting organized by Ozymandias in an attempt to coordinate the new generation of masked superheroes into a group, similar to the Minute Men who were their predecessors. The Comedian, however, openly challenges Ozymandias' logic about the formation of such a group, describing the idea as "bullshit" and accusing

Ozymandias of "getting old" yet still wanting to play "cowboys and Indians" (1986–1987, ch II, p. 10). Unwilling to accept this, Ozymandias argues that "it doesn't require a genius to see that America has problems that need tackling" (1986–1987, ch II, p. 10). In his characteristically cynical fashion, the Comedian explains that while it doesn't take a genius to see America has issues, "it takes a moron to think they're small enough for clowns like you guys to handle" (1986–1987, ch II, p. 10). Ironically, it is the Comedian's madness that inspires Ozymandias's own madness and the formation of his plan to destroy New York City.

As illustrated, while many of the characters in *Watchmen* reflect Woolf's conception of both the cosmic and anguished figure, the narrative also offers an alternative depiction of the mad antihero, one whose ideology and actions are ultimately derived from their insight and understanding of the human condition. For Walter Kovacs, the resulting madness drives him to become the violent vigilante Rorschach. The Comedian, however, as Rorschach notes, "saw the true face of the twentieth century and chose to become a reflection, a parody of it" (1986–1987, p. 27), while Ozymandias, afflicted with the madness derived from the Comedian, focuses his efforts in a plot that would ultimately destroy New York City, killing millions of people, yet paradoxically ushering in a new era of peace. Similar to V, the protagonist of Moore's and Lloyd's *V for Vendetta* (1982–1989), Rorschach, the Comedian, and Ozymandias each represents a natural response to the reality in which they exist and the social, cultural, and political issues with which they are confronted.

Super Transhumans

Despite subverting traditional superhero conventions, the protagonists in *Watchmen* still possess powers and abilities far beyond those acquirable by everyday individuals. For the most part, however, these skill sets might appear, when compared to other protagonists examined throughout this study, largely mundane. Most of the characters, including the second Nite Owl and Silk Spectre, the Comedian, Rorschach, and Ozymandias, demonstrate feats of super strength and agility. However, these have been gained simply through training, which has enabled each to become physically superior to everyday individuals, especially in hand-to-hand combat. In this respect the characters of *Watchmen* may *seem* to reflect a sense of the transhuman, but it is important to realize that it is only Ozymandias and Dr. Manhattan who actually *are* transhuman.

Adrian Veidt, or Ozymandias, is credited with being the world's smartest individual (1986–1987, p. 18). Though born into wealth, Adrian gave away his fortune, only to return as a self-made billionaire some years later. With the exception of his superior intellect, however, Ozymandias' abilities are nothing more than the result of intense personal training. So extreme is the impact of this training that, toward the end of the novel, he is revealed to have the speed and agility to catch a bullet (1986–1987, p. 16). However, it is Ozymandias' combined intellect and fortune that provide him with the capacity to destroy New York City in an attempt to unite the world through a common goal. Logic should clearly indicate that the murder of millions of innocent people, for whatever cause, is demonstrably wrong, if not evil. Even Kant's implementation of the categorical imperative, outlined in the *Groundwork of the Metaphysic and Morals* (1785), would identify Ozymandias' plot as immoral because: (1) Ozymandias is human and thus has an obligation to avoid intentionally inflicting pain or suffering on other individuals, and (2) a morally correct action is one which acknowledges other individuals as ends, within themselves, and not as means. As a result of his intellect, training, and resources, Ozymandias has transcended many of the limitations imposed upon the human condition. As a transhuman, however, Ozymandias' capacity to effect change is, though greater than many of the other characters depicted throughout the narrative, still limited, thus calling into question whether or not he is bound by the same moral and social conventions as other individuals. This is a question of special significance in the context of Dr. Manhattan, a being so powerful that even Ozymandias, in spite of his intellect and wealth, appears pitiful by comparison.

Born Jon Osterman, Dr. Manhattan was created following a lab accident involving an Intrinsic Field Chamber, during which Osterman's physical body was deconstructed at a sub-atomic level (1986–1987, ch V, p. 8). Weeks later, having mastered the ability to reassemble his atomic structure, Osterman reappears as Dr. Manhattan, a being with the capacity to alter his physical appearance, teleport, deconstruct physical matter at will, and perceive multiple time streams simultaneously. For him, the present, past, and future collapse upon themselves, forming a simultaneous stream in which all things have a prefixed destination, an unavoidable, inevitable form: "Things have their own shape in time, not space alone. Some marble blocks have statues within them, embedded within their future" (1986–1987, ch VI, p. 24). During his time on Mars, Dr. Manhattan explains to the Silk Spectre that there is "no future. There is no past ... time is simultaneous"

(1986–1987, p. 6). Existing outside time, however, Dr. Manhattan remains stationary, unchanged, while everything else stays in motion, rushing toward an unknowable, yet predestined, conclusion.

Much like V, Dr. Manhattan is a complex, multifaceted character. As with the monster of Shelley's *Frankenstein* (1818), Dr. Manhattan can be interpreted as a metaphor representative of both the negative and positive ramifications of technoscientific progress. As a being formed of pure atomic energy, Dr. Manhattan is on one hand a clear warning concerning the creation of nuclear weaponry and the militarization of applied science[16]; on the other hand, he is also representative of the potential benefits derived from the progress of science and technology: "The technology Dr. Manhattan has made possible has changed the way we think about our clothes, our food, our travel. We drive in electric cars and travel in leisure and comfort" (1986–1987, p. III). Even these positive remarks, however, are overshadowed by a sense of foreboding:

> Our entire culture has contorted itself to accommodate the presence of something more than human, and we have all felt the results of this. The evidence surrounds us.... One single being has been allowed to change the entire world, pushing it closer to its eventual destruction in the process. The gods now walk amongst us, affecting every man, woman and child on the planet in a direct way rather than through mythology and the reassurances of faith. The safety of the whole world rests in the hands of a being far beyond what we understand to be human. We are all of us living in the shadow of Dr. Manhattan [1986–1987, p. III].

Essentially, Dr. Manhattan offers new insight into the potential consequences regarding the existence of individuals who have somehow, whether biologically or through the use of science and technology, transcended the human condition. What is most interesting, however, is society's reaction to Dr. Manhattan's existence. Many, as the latter quote illustrates, fear his power and hold in trepidation the changes he will inevitably make. Others, however, such as *Watchmen*'s fictional President Nixon, who asks Dr. Manhattan to "intervene in Vietnam" see his power as a potential weapon to be exploited and used toward their own ends (1986–1987, p. 19). Two months following his arrival, "the Vietcong are expected to surrender within the week" (1986–1987, ch II, p. 20). As Dr. Manhattan explains, many of the individuals composing the forces against which he fought hold him in almost sacred awe: "Often, they ask to surrender to me personally, their terror of me balanced by an almost religious awe" (1986–1987, p. 20). So great is his power, and so incomprehensible his presence, he is even exempt from political policy and the law. In 1977, for instance, the American government approves the Keene act, banning "vigilantism," thus returning judicial law to its state prior to its amendment, which accommodated "strategically useful talents" years earlier (1986–1987, p. 28). However, aware of his own significance, Dr. Manhattan explains "they can hardly outlaw me when their country's defense rests in my hands" (1986–1987, p. 23). With such power, however, the question must inevitably be asked: Could such a being be expected to adhere to social and moral conventions or to abide by judicial law?

Through a close reading of *Watchmen* and the role Dr. Manhattan plays throughout the narrative, the answer to the question is clearly a resounding no. Not only has Dr. Manhattan transcended the physical and intellectual limitations imposed upon the human condition, he has broken free of the very bonds placed upon all living things by time and corporeal existence. To this end, Dr. Manhattan is no longer human. He is a transhuman, perhaps one that has reached its logical developmental conclusion. Essentially, Jon Osterman did not die and suddenly become the being Dr. Manhattan. Rather, the accident that cost Osterman his life was simply the origin of Dr. Manhattan's development to a fully realized transhuman, if not posthuman state of being. In the novel, this is reflected through a process of dehumanization, through which Dr. Manhattan is shown to slowly but surely lose both his connection to and interest in humanity.

The most obvious aspect of his dehumanization is revealed aesthetically. In 1960, as Dr. Manhattan is starting to accept that he "shall never feel cold or warm again" (1986–1987, ch IV, p. 12) he is shown wearing a costume that covers his entire body, with the exception of his hands and face. His costume is reduced in 1964, where he is shown wearing an outfit not unlike wrestler's tights, leaving his arms, legs, and part of his chest exposed (1986–1987, ch IV, p. 17). Two years later, during his participation in Saigon, his costume is reduced further, now little more than black briefs (1986–1987, ch IV, p. 20). By 1980, Dr. Manhattan has forgone his costume altogether, unashamed of his nakedness (1986–1987, ch IV, p. 24). His disconnection from social and moral convention is similarly displayed. In 1960, Dr. Manhattan is shown deconstructing a living person who had pulled a gun in a crowded club. In the caption, he explains, "The newspapers call me a crime fighter, so the Pentagon says I must fight crime ... the morality of my activities escapes me" (1986–1987, ch IV, p. 14). When approached by Rorschach during his investigation into the death of the Comedian, Dr. Manhattan reflects a lack of interest: "A live body and a dead body contain the same number of particles ... life and death are unquantifiable abstracts. Why should I be concerned?" (1986–1987, ch I, p. 21). Further, during his time in Saigon, Dr. Manhattan watches as the Comedian pulls a gun and fires upon a young woman pregnant with the latter's child. Afterward, Dr. Manhattan's only comment is observational, rather than emotional: "She was pregnant and you gunned her down" (1986–1987, ch II, p. 15). The Comedian, however, aware of the latter's growing disconnection, retorts: "You coulda changed the gun into steam or the bullets into mercury or the bottle into snowflakes ... but you didn't lift a finger! You don't give a damn about human beings ... you never cared ... you're driftin' outta touch, Doc. You're turnin' into a flake. God help us all" (1986–1987, ch II, p. 15).

When he is left by love interest Laurie, the second Silk Spectre, and the pressure of life amongst everyday individuals becomes too much, he transports himself to Mars, explaining to the reader: "I am tired of this world; these people. I am tired of being caught in the tangle of their lives" (1986–1987, p. 24). While he is immune to death or the slow decay of time, human social reality, to Dr. Manhattan, is simply chaos, "a clock without a craftsman" (1986–1987, ch IV, p. 28). Irrespective of any action he might take, fate is predetermined. For humanity, "It's too late, always has been, always will be too late" (1986–1987, ch IV, p. 28). Dr. Manhattan has the capacity to read atoms, to see the "ancient spectacle governing all things, next to which, human life is brief and mundane" (1986–1987, ch XI, p. 17). When approached by Laurie, his former lover, who asks him to save the world, he explains: "I said often that you were my only link, my only concern with the world.... Don't you see the futility of asking me to save a world that I no longer have any stake in?" (1986–1987, ch XI, p. 8). This is perhaps the most effective example of Dr. Manhattan's antiheroic nature. Despite his capacity to effect change and his identity as a superhero, Dr. Manhattan sees individuals as relatively unimportant. Toward the end of the novel, following his conflict with Ozymandias, who had attempted to destroy Dr. Manhattan by deconstructing him at a molecular level, the latter clearly advocates his nonhuman status when he explains:

> Restructuring myself was the first trick I learned ... did you think it would kill me? I've walked across the face of the sun and seen events so tiny and so fast they hardly can be said to have occurred at all, but you are a man ... and this world's smartest man means no more to me than does its smartest termite [1986–1987, p. 18].

In referring to Ozymandias as just "a man" not more important that the world's "smartest termite" (1986–1987, ch XII, p. 18) Dr. Manhattan rejects his own human identity. The most significant facet of Dr. Manhattan's dehumanization, however, is evident in his name, or more specifically, lack thereof. Nite Owl, for instance, when he removes his mask, is Daniel Dreiberg; even Rorschach has the option to live as Walter Kovacs. Dr. Manhattan, however, having fully transcended the human condition, can live only as Dr. Manhattan. His original identity, Jon Osterman, died in 1959. With only the identity given to him by his handlers, Dr. Manhattan, as a dehumanized being, shares an affinity with the monster of Shelley's *Frankenstein* (1818). As Graham points out, lacking a formal identity, the monster of Shelley's narrative "is placed in an objectified role, as the object of external power" (2002, p. 69). Whereas Victor's monster was objectified as an abomination, a transgression against the natural order, Dr. Manhattan is objectified as a living weapon,[17] a reflection of the potential militaristic power of science and technology. Whether objectified as abomination or living weapon, both the monster of Shelley's *Frankenstein* and Dr. Manhattan of Moore and Gibbons's *Watchmen* lack formal identity, their symbolic value thus being determined by the individuals composing the human social reality against which they are juxtaposed.

Toward the end of the narrative, it is revealed that only Dr. Manhattan has the capacity to save the world and prevent a nuclear holocaust. At this point, the question is inevitably asked: Is Dr. Manhattan morally obligated to intervene and prevent the destruction of the world? According to Christopher Robichaud, the answer is yes (2009). Intoning what is perhaps one of the comic-book industry's most well-known clichés, "With great power comes great responsibility,"[18] Robichaud suggests that neither his superior intellect nor power over individuals is enough to negate Dr. Manhattan's moral obligation to individuals and social reality as a whole (2009, pp. 11–12). To support his claim, Robichaud compares Dr. Manhattan to well-known physicist Steven Hawking, arguing that despite Hawking's knowledge of quantum theory, he does not see humans as being "morally on par with rubble" (2009, p. 7), as does Dr. Manhattan. Further, he argues that many individuals have power over others, such as a parent's power over their children, but do not identify them as being "morally insignificant" (2009, p. 7). What Robichaud's argument overlooks, however, is the notion of dependence and capacity. While Steven Hawking is the leading authority in the field of theoretical physics, it is difficult to ignore the fact that he is also confined to a wheelchair and almost completely dependent on the intervention of human agency to ensure his continued health and well-being. Though Hawking possesses knowledge of subatomic matter, he is unable to manipulate it at will. Hawking also lacks the ability to instantly teleport himself to any destination he chooses, or to walk across the face of the sun, as Dr. Manhattan claims to have done during his confrontation with Ozymandias (ch. XII, p. 18). And while it is true that parents hold an authoritative power over their children, as a general rule, they are unable to deconstruct them at a subatomic level. Essentially, Dr. Manhattan has power and freedom incomprehensible to the individual.

Robichaud draws on Kant's notion of the "Categorical Imperative" outlined in *The Groundwork of the Metaphysics of Morals* (1785) to support his argument. Even this seemingly rational defense, however, is inherently flawed. Irrespective of his power, intelligence, and dehumanization, Robichaud claims Dr. Manhattan is nevertheless "subject to the very same moral mandates, permissions, and restrictions that the rest of us are subject to. Put succinctly, Dr. Manhattan has an obligation to do the right thing" (2009, pp. 10–11). In conclusion, Robichaud stipulates "it's just a brute fact, admitting of no further explanation, that beings like Dr. Manhattan ought to do the right thing and avoid doing the wrong thing, period" (2009, p. 13). Kant's notion of the categorical imperative, however, concerns only autonomous agents. For Kant, this was a self-conscious being with (impure) freedom of choice:

> That which can be determined only by inclination (sensible impulse, stimulus) would be animal choice (arbitrium brutum). Human choice, however, is a choice that can indeed be affected but not determined by impulses, and is therefore of itself (apart from an acquired proficiency of reason) not pure but can still be determined to actions by pure will [1996, p. 13].

If Dr. Manhattan's perception of time, however, is to be accepted, it is to acknowledge that all actions, whether moral, immoral, or otherwise, are predetermined, thus undermining the very principle of free will upon which Kant's theory is based. Further, as previously illustrated, Dr. Manhattan is something far removed from the human condition. It would be unreasonable to assume or even to expect that a being no longer recognizably human, or so far removed from what individuals consider to be the human condition as to be rendered incomprehensible, should conform to moral and social conventions. Barbra Hudson, for example, explains that individuals are confronted with offences and offenders, within their own "geo-political communities," that cannot be understood and thus goes on to question that if they cannot be understood, how it is possible to pass judgment or expectations upon them (2009, p. 237). This notion, however, could be extended to include all of the protagonists depicted in *Watchmen*, whose unique madness and experience within a hostile social reality not only informs their antiheroic identities, but comes to reflect something monstrous, perhaps unknowable to the everyday individual.[19]

Ultimately, Dr. Manhattan no longer recognizes himself as human and has thus transcended not only the human condition, but also what other individuals consider moral and social convention. The ramifications are largely unknowable. Some critics, such as Annas, Andrews, and Isasi, for example, paint a rather bleak picture regarding potential relations between existing individuals and trans- or even posthumans, arguing that it is probable that beings who have transcended the human condition will "likely view the old 'normal' humans as inferior, even savages, and fit for slavery or slaughter" (2002, p. 162). Taking this into consideration, *Watchmen*, then, gives a fairly neutral account of human/transhuman relations when, toward the narrative's conclusion, Dr. Manhattan tells Ozymandias that, yes, he understands and accepts the significance of his plan "without condoning or condemning," but "human affairs" are no longer his concern, as he would be "leaving this galaxy for one less complicated" (1986–1987, ch XII, p. 27).

Through the deconstruction of traditional comic-book conventions, Alan Moore and Dave Gibbons's *Watchmen* (1986–1987), anticipating Victor Brombert's claims regarding the effectiveness of the negative or anti-hero in reflecting a more accurate portrayal of the human condition (1999, p. 3), presents the reader with a more realistic account of the superhero. Essentially, Moore's deconstruction of the superhero takes place upon multiple levels. The most obvious facet of Moore's deconstruction takes place upon the aesthetic level. Far from the embodiments of physical perfection apparent in their forebears, Moore's protagonists are revealed to look and appear just like everybody else. At a deeper level, however, the deconstruction apparent within *Watchmen* aligns the superhero with the human condition so as to explore a number of social and moral issues. In this, *Watchmen* inevitably comes to explore the psychology of the superhero. Unlike other comic-book superheroes, however, Moore's protagonists are marked by a level of mental instability. Although both the comic and anguished figure identified by Woolf in "The Madman as Hero in Contemporary American Fiction" (1976) can be seen within the narrative, many of its characters express a third kind of madness: a madness derived from deeper insight into the human condition and its violent, savage, often perverse nature. Coupled with their own personal reasons for taking up their masks, it is this madness of knowing that ultimately informs many of the protagonists' antiheroic identities.

Though subverted, the protagonists of Watchmen are superheroes nevertheless. This allows for a unique insight into the potential consequences resulting from the existence of trans- or even posthuman beings. As illustrated, this insight is especially apparent in context to Ozymandias and Dr. Manhattan, who both have had a profound impact upon the social realities in which they exist. Despite his identity as the world's most intelligent individual and his accumulated wealth, Ozymandias is nevertheless bound to the same moral and social conventions as everyday individuals. Dr. Manhattan, on the other hand, as a being which has so transcended the human condition as to be rendered incomprehensible, is shown not only to have freed himself of the limitations imposed by time, space, and corporeality, but of humanity itself; he has successfully disposed of his moral and social obligations. The possible implications of this remove, however, remain an area of contest, yet one which will be explored in greater detail throughout the following chapters.

FIVE

Cyberpunk

This chapter examines the development of the cyborg through the cyberpunk subgenre and explores the emergence of paradoxical antiheroes from the integration between biology and technology. As will be demonstrated, cyborg characters and the social realities they inhabit have been largely influenced by the punk-rock subculture of the 1970s, which shapes the physical appearance of the characters (from fashion to body modification and augmentation), determines the social realities in which they are depicted, and is reflected in the ideological foundation underpinning the narrative (manifest as an anarchic philosophy advocating anti-establishment and the rejection of normative social values).

Cyberpunk

Despite its relatively small body of content—little more than a hundred novels and several hundred short stories, most of which can now be found in cyberpunk anthologies such as *Mirrorshades* (Stirling, 1988) and *The Ultimate Cyberpunk* (Cadigan, 2003)—when compared to other genres of science fiction, cyberpunk has had a significant impact on the development of contemporary science fiction and, as this chapter will demonstrate, the paradoxical protagonist.

With a desire to distance itself from the exploratory or "explosive" science fiction of previous decades (the Gernsback era), which frequently spoke of human-kind's adventures upon exotic worlds, victory over galactic aggressors and their conquest of the stars, cyberpunk turned its attention to inner space, exploring instead the metaphysical spaces made possible through the advent of virtual reality, or cyberspace. One of cyberpunk's most defining attributes is its depiction of media-saturated social reality which, for many critics, consolidated cyberpunk's relationship with postmodernism. This is primarily due to Jean Baudrillard's *Simulacra and Simulation*[1] (1981) which discusses the notion of a self-perpetuating alternative reality derived from simulation. According to Jonathan Epstein, cyberpunk's success is primarily due to the "plausibility with which the genre portrays the near future" and that the worlds envisioned by authors such as Gibson and Effinger "are essentially extrapolations of the late twentieth century world their readers inhabit" (1998, p. 232).

Concerned with issues relevant to the philosophical climate of the 1980s (including disembodiment, deconstruction, identity, metaphysics, and the potential social impact of computer-based technology), cyberpunk, for critics including Jameson, McHale, and Suvin, came to be synonymous with the concept of postmodernism, or perhaps more accurately, with the postmodern condition as defined by Jean-François Lyotard in his publication of the same name. The inherent relationship between postmodernism and cyberpunk was perhaps most effectively expressed by Fredrick Jameson, who regrets having been unable to include a cyberpunk chapter in *Postmodernism or the Cultural Logic of Late Capitalism*, describing the genre as the supreme literary expression "if not of postmodernism, then of late capitalism itself" (1991, p. 417). Expanding on Jameson's comments regarding the relationship between fiction and philosophy, Brian McHale writes that cyberpunk or science fiction, in general, is to "postmodernism what detective fiction was to modernism: it is the ontological genre par excellence (as the detective story is the epistemological par excellence)" (1987, p. 16). Taking this into consideration, it is perhaps little wonder that cyberpunk should have gained such attention. If all science fiction is a "literature of cognitive estrangement" as Darko Suvin suggests (1979, pp. 7–8), then it is perhaps not unreasonable to claim that cyberpunk, in responding to the ideological stance of postmodernism and the crisis of an increasingly technological age, has come to represent a literature not only of "cognitive estrangement" but of physical, metaphysical, and moral ambiguity, a literature in which, for the first time, the crimes of the body are separated from those of the mind.

As previously mentioned, the influence of the punk-rock counterculture[2] upon cyberpunk can be perceived upon an aesthetic and ideological level. The aesthetic of punk, specifically in the context of fashion, was typified by tartan trousers, animal-print, "black, straight-leg pants ... and torn T-shirts held together with safety pins," black leather jackets, studded and emblazoned with graffiti, spiky hair, and mohawks[3] (Hannon,

2009, p. 49). Such a description, however, is somewhat reductive, as the punk subculture denotes more than a music subgenre or a specific, albeit eclectic, fashion sense. As Hannon points out, punk is also affiliated with a resistance to mainstream culture and rebellion against "conformity ... and society at large" (2009, p. 2). The anti-conformist stance adopted by punk was driven by an anarchic ideology.

Subculture theorist Raymond Calluori argues that punk subculture is characterized by "senseless violence, masochism, bondage, anarchy, and nihilism" (1985, p. 53). The relationship between the punk subculture and anarchy is further supported by Craig O'Hara, who points out that punks are, perhaps with the exception of Skin Heads, ideologically, politically, and philosophically anarchists (1995, p. 56). The anarchic ideology to which the punk subculture subscribes is not one founded on a notion of lawlessness, but rather one devoid of leaders. According to O'Hara, an anarchic society requires cooperation within the community and for "individuals to behave responsibly" (2009, p. 78). As mentioned in Chapter Three's examination of Moore and Lloyd's *V for Vendetta*, the ideological foundation of anarchy, as a philosophy, can be identified as an important facet in contributing to the development of the antihero within speculative fiction.

Cyberpunk Aesthetics

The punk-inspired aesthetic depicted within cyberpunk denote the counterculture's most obvious contribution to the subgenre. This contribution can be identified upon two separate, albeit linked, levels. On one level, it informs the appearance of the characters themselves, which is especially important in relation to cyberpunk's contribution to the notion of the cyborg. On the other, however, the punk aesthetic determines the appearance of the social reality depicted throughout the narrative. As shown through the discussion of *V for Vendetta*, the narrative's social reality is especially important in relation to the antihero because it has the capacity to position readers to accept, though not necessarily condone, actions or perspectives they would otherwise condemn.

Anarchy can be interpreted as the foundation of punk, informing every facet of the counterculture, including its aesthetics. The notion of an anarchic aesthetic is clearly visible within the social realities depicted throughout cyberpunk. In William Gibson's *Neuromancer*, a sense of anarchic urbanism clearly prevails over the presented social reality:

> Now he slept in the cheapest coffins, the ones nearest the port, beneath the quartz-halogen floods that lit the docks all night like vast stages, where you couldn't see the lights of Tokyo for the glare of the television sky, not even the towering hologram of the Fuji electric company, and Tokyo Bay was a black expanse where gulls wheeled above drifting shoals of white Styrofoam [1984, p. 13].

This sense of extreme, anarchic urbanism is synonymous with both punk and cyberpunk. The noisy, crowded streets of inner-city night-life provide the foundation and mood for the narrative and provide a sense of the social reality in which the protagonist exists. In *Metrophage* (1988), Richard Kadrey expertly conveys this mood through the "nervous glare of neon signs and halogen street lamps" that "domed Sunset in a pulsing nimbus of come-on colors" (1988, p. 4). The cityscape presented in cyberpunk, however, is almost always in a state of decay, often alluding to some unknown ecological or environmental catastrophe. As Claire Sponsler points out in "Beyond the Ruins," the realities depicted within cyberpunk often look highly similar to the setting of any post-disaster story: "Blighted, rubble-strewn, broken-down cityscapes; vast terrains of decay, bleakness, and the detritus of civilization; and the nearly complete absence of a benign or beautiful nature" (1993, p. 253). This resonates within the now famous opening passage of Gibson's *Neuromancer*: "The sky above the port was the color of television, tuned to a dead channel" (1984, p. 9). Mingolla, the protagonist of Lucius Shepard's *Life During Wartime* (1987), describes the corridors of his hotel as "stinking of urine and disinfectant" where a "drunken Indian man with his fly unzipped and a bloody mouth" pounds away at a door (1987, p. 24). In *Snow Crash* (1992), Neal Stephenson offers a more individual, though equally urbanized perspective through the protagonist, Hiro Protagonist, who describes his residence as:

> a spacious 20-by-30 in a U-Stor-It in Inglewood California. The room has a concrete slab floor, corrugated iron walls separating it from neighbouring units and—this is a mark of distinction and luxury—a roll-up steel door that faces north-west, giving them a few red rays at times like this, when the sun is setting over LAX [1992, p. 18].

Much like the characters themselves, the urban environments depicted within cyberpunk exist at a metaphorical junction between what is real and unreal, natural and unnatural, biological and technological. In drawing parallels between the body and the urban environment, Dani Cavallaro elaborates upon this concept: "Like the biological, erotic body, the body of the cybercity combines materiality and immateriality. Digital technology tends to ideate the city in immaterial terms as an abstract map or network of computer processed data" (2000, p. 133). For Sabine Heuser, the junk and refuse that clutter the cityscapes parallel the body of the cyborg, both equally natural and unnatural (2003, p. 33).

As the punk movement was one primarily related to the working social class, depictions of urbanism, the cityscape, and "street living" evoke a sense of community amongst members and reflect the subculture's origins and ethos. Within cyberpunk, however, similar depictions of extreme urbanism are used to illustrate a social reality stretched to its limits, where notions of community have been stripped away. Environmental catastrophes reflect the grim, yet all too real potential ramifications of an increasing population driven by a post-industrial capitalist society. Drugs, violence, theft, and vice are prolific. Though the police and other law-enforcement agencies are active, their numbers are limited and their ability to enforce the law dramatically undermined. Governmental bodies, when present, have been sidelined, their power and influence gone to feeding the growing corporate entities and international conglomerates that form a new ruling class.

The social realities depicted within cyberpunk are often openly hostile, the only law seemingly that of survival. Sharon O'Toole argues in *Cyberpunk Visions* that such realities draw on a theme of "scrap culture— of making do" that parallels the punk subculture's "DIY" ethos and reinforces cyberpunk's representation of society surviving on the "coattails and table droppings of a quickly moving transnational corporate culture" (2004, p. 131). Survival, however, as Michael Woolf points out in "The Madman as Hero in Contemporary American Fiction," is seldom a heroic objective (p. 261). In this, cyberpunk's urbanism, influenced visually and ideologically by the aesthetic derived from the punk subculture, not only informs the appearance of the social reality in a given narrative, but also provides a frame in which the antiheroic protagonist might act, as will be discussed later in this chapter.

The anarchy-inspired aesthetic derived from the punk counterculture also informs the appearance of the characters that populate the social realities depicted throughout cyberpunk. It is at this individual level, however, that the often violent aesthetic championed within the punk subculture comes into direct contact with cybernetics and advanced technology. This contact marks an intersection at which biology and technology collide. However, this intersection is not an area of conflict in which one threatens to engulf the other, but rather a site of integration—a reflection of biology's willing acceptance of technology. It is this integration of biology and technology that informs cyberpunk's most controversial image: the cyborg. According to Cavallaro, the cyborg embodies much of the contemporary fear and anxiety surrounding the integration between biology and technology and the notion that "there are no clear divisions between the nonhuman and the human … the original and the copy" (2000, p. 4).

More often than not, many of the protagonists depicted throughout the cyberpunk subgenre can be regarded as cyborgs. Gibson's *Neuromancer* offers an effective example through female protagonist Molly Millions, whose body has been augmented in a number of different ways:

> The glasses were surgically inset, sealing her sockets. The silver lenses seemed to grow from smooth pale skin above her cheekbones, framed by dark hair cut in rough shag. The fingers curled around the Fletcher were slender, white, tipped with polished burgundy. The nails looked artificial…. She held out her hands, palms up, the white fingers slightly spread, and with a barely audible click, ten double-edged, four-centimeter scalpel blades slid from their housings beneath the burgundy nails [1984, p. 37].

In *Snow Crash*, Neal Stephenson offers a similar, albeit more subtle version of the female cyborg through YT (Yours Truly) who, like Molly, has become integrated with technology:

> The Kourier is not a man, it is a young woman. A fucking teenaged girl. She is pristine, unhurt…. She is holding her [harpoon] in her right hand, the electromagnet reeled up against the handle so it looks like some kind of strange wide-angle intergalactic death ray. Her chest glitters like a general's with a hundred little ribbons and medals, except each rectangle is not a ribbon, it is a bar code [1992, p. 16].

Just as the ideology underpinning the antihero seeks to challenge the reader's perception of normative moral and social convention, so too does the appearance of such characters often defy, subvert, and in some cases, destroy completely preconceived values and assumptions held by the reader. When exploring punk and cyberpunk, this is especially true in relation to beauty. As Shannon points out, the punk aesthetic was deliberately implemented in an attempt "not to conform" and a desire to appear "different or threatening" (2009, p. 49). Cyberpunk mirrors punk's use of aesthetics to serve as an indicator for non-conformity. In *Neuromancer*, this is first reflected through Ratz,[4] whose "ugliness" is described as being the "stuff of legend" (1984, p. 9). According to the protagonist, Case, in an "age of affordable beauty, there was something heraldic about his lack of it" (1984, p. 9). Later in the narrative, the shock-factor often associated with the punk aesthetic is displayed through Angelo, a member of a technologically sophisticated minor terrorist group called the Panther Moderns:

> Case met his first Modern.... The one who showed up at the loft ... was a soft-voiced boy.... His face was a simple graft grown on collagen and shark-cartilage polysaccharides, smooth and hideous. It was one of the nastiest pieces of elective surgery Case had ever seen. When Angelo smiled, revealing the razor-sharp canines of some large animal, Case was actually relieved. Toothbud transplants. He'd seen that before [1984, pp. 75–76].

While Angelo's appearance fulfills the punk aesthetics' desire to shock, it also functions by presenting the reader with an alternative image of technological integration or the transhuman cyborg. This is to suggest that through the implementation of body modification and elective surgery, Angelo has essentially transcended, at least aesthetically, the human condition. Cyberpunk implements the punk counterculture's depiction of body modification, specifically tattooing, branding, scarification, and piercing, in its presentation of the cyborg.

Cyberpunk Cyborgs

The protagonists in cyberpunk can more often than not be interpreted as cyborgs. In the now famous "A Cyborg Manifesto," Donna Haraway describes the cyborg as a cybernetic organism, a "hybrid of machine" and biology (1991, p. 149). As noted by both Clark (2003) and Hayles (2010), a cyborg is essentially a transhuman and thus superior to existing human individuals. Within cyberpunk, the cyborg is often the result of body modification, which, as previously explained, is itself a facet of the punk aesthetic. That is to say, within cyberpunk, body modification, especially piercing, augmentation, and elective surgery, provides the means by which the individual might transcend the human condition.

For Sheila Jeffreys, modification of the body, especially by tattooing and piercing, has become a "prevalent artifact in modern social reality" (2000, pp. 409–410). While body modification within contemporary popular culture might be defined as simply aesthetic or cosmetic, Heuser argues that deliberate and elective body modification is seldom devoid of some symbolic value; "they are statements, markers for a social group, even tribal insignia" (2003, p. 36). It is perhaps important to note however, that body modification, specifically piercing and tattooing, has long been affiliated with subversive subcultural groups, some social, others criminal. As Jenks argues, the primary function of the specific style or aesthetic characteristics adopted by a social or subcultural group is to provide a visual guideline for membership and to allow members of one group to differentiate from others, thus reinforcing the collective identity shared by individual members (2005, p. 43). Inevitably, such factors lead to the development of group or collective identities. Where the punk counter-culture is concerned, however, it is safe to assume that any collective iden-tity has far less to do with acceptance (specifically intergroup camaraderie) than with rejection of normative moral, social, and aesthetic convention and socio-political ideologies in general.

For the most part, however, the punk aesthetic evokes a sense of anar-chy while simultaneously attempting to reflect the anger and frustration experienced by its members who see existing society, or at least the con-ventions by which it is underpinned, as having failed them. According to Daniel Wojcik, the punk counterculture, successfully and effectively, "cre-ated a coherent and elaborate system of body adornment" that expressed its members' "estrangement from mainstream society" and "horrified the general public" (1995, p. 11). For individuals affiliated with the punk coun-terculture, body modification thus became another way of expressing their rejection of social expectations, simply another "form of adornment that transgressed conventional notions about proper appearance of the body" (1995, p. 10). The Panther Modern Angelo of Gibson's *Neuromancer* again serves as an effective example, reflecting punk's use of aesthetics to achieve estrangement, while at the same time illustrating how terms such as oth-erness come to be attached to groups whose beliefs or practices fall beyond social convention, becoming instead a source of grotesque curiosity. This point is expressed by anthropologist Alphonso Lingus, who explains:

> They paint, puncture, tattoo, scarify, cicatrize, circumcise, subincise them-selves. They use their own flesh as so much material at hand for—what? We hardly know how to characterize it—Art? Inscription? Sign-language?… All that excites some dark dregs of lechery and cruelty in us, holding our eyes fixed with repugnance and lust [1995, p. 22].

On the other hand, Victoria Pitts suggests that Lingus' study serves to reflect how "foreign bodies" have come to be "exoticized and fetishized" within western, post-colonial society and thus work to reinforce "symbolic boundaries" separating mainstream society from the other (2003, p. 120). In relation to cyberpunk, however, Pitts argues that the "limitlessness" depicted by the genre, in conjunction with "dissolution of all material and symbolic barriers," provides a freedom in which individuals have the capacity to choose both "body and identity" (2003, p. 152).

In cyberpunk, body modification transcends the aesthetic, generating a level of symbolism not unlike that which is claimed through traditional ritual practices. This is to say, the symbolic and ideological value underpinning cyberpunk's depiction of body modification mirrors cultural practices pertaining to rites of passage. Terrence Turner suggests that ritual body modification serves as a means of social production that reinforces the relationship between the natural environment, the individual, or "the human subject, and the socialized body" (1995, p. 167). Similarly, for anthropologist and ethnologist Claude Levi-Strauss, such practices, specifically tattooing, are not simply the gaining of aesthetic adornment but rather the means through which "all the traditions and philosophies of the group comes to be imprinted upon both the body and mind of its individual members" (1963, p. 257). Most significant, however, is that body modification allows the individual to negotiate the liminal, often ambiguous spaces of social reality. As Enid Schildkrout points out, modification not only allows for the establishment of relations between "the individual and society" and "between different social groups" but at the same time "mediates relations between persons and spirits, the human and the divine" (2003, p. 321). Thus body modification works to reduce the liminal capacity separating the individual (physical) from the divine (metaphysical). In cyberpunk, body modification, especially piercing and augmentation, similarly reduces the liminal space between physical and metaphysical and acts as an interface, allowing the individual to bridge the gap between biology and technology.

The integration between biology and technology reinforces the paradoxical nature of the protagonists within cyberpunk in that they exist as both individuals and technological objects. Here, however, they obtain a level of functionality. Heuser argues that in cyberpunk, body modifications are "never merely decorative: they are statements, markers for a social group, even tribal insignia" (2003, p. 35–36). Further, he goes on to explain, here in reference to Gibson's *Neuromancer*, that the ports and sockets—which reflect a continuation of the aesthetic piercing—with which many cyberpunk protagonists are equipped, represents a "gateway … between man and machine, through which the body truly becomes a cyborg or cybernetic organism" (2003, p. 36). Perhaps as a result of its affiliation with postmodernism—an area already synonymous with deconstruction—the implementation of body modification not only allows individuals to negotiate or reduce but, in some instances, to destroy completely the liminal space between physical and metaphysical. This is especially true in relation to cyberpunk's exploration of virtual reality. Both Case and Hiro of Gibson's *Neuromancer* (1984) and Stephenson's *Snow Crash* (1992) respectively, are equipped with physical augmentations that allow them to pass from the physical into the metaphysical, reality into virtual reality. In cyberpunk, the implementation of body modification serves as the means by which the individual—by becoming a cyborg—might transcend the human condition and, as a matter of consequence, be identified as transhuman.

Marid Audran, the protagonist of George Alec Effinger's *When Gravity Fails*, accurately reflects cyberpunk's implementation of body modification as a means of both transcending the human condition and reducing the liminal space between biology and technology, physical and metaphysical. Initially Marid takes pride in the fact that he is one of the few individuals who has not undergone cranial modification[5]:

> Almost everyone around me ... is modified somehow, with personality modules and add-ons wired down deep into their brains, giving them skills and talents and inputs of information; or even, as with the Honey Pilar moddy, entirely new personalities. I alone walked among them unaltered, relying on nerve and stealth and savvy. I outhustled the hustlers, putting my native wits against their computer- boosted awareness [1987, p. 53].

When Marid is later hired by Friedlander Bey (the Budayeen's most powerful and influential citizen) to hunt down a psychopathic serial killer responsible for murdering a number of Bey's associates, the protagonist quickly comes to understand that he is essentially outclassed. If he is to stand a chance, he will have to undergo the augmentation he had been so desperate to avoid. Fearing that the augmentation might alter his individuality, Marid at first rejects Bey, who pledged to cover the cost of the necessary operation. Bey counters by telling the protagonist that things "have moved beyond your wishing" and that:

> "You will do as I say. You cannot hope to succeed against our enemies unless your mind is improved. We know that at least one of the two has an electronically augmented brain. You must have the same, but to an even greater degree. My surgeons can give you advantages over the murderers" [p. 133].

Following the procedure, Marid realizes that his fears concerning augmentation had been misplaced. He explains, "Maybe I ought to have had my brain boosted a long time ago. I suspected that I'd been missing a beat, that I'd been wrong and everybody else had been right" (p. 199).

Similarly concerned with the process by which the liminal space separating juxtaposed concepts might be reduced, Gibson's *Neuromancer* offers further examples of the cyberpunk cyborg and how body modification serves in the development and potential creation of transhuman beings. Through its protagonist, Case, *Neuromancer* moves to illustrate the significance of body modification in the creation of cyborgs by depicting the process in reverse. At the same time, the narrative also draws attention to some of the antiheroic characteristics reflected by a majority, if not all cyberpunk protagonists. Essentially, Case is described as a thief in the employ of other "wealthier thieves":

> At twenty-two, he'd been a cowboy, a rustler, one of the best in the Sprawl. He'd been trained by the best ... legends in the biz. He'd operated on an almost permanent adrenaline high, a byproduct of youth and proficiency, jacked into a custom cyberspace deck that projected his disembodied consciousness into the consensual hallucination that was the matrix [1984, p. 12].

When he is caught stealing information, however, he is injected with mycotoxin, which damages his central nervous system, effectively removing his ability to access the matrix. The detrimental impact of Case's loss is reflected following his relocation to Chiba, where he had hoped to find a cure:

> A year here and he still dreamed of cyberspace, hope fading nightly. All the speed he took, all the turns he'd taken and the corners he'd cut in Night City, and still he'd see the matrix in his sleep, bright lattices of logic unfolding across the colorless void ... [1984, p. 11].

Case attempts to return to pre-augmented life by becoming "just another hustler trying to make it through" (1984, p. 11) but is unable to cope with his loss:

> The dreams come on in the Japanese night like livewire voodoo, and he'd cry for it, cry in his sleep, and wake alone in the dark ... his hands clawed into the bedslab, temperfoam bunched between his fingers, trying to reach the console that wasn't there [1984, p. 11].

Body modification evokes a level of symbolism that, within the punk counterculture, acts to reinforce the group's collective identity by distancing them from other members of society. Within cyberpunk, however, the symbolic value affiliated with body modification becomes twofold. On one hand, it shares with traditional punk aesthetics the desire to shock and to reject normative social and moral values and assumptions, specifically in context to beauty. On the other, it evokes a sense of almost mystic symbolism, not unlike that affiliated with ritualistic ceremonies pertaining to rites of passage, and acts as an interface through which the liminal space separating physical from metaphysical is reduced and the boundaries between human and machine become blurred. However, through the implementation of body modification, especially augmentation, the integration of biology and technology not only leads to the creation of cyborgs, but also represents the means by which the individual might gain the capacity to transcend the human condition.

Punk Ideology

Although punk is often associated with the punk-rock counterculture of the 1970s, in colloquial American discourse the term can also be used to refer to individuals who engage in acts of low-level criminality. The application of the term "punk" to describe a petty criminal is not without its relevance, as Heuser points out (2003, p. 30), to the protagonists depicted throughout the cyberpunk subgenre. Gibson's Case, for example, is described as a "thief" (1984, p. 12) and Marid Audran could be easily identified as a low-level, anything-for-money hustler (1987, pp. 1–20). Similarly, Jonny Qabbala of *Metrophage* is a "drug dealer, ex–Committee for Public Health bounty hunter, and self-confessed loser" (1988, p. 1).

Within cyberpunk, the anarchy-inspired philosophy derived from the punk counterculture can be identified as informing the protagonists' actions and perspectives. This is especially true in relation to cyberpunk's depiction of self-destruction, drug use, nihilism, and anti-capitalist, anti-establishment ideology. More often than not, it is their adoption of punk's anarchic philosophy that determines the protagonists' antiheroic identity.

The nihilism inherent to the early days of the punk subculture, particularly in the English punk movement, is clearly reflected in the lyrics of the Sex Pistols' song "No Future" (alternatively titled "God Save the Queen"):

> When there's no future how can there be sin
> We're the flowers in the dustbin
> We're the poison in your human machine
> We're the future your future [1977].

Punk's nihilism—manifest as a lack of concern for either the self, other individuals, or society as a whole—is aptly shown through its affiliation with self-destruction, a sentiment which comes to be expressed in several areas. Many performers in the counterculture's music scene, such as Johnny Rotten, Sid Vicious, and G.G. Allin, would deliberately injure themselves, or other band-members, break props, demolish the stage, and even destroy their own instruments. Audience members were encouraged to yell, scream abuse, spit, and pelt the band with objects, especially cans and bottles. Further, as William Tsitsos notes, audience members would also engage in moshing or slamdancing, wherein participants would "violently hurl their bodies at one another" (1999, p. 397). Self-mutilation, well beyond that associated with body modification, is also observed. The most obvious, or at least recognizable facet of the punk counterculture's affiliation with nihilism is manifest within self-destructive behaviors, especially excessive consumption of alcohol and/or illicit substances.

A quick sampling of the cyberpunk subgenre reveals a great deal of excessive drug-consuming, alcohol-guzzling protagonists who are all too aware of their self-destruction; as fictional examples of the subculture's nihilism, they simply don't care. Case is a heavy narcotics user; after being robbed of his ability to access the matrix, the former console-cowboy turns to drugs in an attempt to avoid the reality of being imprisoned within his own body: "Case washed down the night's first pill with a double espresso. It was a flat pink octagon, a potent species of Brazilian dex" (1984, p. 13). Case, however, remains fully aware of his self-destruction, as revealed through flashes of internal dialogue:

> Case knew at some point he'd started to play a game with himself, a very ancient one … a final solitaire…. He no longer took basic precautions. He ran the fastest, loosest deals on the street…. A part of him knew the arc of his self-destruction was glaringly obvious … but that same part of him basked in the knowledge that it was only a matter of time [1984, pp. 14–15].

For Case, drugs have simply come to replace the exhilaration and sense of disembodiment associated with accessing the matrix, which might be interpreted as his primary drug of choice (1984, p. 12). This is perhaps most accurately reflected following the repair of his neurosystem, when he is able to access the matrix for the first time in two years:

> He closed his eyes…. And in the bloodlit dark behind his eyes … symbols, figures, faces, a blurred fragmented mandala of visual information. Please, he prayed, *now*—A grey disk, the color of Chiba sky. *Now*—Disk beginning to rotate, faster, becoming a sphere … expanding…. And flowered … flowered for him, fluid neon origami … the unfolding of his distanceless home, his country…. And somewhere he was laughing, in a white-painted loft, distant figures caressing the deck, tears of release streaking his face [1984, pp. 68–69].

Marid Audran, on the other hand, is completely dependent on drugs, having come to use and depend on them as other individuals have upon their "daddies" and "moddies."[6] He uses "tri-phets" or triamphetamine for stimulation: "I ... reached for my pill case ... fumbled it open and took out a couple of little blue triangles. They'd wake me up fast" (1987, p. 20); bataqualide HCI or "beauties" as a euphoric and sedative: "I saw that my entire stash of beauties—bataqualide HCI—was gone. They were illegal as hell all over.... I'd had eight last night. I must have taken a handful to get me to sleep over the screaming tri-phets" (1987, p. 46); and Sonneine, or "sunnies," an opiate, to ease pain and discomfort: "I had seven tabs.... When I got them down, it would be like the sun breaking through the gloomy clouds. I would bask in a buzzy, warm respite, an illusion of well-being rushing to every hurt and damaged part of my body" (1987, p. 46).

Unlike Case, Marid does not acknowledge his drug-use as self-destructive; drugs for Marid are to be enjoyed and respected, like the company of a good friend:

> Drugs are your friends, treat them with respect. You wouldn't throw your friends in the garbage. You wouldn't flush your friends down the toilet. If that's the way you treat your friends or your drugs, you don't deserve to have either. Give them to me. Drugs are wonderful things. I won't listen to anybody trying to get me to give them up. I'd rather give up food and drink—in fact, on occasion, I have [1987, p. 150].

Even so, with an increased chance of permanent neurological damage following his augmentation, Marid does abstain from the consumption of narcotics, for a short time, at least. Unable to cope with life, Marid soon comes to depend on the effects of his augmentation, simply replacing one addiction for another. After his first experience using the augmentation, he concludes that he should have done it a long time ago (1987, p. 199). At the same time, however, his augmentation allows him to achieve results similar to those offered by the narcotic substances he had used previously. This includes the ability to suppress his appetite and thirst, the negation of basic bodily functions such as urinating or sleeping, and the ability to increase his natural cognitive function, thus improving attention, focus, and working memory.

In Kadrey's *Metrophage*, Jonny Qubbala is yet another drug-user:

> He swallowed two tabs of Desoxyn, hijacked from a Committee warehouse ... good stuff. Very soon, a tingling began in his finger-tips and moved up his arms, filling him with a pleasantly tense, almost sexual energy [1988, p. 3].

Though other cyberpunk protagonists often participate in illegal activities, such as Case's hacking or Marid's questionable hustling, seldom are their occupations as deliberately immoral as Jonny, a drug dealer who

> had chosen his own brand of survival when he walked away from the Committee for Public Health and threw in with the pushers.... Now he worked the black market, selling any drugs the smuggler lords could supply—antibiotic, LSD analogs, beta-endorphins, MDMA [1984, p. 3].

In *Software*, Rudy Rucker offers a more optimistic, though no less drug-addled example through protagonist Stanley Hilary Mooney, Jr., who changes his name to Sta-Hi (stay-high) so as to reflect his favorite pastime:

> Riding his hydrogen-cycle home ... Sta-Hi began to feel sick. It was the acid coming on. He'd taken some Black Star before turning his cab in.... That was an hour? Or two hours ago.... He had to keep moving or he'd fall through the crust [1982, p. 23].

Another facet of cyberpunk's nihilism is manifest is its disregard for physicality or embodiment, advocating instead the disembodied state of being associated with virtual reality. In this, cyberpunk inevitably evokes a sense of the Cartesian paradigm or duality and places an emphasis upon computer-generated reality and cybernetics over physicality and biology. Like a number of cyberpunk protagonists, Case, for instance, has nothing but "contempt for the flesh," seeing the body as "meat" (1984, p. 12). For him, the body, or more specifically, physicality in general, is simply a "prison of his own flesh" (1984, p. 12), which he would happily escape for the cold confines of cyberspace. Both Case and his former mentor, Dixie, have flat-lined, literally died, during separate hacking attempts, yet insist on continuing. In Rucker's *Software*, the protagonist, Cobb Anderson, willingly allows both his body and brain to be destroyed by the "boppers"[7] so that his personality and consciousness can be transferred into an artificial (robot) body in order to obtain a form of immortality:

> They had already flayed Cobb's torso. His chest was split down the sternum. Two arms held the ribcage open, while two others extracted the heart, and then the lungs. At the same time Ralph Numbers was easing Cobb's brain out of the top of the opened-up skull.... He ... then dropped the brain into something that looked like a bread-slicer connected to an X-ray machine [1982, p. 85].

While this reflects cyberpunk's interest in self-destruction, it also provides a more direct example of the integration between biology and technology and the development of the cyborg.

Although self-destruction is inarguably an obvious correlation between punk counter-cultural ideology and cyberpunk, the most important correlation concerns the foundation upon which punk was based: anarchy and rebellion through resistance and the rejection of normative social and moral conventions. The punk counterculture's anarchic foundation also belies its implementation of anti-establishment and anti-conformist ideology. Inevitably, the subcultural ethos advocated by the punk counterculture, specifically in context to its anarchic, philosophical roots, evokes a sense of struggle or conflict. It is the adoption of punk's anarchic ideology and participation in its struggle that, more often than not, determines the cyberpunk protagonist's antiheroic identity.

Counter-Cultural Ideology

The punk counterculture emerged in response to the increasingly capitalist stance adopted by major record companies. Essentially, punk sought to destabilize the consumer-driven ideologies prevailing over the music industry by providing an alternative to the highly commercialized pop and rock groups whose work saturated the music charts during the 1970s and 1980s (Sabin, 1999, pp. 1–4). Typified by a sense of raw, politically motivated anger, punk music was far more concerned with having a message and sense of purpose than individual musical talent (Dale, 2012, pp. 23–24; Sabin, 1999, pp. 2–3). This do-it-yourself ethos strongly resonated with the working class, especially in the London scene, and reinforced the punk counterculture's attempts to destabilize major record labels. As Jon Purkis and James Bowen explain, in allowing everyday individuals to pick up instruments, form bands, and produce and distribute their own music, punk rock challenged elitist conceptions of the artist and succeeded, to some extent, in breaking down the "barrier between producers and consumers of music" (1997, p. 99). By taking up and implementing the music industry's own technology as a weapon, the punk counterculture became synonymous with the notion of subversion, specifically subversion of the mechanisms of control. As Heuser rightly observes, punk's use of the music industry's technology as a weapon is indicative of what he describes as an "iconography of disrespect" that was "directed against present social and cultural systems, as well as against the past systems of value that originally produced them" (2003, p. 41). Punk's seizure and implementation of the mechanisms of control (technology) as a weapon to be used against the establishments by which they were produced is a practice clearly adopted by cyberpunk. As Larry McCaffery notes in *Storming the Reality Studio*, both punk and cyberpunk aim to seize control of technology from the "banalizing effects of the media industry" (producers) so as to "re-establish a sense of menace, intensity" (1991, p. 289).

This sense of implementing technology as a weapon against itself, or more specifically, the mechanisms of control, is acknowledged in Gibson's *Neuromancer* through the Panther Moderns, whom Case describes as "mercenaries, practical jokers, nihilistic technofetishists" (1984, p. 75). The Panther Moderns, it is explained, differ from other anarchist groups "in their degree of self-consciousness" and in their "awareness of the extent to which media divorce the act of terrorism from the original sociopolitical intent" (1984, p. 75). In preparation for their assault upon the "Sense/Net building" (1984, p. 80), for example, Case, Molly, and Armitage[8] enlist the help of the Panther Moderns, who aptly reflect their capacity to subvert the mechanisms of control for their own purposes:

> The Panther Moderns allowed four minutes for their first move to take effect, then injected a second carefully prepared dose of misinformation. This time, they shot it directly into the Sense/Net building's internal video system. At 12:04:03, every screen in the building strobed for eighteen seconds in a frequency that produced seizures in a susceptible segment of Sense/Net employees [1984, p. 80].

The subversion of the mechanisms of control is often directly linked to the protagonist's capacity to effect change. In short, the potential power of the cyberpunk protagonist is limited to his technological or, more specifically, computer know-how. In *Neuromancer*, for example, Case is a hacker who is hired by Armitage to emancipate a rogue artificial intelligence, Wintermute,[9] from the systems of Tessier-Ashpool SA.[10] In order to enter Tessier-Ashpool's computer systems, Case implements other computer-based programs to break through their ICE[11]: he enlists the help of a computer construct named Dixie Flatline[12] and implements "Kuang Grade Mark eleven" to penetrate the ICE protecting Tessier-Ashpool's systems (1984, p. 240).

A more direct example can be observed through Marid in *When Gravity Fails*, who is forced to undergo augmentation when hired to hunt down an augmented serial killer (1987). A similar example can also be observed in *Software*, where Cobb Anderson willingly allows his body and brain to be destroyed so that his consciousness can be transferred into a cybernetic body (1982). While Cobb's initial decision is motivated by self-preservation, his consciousness is later used to assist boppers in gathering human brains for taping.[13] In the latter narrative's sequel, *Wetware*, Cobb, now a facet of technology himself, assists an Edgar Allan Poe–obsessed bopper named Berenice by raising Manchile, a human/bopper hybrid that carries the genetic material that will inevitably bring about the next stage of biological and cybernetic evolution, respectively (Rucker, 1988).

Another facet of cyberpunk's anarchic ideology comes through its depiction of large multinationals and consumer-driven corporations as evil, hegemonic institutions of oppression against which the protagonist must rebel. Further, the individuals who run these corporations are, like the individuals they suppress, no longer completely human.

The representation of multinationals and corporations as evil regimes, however, can be identified in precursory works of cyberpunk fiction, such as *The Stars My Destination*, discussed in Chapter Two. In *Watchmen*, discussed in the previous chapter, it is the antihero Ozymandias' corporate influence and economic power that enables him to fulfill his plans of achieving world-peace by destroying New York City, effectively killing millions of people. During an interview, Moore affirms that *Watchmen*'s depiction of the evil multinational was a deliberate strategy wherein the stereotypical comic-book super-villain was replaced by what, to Moore's mind, was far more terrifying: a modern businessman (Iannucci, 2008).

Cyberpunk illustrates the inseparable relationship between technology and economy.[14] On an aesthetic level, corporate logos, company slogans, and brand advertising saturate every surface of the cityscape. In this, cyberpunk often reflects social realities wherein the very concept of democracy has been reduced and superseded by consumerism. Multinationals, or the zaibatsu,[15] to borrow from Gibson's use of the Japanese term, are no longer governed by either international restrictions or the notion of moral practice and have gained such power that they have been successful in carrying extreme capitalist ideology to what might be interpreted as its logical conclusion: total hegemony. The hegemonic influence derived through capitalist ideology and distributed through multinational entities is an idea discussed by Jean Baudrillard, who sees contemporary society as having become dominated by the "remarkable conspicuousness of consumption and affluence," derived from "the multiplication of objects, services, and material goods" (1998, p. 32).

In *Neuromancer*, Gibson acknowledges the relationship between capitalist ideology, power, and hegemony when the protagonist reflects:

Power, in Case's world, meant corporate power. The zaibatsus, the multinationals that shaped the course of human history, had transcended old barriers. Viewed as organisms, they had attained a kind of immortality. You couldn't kill a zaibatsu by assassinating a dozen key executives; there were others waiting to step up the ladder, assume the vacated position, access the vast banks of corporate memory [1984, p. 242].

The influence of capitalist ideology and the technology, or more specifically, the media it produces can be observed in facets of contemporary society, acting to shape the way individuals interact with others and perceive themselves. According to Baudrillard, this marks a "fundamental mutation in the ecology of the human species" wherein the economic elite, as a result of their wealth, are "no longer surrounded by other human beings, but by objects" (1998, p. 32). In *Neuromancer*, Case explains that he had always assumed that individuals of power—"the real bosses and kingpins of a given industry"—would be "both more and less than people," and their transformation or assimilation into the elite class would be marked by "a gradual and willing accommodation of the machine, the system, the parent organism" (1984, p. 243). Baudrillard makes a similar observation, suggesting that the individual is taking on characteristics of technology so as to adapt to an increasingly technological, media-driven social reality (1998, p. 32). Thus the relationship between capitalism, technology, and the individual can be identified as giving rise to a new form of cyborg or transhuman, one specifically suited to the increasingly technological and media-saturated social realities in which they exist. This is something clearly reflected throughout a majority of cyberpunk narratives.

In *Neuromancer*, for example, this is reflected through the plutocratic Tessier-Ashpool family, wherein individual members are cloned and used to replace their predecessors upon death, thus giving rise to an immortal hive-mind–like entity (1984, p. 242). Gibson's allusion to the Tessier-Ashpool family as a hive mind is affirmed in Case's deranged vision of "hatching wasps" in a "time-lapse machine gun of biology" where hives have acquired "cybernetic memories" derived from "vast single organisms," their "DNA coded in silicon" (1984, p. 242). A similar, albeit more subtle image can be identified in *When Gravity Fails* through Friedlander Bey, the two-hundred year old Islamic godfather whose empire—founded on prostitution, drug-trafficking, extortion, and black-market weapons and technology—extends throughout the entire city of Budayeen, his life having been radically extended through the use of technoscientific development. In Bruce Sterling's *Schismatrix* (1985), protagonist Abélard Lindsay undergoes diplomatic training and pledges his allegiance to the Shapers in their conflict against the Mechanists, who have used their technology to achieve economic dominance over other factions. Later, however, another capitalist-based hegemonic power emerges through the Investors, an economics-obsessed alien race that encourages both factions to set aside their differences and to consolidate their efforts by concentrating on business rather than war. Taking a more humorous approach, *Snow Crash* depicts a social reality in which capitalism has led to the cannibalization of the CIA by the CIC, a for-profit organization that deals in information, most of which is purchased from street-level criminals and hackers, such as the protagonist Hiro (1992). Aside from their various illegal activities, the Italian mafia run by Uncle Enzo also runs a pizza delivery service that is currently at war with an emerging religious cult organized by L. Bob Rife and founded on an eclectic mix of Sumerian mythology, biblical stories pertaining to the Tower of Babel, linguistic theory, and computer science. In the text, the cult has gained power enough to mass-produce a virus whose effects are experienced in both virtual and physical reality and later hijack the USS *Enterprise* (CVN-65), which they plan on using to safeguard the faithful in a Noah's Ark–like scenario (1992).

What comes to be revealed throughout cyberpunk's social realities is a sense of oppression derived from the multinationals and corporate giants whose hegemonic dominance is perpetuated and reinforced through media and technology. With traditional political bodies superseded by the multinationals and the presence of law-enforcement organizations diminished if not completely eradicated by the influence of capitalist ideology, the cityscape, as cyberpunk's iconic topographical environment, is largely hostile. Traditional concepts pertaining to heroic action are rendered inappropriate and survival "underground at the interstices of corporate capitalism" can only be ensured through "guerrilla tactics" (Heuser, 2003, p. 37), or more specifically, subverting the mechanisms of control. To this end, the anarchic ideology underpinning the punk subculture strongly resonates within cyberpunk. The specific brand of anarchy evoked by cyberpunk, however, is not one of chaos, or even lawlessness, but an advocacy of independence and a rejection of the "all-consuming economic climate of corporate capitalism" (2003, p. 38). As Heuser points out, "The hero's world-view is continually overshadowed by larger-than-life conspiracies trying to contain [his] free will.... The hero's range of action consists primarily of acts of sabotage, turning the system against itself"

(2003, p. 38). The cyberpunk protagonist's struggle against the multinationals mirrors that of the early punk band's struggle against the oppressive influence of major record companies.

The punk-rock counterculture that arose in the 1970s was typified by a specific aesthetic and anarchic ideology, both of which can be identified within cyberpunk. The countercultural aesthetic derived from punk can be observed shaping the social realities depicted throughout the cyberpunk subgenre. This is especially true in relation to the harsh, neon-lighted, rubbish-strewn and media-saturated cityscape. These hostile, sprawling urban environments not only provide the foundation for a majority of cyberpunk narratives, but in conveying a sense of desolation also exist in sharp contrast to the rich affluence reflected by the multinationals, whose power and influence have allowed them to supersede traditional forms of governance and carry extreme capitalist ideology to what might be interpreted as its natural conclusion: complete social and economic hegemony. Upon an individual level, however, the punk aesthetic also informs the appearance of the protagonists themselves, which, in relation to the latter's affinity with body modification, marks a significant contribution in the development of the cyborg. While fulfilling punk's initial desire to shock, within cyberpunk, body modification gains a level of functionality which marks not only the integration between biology and technology, but also how this integration might also provide individuals with the capacity to transcend the human condition. The ideology underpinning the punk counterculture can also be observed through the protagonist's actions, attitude, and perspectives, and it is usually the protagonist's adoption of such ideology that determines their antiheroic identity.

Six

Reinterpreting Cyberpunk

The emergence of transhuman theory and predictions regarding the development of science and technology largely problematize the concept of identity and further complicate notions relating to dualism or the Cartesian paradigm. This is especially true in relation to the integration of biology and technology, wherein the liminal space separating previously juxtaposed terms such as human and machine are significantly reduced. Further issues arise when considering that technoscientific development might also allow for the existence of multiple realities—virtual and physical—and for consciousness to exist independent of the body or within other, non-biological states, such as data. In order to substantiate such a claim, this chapter will focus on Richard Morgan's Takeshi Kovacs trilogy—*Altered Carbon* (2002), *Broken Angels* (2003), and *Woken Furies* (2005).

To illustrate the development of the paradoxical protagonist within speculative fiction, the following builds upon arguments raised in Chapter Five and demonstrates how Morgan's work shares with movement-era cyberpunk a number of thematic, aesthetic, and ideological similarities that not only inform the atmosphere and appearance of the worlds in which the narratives are set but also reinforce the antiheroic identity of the trilogy's protagonist. Significantly, Morgan's largest contribution in relation to the development of both speculative fiction and the paradoxical protagonist stems from the subversion of cyberpunk's most recognized themes, specifically the existence of virtual reality, the integration between biology and technology, and the possibility of disembodied states of existence. At the same time, however, Morgan's treatment of the subjective self highlights a number of paradoxes concerning identity and embodiment.

Postcyberpunk: Aesthetics and Ideology

As demonstrated in the previous chapter, cyberpunk is a subgenre of speculative fiction largely informed both aesthetically and ideologically by the punk-rock counterculture of the 1970s. Morgan's trilogy shares with cyberpunk a number of aesthetic, ideological, and thematic similarities. The appearance of such cyberpunk-derived rhetorical devices and their subsequent reinterpretation throughout Morgan's work act to highlight how the genre has developed in response to technoscientific progress and the emergence of transhuman theory.

The similarities between Morgan's Takeshi Kovacs trilogy and canonical cyberpunk have also been noted by Pawel Frelik, who contends that Morgan's work is "firmly rooted in the cyberpunk aesthetic, because of both its construction of human subjectivity and its focus on the areas which have been traditionally asserted to be emblematic of cyberpunk" (2011, p. 174). Further, the implementation of cyberpunk's most recognized tropes, such as virtual reality, cyborgs, disembodied states of existence, and the potential threat posed by large multinational corporations in an increasingly technologized, consumer-driven social reality aid in the resurrection of what Graham Murphy and Sherryl Vint define as the genre's premature termination (2011, p. xii). For critics such as Murphy, Vint, and Person, the reappearance of such themes marks the emergence of a new literary genre: postcyberpunk. For all that, however, as Murphy and Vint correctly point out, postcyberpunk nevertheless continues from where its predecessor left off, namely by contributing to the discussion of "how to negotiate exchanges among information technologies, global capitalism and human social existence" (2011, p. xiii).

The influence of canonical cyberpunk is clearly recognizable throughout the Takeshi Kovacs trilogy, both aesthetically and ideologically. At an aesthetic level, Morgan's implementation of cyberpunk evokes a sense of progressive technological development. Unlike the media-saturated settings of traditional cyberpunk, the Takeshi Kovacs trilogy presents readers with a social reality supported, rather than dominated by the technologies it has produced. In many ways, the aesthetic depicted within Morgan's work, though cyberpunk in origin, subverts the almost post-apocalyptic images manifest in narratives such as *Neuromancer*, *Metrophage*, and *Snow Crash*.

In *Altered Carbon*, for example, Kovacs reflects upon the environment into which he has emerged:

I ... made out angular buildings behind real wire fences on the other side of a badly-kept landing lot. Sterile, off-white, quite possibly original pre-millennial structures. Between the oddly monochrome walls, I could see sections of a grey iron bridge that came vaulting in to land somewhere hidden from view. A similarly drab collection of sky and ground cruisers sat about in not particularly neat lines. The wind gusted abruptly and I caught the faint odour of some flowering weed growing along the cracks in the landing lot [2001, p. 20].

While Morgan's use of technological extrapolation is clearly evident, description nevertheless succeeds in evoking a sense of familiarity—set apart from the alienating presence of cyberpunk's extreme urban environments—through its alteration of existing social reality wherein chain-link fences have been replaced by "real wire" and cars by "ground cruisers" (2001, p. 20). However, this is not to suggest that the Takeshi Kovacs trilogy is in any way more utopian in its image of future society than was movement-era cyberpunk. Nor is this to suggest that it fails to acknowledge the irrevocable significance of the cityscape by which the latter genre was essentially typified. In *Woken Furies*, for example, Takeshi describes Kompacho as "all light, ramp after sloping evercrete ramp aswarm with Angier lamp activity around the slumped and tethered forms of hoverloaders.... Loading hatches gleamed open on their flaring flanks and illuminum painted vehicle maneuvered back and forth.... There was the constant backdrop of machine noise" (2005, p. 33).

As with other authors writing within and around cyberpunk, Morgan does not shy from the sordid underbelly of the urban environment and is highly critical of the human subject and its susceptibility to vice and violence. This is illustrated in *Woken Furies* when Takeshi makes his way through a docking area, "tracking between a couple more whores, one a woman, the other of indeterminate gender" (2005, p. 9) before having to sneak past a street brawl: "The pipe houses on Muko had just turned out and their synapse-fried patrons had met late-shift dock workers coming up through the decayed quiet of the warehouse quarter" (2005, p. 11).

Apart from the social reality in which the narratives take place, Morgan's implementation of the cyberpunk aesthetic can also be seen to inform the appearance of the characters. Throughout the trilogy it is shown that technoscientific advances in cybernetics and biological and genetic engineering have provided individuals with the capacity to alter their physical appearances. Perhaps inspired by the punk aesthetic's desire to shock, some individuals presented throughout the narratives have taken this freedom to the extreme, the freak-fighters being one example. Such individuals have augmented their bodies, not only for combat purposes, but to make a spectacle of their physical appearances, altered to such an extent as to no longer be recognizably human. In *Altered Carbon*, Takeshi describes one freak-fighter as:

> a two-and-a-half-meter giant naked to the waist with what looked like Naka-mura's entire muscle graft sales for the year wrapped around his arms and trunk. There were red illuminum tattoos under the skin of his pectorals so his chest looked like a dying coal fire.... The hands that hung open at his sides were tipped with filed talons. His face was seamed with scar tissue from the freak fights he had lost ... a cheap prosthetic magnilens screwed into one eye[1] [2001, p. 139].

While more subtle, the extremes of aesthetic alteration can also be seen in *Woken Furies*, reflected through Orr, to whom Takeshi is introduced when a friend stops to look at "the shaven-headed giant" (2005, p. 34). At the time of this encounter, Orr is in the process of having his augments enhanced: "They were doing something to the bones in the right shoulder—a peeled-back flap of neck and collar hung down on a blood-soaked towel.... Carbon black neck tendons flexed restlessly in the gore within" (2005, p. 33). Both Orr and the freak-fighter described by Kovacs illustrate the extremes to which individuals are able to alter their physical appearances.

The influence of the cyberpunk aesthetic also translates into other areas, external to the physical body, such as fashion. Mirrorshades, that most iconic of cyberpunk accessories, make a return in *Altered Carbon* upon the faces of the Bay City Police (2001, p. 19), and the punk aesthetic's desire to shock is expressed more subtly through Isa[2] in *Woken Furies*, who flaunts some "eye-opening embedded body jewelry" (2005, p. 359) and is described as follows by Takeshi earlier in the narrative:

> Her hair was a savage crimson today, and a little longer than it had been. She'd greysprayed opposing quadrants of her face for a harlequin effect and her eyes were dusted with some haemoglobin-hungry luminescent glitter that made the tiny veins in the whites of her eyes glow as if they were going to explode. The datarat plugs were still proudly on display in her neck, one of them hooked up to the deck she'd brought with her [2005, pp. 332–333].

As explained in the previous chapter, the term punk was and is to some extent still used in reference to low-level criminality, contempt for authority, and a nihilistic lack of concern regarding the self. Unlike canonical cyberpunk protagonists such as Case or Marîd Audran, who are not only described as being predisposed to criminality as a result of their origins but are shown engaging in criminal activities of escalating immorality, Kovacs has not always been a criminal. While he shares with Case and Audran an impoverished upbringing and early exposure to criminality that saw him "running with gangs" by the age of fourteen and having first killed someone at sixteen (2003, pp. 247–248), Morgan's protagonist ultimately departs from the canonical cyberpunk protagonist. Kovacs, who has grown tired of his current life and wants to support his family, joins the military at eighteen, thereby contributing to and reinforcing the existence of the very mechanisms of control—primarily political and economic establishments—against which previous cyberpunk protagonists so desperately struggled. As recognition for his borderline psychopathic tendencies while retaining the ability to take orders, Kovacs is soon selected for Envoy Corps[3] training. Later, however, following years of politically sanctioned violence and the events that took place upon Innenin[4] during which he lost a number of close personal friends, Kovacs is discharged from the military and Corps service, deemed psychologically unfit for duty. Unsure of where to go, Kovacs returns home to Harlan's World, but as he explains to Detective Kristin Ortega, his partner and love interest in *Altered Carbon*, with the exception of criminality, there are few other options left open to individuals once outside the Corps:

> There's not much else to do once you've been discharged from the Corps. They won't let you into anything that might lead to a position of power or influence. On most worlds you're barred from holding public office. Nobody trusts Envoys ... and the stuff we've been trained to do is so close to crime, there's almost no difference. Except that crime is easier. Most criminals are stupid, you probably know that. Even the organised syndicates are like kid gangs compared to the Corps. It's easy to get respect. And when you've spent the last decade of your life jacking in and out of sleeves, cooling out on stack and living virtual, the threats that law enforcement has to offer are pretty bland [2001, p. 270].

For Kovacs and others like him, criminality, albeit a more organized version than that orchestrated by traditional cyberpunks, is simply the next logical step. In this Morgan borrows from cyberpunk its portrait of the relationship between punk and criminality, yet at the same time reinterprets the traditional pathos to produce a protagonist whose engagement with criminality is altogether different. Even so, the protagonist's participation in criminal activity works to highlight his rejection of normative moral and social convention and antiheroic identity.

Another facet of the punk counterculture that Morgan implements is the use of narcotics. Like other cyberpunk protagonists such as Effinger's Marîd and Sta-Hi Mooney of Rudy Rucker's *Wetware*, Kovacs is no stranger to illicit substances and throughout the trilogy is depicted consuming a variety of narcotics. In *Altered Carbon*, for example, Kovacs and hired mercenary Trepp go on a drug-fueled bender while awaiting orders: "We started in a hotel room on a street I could not pronounce. Some tetrameth analogue fired through the whites of our eyes by needlespray" (2001, p. 295) and later, more "meth, eye-shot on a street corner, leaning against a wall" (2001, p. 297). In the same novel, Kovacs uses a synthetic substance in preparation for his assault upon Head in the Clouds[5] in order to trick the facility's advanced security systems by lowering his body temperature and thus concealing his presence. While Kovacs's use of the drug might seem necessary in relation to the situation, it does not prevent him from enjoying the experience, describing its immediate effects as both euphoric and mildly hallucinatory: "The cabin of the transport and the people in it were suddenly like a coded puzzle that I had the solution for if I could just…. I felt an insane grin eating its way across my features" (2001, p. 422). Further, he ensures his partner, Detective Ortega, "Whoooh, Kristin, this is … good stuff" (2001, p. 422).

Although Kovacs is no drug addict, nor is his use of narcotics even habitual—unlike a number of canonical cyberpunk protagonists such as Case, or the often psychotropically-fried Marîd—he has nevertheless constructed a personal philosophy around the consumption of narcotics, weighing up the positive and negative effects. Following a night of celebration in *Broken Angels*, he describes tetrameth as being one of his favorites because:

> It doesn't ride as savagely as some military stimulants, meaning you won't lose track of useful environmental facts like *no, you can't fly without a grav harness or punching this will smash every bone in your hand.* At the same time, it does allow you access to cellular-level reserves that no unconditioned human will ever know they possess. The high burns clean and long…. You can hallucinate mildly, if you really want to, but it takes concentration. Or an overdose, of course. The come down is no worse than most poisons [2003, p. 376].

Morgan's portrayal of drug use not only reinforces the antiheroic aspects of his protagonist, but also reflects punk counterculture's affinity for nihilism, self-destruction, and a general lack of concern for the physical body. Within traditional cyberpunk, the sense of nihilism is chiefly expressed through the genre's emphasis upon disembodied states of existence, as will be discussed later in the chapter. Throughout the Takeshi

Kovacs trilogy, Morgan takes this lack of concern for the physical body (or perhaps more specifically for the body in which the individual currently resides) to the extreme, as reflected by The Little Blue Bugs, a crime gang to which Kovacs once belonged, who purposely infect themselves with various pathogens and viruses as a replacement for illicit substances. When Kovacs asks Jack Soul Brasil, the Bugs leader, whether he is still indulging in old habits, Brasil explains:

> That chemical shit is Stone-Age stuff. I ran Hun Home flu against a spec-inhibited immune system for ten years and all I got was a buzz and some really cool delirium dreams. Real wave climbers. No headaches, no major organ damage, not even a runny nose once the inhibitors and the virus meshed. Tell me one drug you could do that with [2005, p. 285].

This nihilistic approach to the body is compounded by what the narrative describes as an oft-cited piece of street-based philosophy regarding the storage of the body during incarceration. This is first expressed in the first chapter of *Altered Carbon*, when Kovacs, having just been removed from storage, remembers his last encounter with his former Envoy trainer Virginia Vidaura—then facing over a hundred years' storage—who tells him: "'*Don't worry kid, they'll store it.*' Then she bent her head to light a cigarette, drew the smoke hard into lungs she no longer gave a damn about and set off down the corridor as if to a tedious briefing" (2001, p. 9).

While it is clear Morgan borrows from cyberpunk a number of aesthetic and ideological features, which shape the appearance of the characters and the social realities in which they exist and reinforce the protagonist's antiheroic identity, other aspects of the cyberpunk canon are radically subverted. This is particularly apparent in relation to Morgan's treatment of the political ideology expressed by movement-era cyberpunk.

Taking Politics Personally

Prototypical cyberpunk protagonists such as those presented in *Neuromancer* and *Snow Crash* reflect a linear model and sameness of personality that, according to Andrew Ross, sees them portrayed as "youthful male heroes with working-class chips on their shoulders and postmodern biochips in their brains" (1996, p. 152). Although the "postmodern" biochip fails to resonate with Kovacs—unless of course it was to be interpreted as his Envoy conditioning—the protagonist of Morgan's trilogy is one whose central ideological outlook and general perspectives concerning the world in which he exists are undeniably shaped by the "working-class chip" on his shoulder. This is reflected through his contemplation of the impoverished, lower working-class environment in which he was brought up, yet more importantly through his not infrequent citation of Quellist philosophy, an ideological doctrine devised by Quellcrist Falconer—a revolutionary figure who rose up against the ruling class of Harlan's World. Quellist philosophy or Quellism is a critical ideology clearly informed by Marxist theories of economic hegemony and is similarly critical of the disparity manifest between the working and ruling class.

In both the first and second narratives, however, Kovacs appears to resist adherence to any political doctrine, governmental, revolutionary, or otherwise. As Frelik points out, there are few protagonists within cyberpunk, or speculative fiction in general, who are so ruthlessly critical of "inhuman mechanisms of control" and contemptuous of the hierarchies by which they are maintained (2011, p. 177). Further, while canonical cyberpunk protagonists were never "law-abiding model citizens" and frequently sought to undermine—however subtly—political ideology, the intensity and frequency of Kovacs's "acidic remarks and judgments concerning authority and mechanisms of governance ... is more than a token rebellious spirit would require" (2011, p. 177).

Kovacs's contempt for political systems is presented throughout each of the three narratives. When attempting to retrieve a Martian artifact in *Broken Angels*, Kovacs and his affiliates find themselves caught in the middle of a war between the Wedge—a suppression force deployed by the Protectorate[6]—and Revolutionaries under the command of Joshua Kemp. While recruiting his team, Kovacs engages with Jing,[7] asking "You're not a big Kemp fan, are you Jing?" to which Jing responds by posing a question: "The Kempists preach a revolution ... [b]ut what will change if they take power on Sanction IV?" Kovacs responds sarcastically: "Well, there'll be a lot more statues of Joshua Kemp in public places, I imagine. Apart from that, probably not much" (2003, p. 140). In *Woken Furies*, however, Kovacs's view of revolution is revealed to be not dissimilar from his perspective on the Corps and its role within the Protectorate's arsenal of deployable weaponry: "We just used to go silently, crush the odd planetary uprising, topple the odd regime and then plug in something UN–compliant that worked" (2005, p. 24). Thus both the forces of revolution and existing hegemonies are viewed as intrinsically the same and as equally naïve in their implementation of violent action. The only difference is that, under orders of the Protectorate, suppression is politically sanctioned: "Slaughter and suppression across the stars, for the greater good—naturally—of a unified Protectorate" (2005, p. 24).

In spite of having once held a place within the elite Envoy Corps, Kovacs is equally cynical about the military, as shown in *Broken Angels* during his conversation with Jing, to whom he explains that while it might be hard for a soldier to hear, "[w]hen you put on that uniform, you're saying in effect that you resign your right to make independent decisions about the universe and your relationship to it" (2003, p. 207). Kovacs explains that soldiers essentially "follow orders. Regardless. The moment you refuse to carry out an order, you're no longer a soldier. You're a paid killer trying to renegotiate your contract" (2003, p. 208). In his mind the facilities by which power is maintained demand uniformity; the individual must forgo individuality or subversive reasoning if they are to exist within the system. In *Woken Furies*, however, Kovacs is forced to reevaluate his own personal beliefs in relation to political agendas and the possibility of social reform when he becomes an unwilling participant in a sociopolitical conflict that has been taking place for centuries on his home planet of Harlan's World. This not only marks the site of Kovacs's transformation, but, significantly, the point at which Morgan's narrative departs from canonical cyberpunk's ideological foundation. Kovacs, not simply an accessory, becomes an active participant in the destabilization of the mechanisms of control.

That Kovacs changes so radically in the third narrative should come as little surprise when considering the apparent similarities between the philosophical ideologies underpinning the revolution taking place upon Harlan's World and the protagonist's own personal beliefs. The relationship between the two is first evidenced in *Altered Carbon*, the parameters given substance by the Quellist epigraph "Make it Personal," documented in *Things I Should Have Learnt by Now*:

> The personal, as everyone's so fucking fond of saying, is political. So if some idiot politician, some power player, tries to execute polices that harm you or those you care about, TAKE IT PERSONALLY.... The machinery of Justice will not serve you here—it is slow and cold, and it is theirs.... Only the little people suffer at the hands of Justice; the creatures of power slide out from under with a wink and a grin. If you want justice, you will have to claw it from them [2001, p. 168].

Solidification of Kovacs's personal belief system and Quellist philosophy can clearly be perceived in his justification for leading an assault upon Head in the Clouds and in his decision to kill its owner, Reileen Kawahara[8]:

> But this was worse than personal. This was about Louise, alias Anenome, cut up on a surgical platter; about Elizabeth Elliott stabbed to death and too poor to be re-sleeved; Irene Elliott, weeping for a body that a corporate rep wore on alternate months; Victor Elliott, whiplashed between loss and retrieval of someone who was and yet was not the same woman. This was about a young black man facing his family in a broken-down, middle-aged white body; it was about Virginia Vidaura walking disdainfully into storage with her head held high and a last cigarette polluting lungs she was about to lose, no doubt to some other corporate vampire. It was about Jimmy de Soto, clawing his own eye out in the mud and fire at Innenin, and the millions like him throughout the Protectorate, painfully gathered assemblages of individual human potential, pissed away into the dung-heap of history. For all these, and more, someone was going to pay [2001, p. 393].

The fundamental reason behind the protagonist's transformation and his decision to take an active role in the revolution unfolding upon Harlan's World is revealed in *Woken Furies* (2005). Here the revolutionary figure of Quellcrist Falconer, who was thought to have died over three hundred years prior to the events of *Woken Furies*, returns, manifest in the body of Sylvie Oshima, a "command head"[9] who accidently downloads Quell's personality while working in the Uncleared.[10] Initially, Kovacs's involvement could be interpreted as being derived from his interest in Sylvie, who is taken captive by the First Families—the planet's economic elite— when they discover that the command head is carrying the consciousness of Quellcrist Falconer. As the novel progresses, however, Kovacs is forced to accept or at least begrudgingly acknowledge the possibility of the social reform that Quellist philosophy aims to achieve. Essentially, Quellism seeks to establish a "new revolutionary ethic which borrowed from existing strands of extremist thought but was remarkable for the vitriol with which said strands were themselves savagely critiqued almost as much as ruling class policy" (2005, p. 172). The governing principle of Quellist philosophy, however, is its perception of power, which is perceived as a flow system rather than a structure: "It either accumulates at the top or it diffuses through the system" (2005, p. 542).

Seeking reform through the destabilization, if not utter destruction, of existing systems of hegemonic power, the Quellist philosophy to which Kovacs comes to adhere is more associated with anti-establishment anarchic philosophy than those philosophies depicted in canonical cyberpunk.

This is especially evident when considering Emma Goldman's definition of anarchic political ideology:

> Anarchism ... really stands for the liberation of the human mind from the dominion of religion; the liberation of the human body from the dominion of property; liberation from the shackles and restraint of government. Anarchism stands for a social order based on the free grouping of individuals for the purpose of producing real social wealth; an order that will guarantee to every human being free access to the earth and full enjoyment of the necessities of life, according to individual desires, tastes, and inclinations [1972, p. 59].

The freedom Goldman describes correlates with the desire to effect change expressed by Takeshi and the inhabitants of Harlan's World, who, according to Steven Shaviro, have been "offended beyond endurance by the exploitation, torture, and murder that are continually being inflicted on Harland's World (and all the other human-inhabited planets) for reasons of economic gain, or self-righteous religious dogma" (2005). The apparent relationship Quellist philosophy shares with anarchic ideology is evident when Kovacs questions what will happen should their revolution actually succeed and Quellcrist tells him that they would simply

> Run things ... take control. Look after social systems. Keep the streets safe, administer public health and education. Build stuff. Create wealth and organize data, and ensure they both flow where they're needed.... You've got to build structures that allow for diffusion of power, not re-grouping. Accountability, demodynamic access, systems of constituted right, education in the use of political infrastructure [2005, p. 446].

Kovacs' transformation from an individual with a vested interest—primarily his affection for Sylvie—to an active participant in revolutionary social reform is derived from his own personal belief system, his begrudging acknowledgment of Quellist philosophy, and the events that occur throughout *Woken Furies*. This provides the final narrative in Morgan's trilogy with a sense of optimism—one that acknowledges the possibility of change—that was entirely absent from the previous two novels. Further, Kovacs' shift also indicates Morgan's willingness to offer direct political commentary and criticism (which, as Frelik points out, had been completely "absent in Movement-era cyberpunk narratives") while also contributing to, if not reinterpreting, existing canonical trends such as the focus on "anti-corporatism" (2010, p. 181). At the same time, however, the protagonist's decision to actively participate in Quell's revolution is also indicative of the emphasis Morgan's trilogy places upon direct action and the significance of embodiment, or the body, in general. Essentially, this not only marks part of Morgan's subversion of canonical cyberpunk conventions but also acts as a foundation for the development of the antiheroic identity by which the protagonist is underpinned.

Violence and Physicality

Morgan's application of the punk-cum-cyberpunk subcultural ethos reinforces the protagonist's antiheroic identity through a predisposition to criminality, nihilism, and self-destruction, especially in relation to drug use. Unlike canonical cyberpunk protagonists whose primary mode of action is limited to their hacking capabilities, as a former member of the Envoy Corps, Kovacs frequently uses physical violence to achieve a desired goal. As such, he is a protagonist shown to be firmly rooted in both his body and physicality. Significantly, the emphasis Morgan places upon physicality largely reinterprets the role and mode of action employed by movement-era cyberpunk protagonists.

According to Person, prototypical cyberpunk protagonists were often "stereotypically marginalized, alienated loners who lived on the edge of society in generally dystopic futures where daily life was impacted by rapid technological change" (1998). The cyberpunk protagonist is thus something of an urban-outlaw, or the Robin Hood of an increasingly technologized social reality. What is most important, however, is that cyberpunk protagonists such as Case of *Neuromancer*, Sam of Pat Cadigan's *Synners* (1991) or the aptly named Hiro Protagonist of *Snow Crash* were not just "marginalized, alienated loners" (1998) as Person observes, but figures whose identity, main concern, and primary mode of action were manifest in and conducted through cyberspace. The cyberspaces in which such protagonists operate, it should be pointed out, are virtual or artificial constructs that do not exist in the physical reality inhabited by the protagonists themselves, but within computer-generated grids or networks of digitized information.

While a number of cyberpunk protagonists are depicted as becoming entangled in real-world events, their capacity to effect change is severely limited, if not restricted, to their ability to manipulate the metaphysical and virtual realities through which they operate. Networks and computer simulated realities exist as the battlegrounds upon which the cyberpunk fights, while information, data, and the technology through which they engage reflect their weapons of choice. As Case, who lived for the "bodiless exultation of cyberspace" (1984, p. 12) reflects, and as a number of critics have pointed out,[11] the traditional cyberpunk protagonist is one who expresses contempt for the flesh and rejects the significance of embodiment in what Kirby defines as the acquisition of perfection "through an annihilation of the flesh" (1992, p. 132). Canonical cyberpunks' emphasis on disembodiment evokes a sense of the mind/body duality or Cartesian paradigm wherein the mind, or consciousness at least, is depicted as being superior to the body and the true seat of what defines an individual's identity (Howard, 2003). Within the Takeshi Kovacs trilogy, Morgan subverts cyberpunk's emphasis on disembodied existence by presenting a protagonist firmly rooted in physicality. Much of the action that takes place throughout the narratives is highly visceral, placing further focus upon the body and embodiment.[12] Simply put, where movement-era cyberpunk protagonists restricted their involvement to a casual, almost observational capacity, Kovacs is shown to be actively engaged with physical reality, irrespective of the situation.

Morgan's emphasis upon physicality and embodiment is most effectively illustrated through Kovacs' use of violence and brute force to achieve goals that further reinforce the protagonist's antiheroic identity. While the visceral aspect of Morgan's emphasis upon physicality and embodiment can be perceived throughout the series as a whole, it is perhaps most evident in *Altered Carbon* when Kovacs is removed from storage[13] at the request of Laurens Bancroft (whose death he is charged with investigating). Accepting the terms of his release, Kovacs starts following leads but is soon abducted and brought in for interrogation, having come to the attention of individuals who would prefer Bancroft remain oblivious to the events surrounding his death. Kovacs is thus uploaded into a virtual construct[14] where he is sleeved into the body of a young woman[15] and tortured repeatedly. "There's no kind of conditioning in the known universe that can prepare you for having your feet burnt off. Or your nails torn out. Cigarettes stubbed out on your breasts. A heated iron inserted into your vagina. The pain. The humiliation. The damage" (2001, p. 154). While the reality in which Kovacs's torture takes place is virtual and non-physical, the pain, fear, and psychological impact he experiences are all too real. Drawing on his former association with the Corps, however, he is able to negotiate his release and manages to escape his captors during transport.

Back on the streets, Kovacs starts asking questions and following leads and soon discovers the location of the Wei-clinic, the facility where he was interrogated. Once armed, he returns to the clinic and, in an especially bloodthirsty scenario, kills everyone he can get his hands on:

> I stamped a foot down between her shoulders to stop her and then kicked her onto her back.... I lifted the blaster for her to see. "Real death," I said and pulled the trigger. I walked back to the remaining medic who had seen and was now scrabbling desperately backwards away from me. I crouched down in front of him.... "Jesus Christ," he moaned, as I pointed the blaster at his face. "Jesus Christ, I only work here." "Good enough," I told him. The blaster was almost inaudible against the alarms.... On my way out along the screaming corridors of the clinic, I killed every person that I met, and melted their stacks to slag [2001, p. 180].

Ironically, while Kovacs is so infuriated by his capture and the torture that took place during his interrogation that he was driven to kill all those involved, it is later revealed that he is not above using the exact same methods to achieve a goal. In preparation for his assault upon Head in the Clouds, Takeshi captures Miller, one of Kawahara's associates working at the Wei-clinic, in order to obtain information regarding the security and layout of the latter facility. Kovacs uploads Miller into a virtual construct, where he is to be tortured. Before exiting the construct, Takeshi hands Miller a phone, telling him, "When you've had enough, let me know. It's a direct line" (p. 365). Before long, the Hendrix[16] informs Kovacs that the "subject is showing signs of psychological stress" (2001, p. 365).

As with other paradoxical protagonists examined throughout this study, Morgan's Takeshi Kovacs is revealed to be a character whose actions are often informed by a personal sense of morality and justice.[17] During his assault upon Head in the Clouds, for example, Kovacs pauses when confronted with a particularly disturbing scenario involving a dog by which he is so outraged that he moves to kill the patron:

> "Jack? You finished al—." He stared at the gun in my hands without comprehension, then as the muzzle came to within half a meter of his face a note of asperity crept into his voice. "Listen, I didn't dial for this routine." "On the house," I said dispassionately and watched as the clutch of monomolecular shards tore his face apart. His hands flew up from between his legs to cover the wounds and he flopped over sideways on the bed, gut-deep noises grinding out of him as he died [2001, p. 431].

Kovacs's capacity for violence is shown to be linked with his early childhood experiences and the impoverished conditions in which he was raised. The link between Kovacs' use of violence and early-life experience is first evidenced in *Altered Carbon* where, following his assault against Warden Sullivan,[18] he reflects that "something cold was rising in me, something born on the benches of the Newpest justice facility and tempered with years of pointless unpleasantness I had been witness to" (2001, p. 276). As he tells a fellow soldier in *Broken Angels*, along with a predisposition to criminality, these experiences also made him "sociopathic from an early age, sporadically and violently resistant to authority and emotionally unpredictable" (2003, p. 247). Despite the highly visceral approach adopted by Morgan throughout the series, Kovacs' relationship with violence is later revealed to be more complicated than just hyper-masculine posturing.

As a former member of the elite Envoy Corps—a group whose name has become synonymous with brutality and slaughter—Kovacs is perfectly comfortable engaging in wars in which he has no vested interest and murdering individuals for reasons that, as a soldier, he may never understand (2001, p. 34). In both *Altered Carbon* and *Broken Angels*, Kovacs engages in bloody conflicts in which he has no personal or emotional investment. Although he stands to gain substantial economic compensation for his efforts, specifically in *Broken Angels*, Kovacs implements violence and brutality, not for his own sake, but for others. Essentially, it is impersonal. This changes drastically in *Woken Furies*, when the protagonist returns home to Harlan's World to discover that his former lover and partner in crime, Sarah Sachilowska, has been killed along with her daughter due to their affiliation with the fanatical religious members of the New Revelation.

Akin to other paradoxical protagonists such as V or Gully Foyle, Kovacs turns to revenge. The scenes in which Kovacs is depicted executing members of the New Revelation are highly visceral, thus placing further emphasis upon the body and physicality. Early in the novel, for example, Takeshi encounters several members harassing a young woman, Sylvie, in the Tokyo Crow:

> A robe straining belly offered itself. I stepped in and the Tebbit knife leapt upward, unzipping. I went eye to eye with the man I was gutting. A lined, bearded visage glared back.... I jerked a nod, felt the twitch of a smile in one clamped corner of my mouth. He staggered away from me, screaming, insides tumbling out [2005, p. 27].

For Kovacs, however, the act of murder is not enough: later it is revealed that after killing a member of the New Revelation, he removes the deceased's stack and hands it to an old friend who, for a price, places the stack in an older swamp-panther.[19] The newly installed consciousness is then given time to adjust to its new body before being thrown into the fight-pits, where it are forced to fight for its life against other panthers. Kovacs explains that it's more than likely the individuals uploaded into the panthers are "pretty much insane by now. Can't be much fun being locked up inside the mind of something that alien in the first place, let alone when you're fighting tooth and nail for your life in a mud pit" (2005, p. 314).

Even in his quest for revenge, Kovacs remains methodical in his approach, first targeting and killing every individual who resided in the same village as Sarah and her daughter—anyone who might have had the chance to intervene but failed. He then goes on to hunt down "the ones who were serving members of the Ecclesiastical Mastery when she was murdered. The ones who wrote the rules that killed her" (2005, p. 315), explaining that he doesn't plan on stopping at all because "They can't give her back to me, can they? So why should I stop?" (2005, p. 315). The single-mindedness with which Kovacs pursues and kills those individuals he perceives as being accountable for the death of Sarah and her child inevitably leads to his alienation from both social reality and other individuals. Nevertheless, revenge remains his only concern throughout the events which take place early in the novel. This is clearly expressed when Kovacs considers the stacks removed from the priests he had killed, which he carries around in his pocket:

> I'd been able to reach into my pocket and weigh its varying contents in my palm with a dark, hardened satisfaction. There was a sense of slow accumulation, an assembly of tiny increments in the balance pan that sat opposite the colossal tonnage of Sarah Sachilowska's extinction. For two years I'd needed no purpose other than that pocket and its handful of stolen souls. I'd needed no future, no outlook that didn't revolve around feeding the picket and the swamp-panther pens at Segesvar's place out on the Expanse [2005, p. 399].

With the exception of his former trainer, Virginia, Kovacs' capacity for violence is not understood by those around him, something which further contributes to his alienation. When Kovacs is rejected by Sylvie, the command-head carrying the disembodied consciousness of Quellcrist Falconer, whom he had jokingly propositioned, she tells him:

> You're locked up … tighter than anyone I've ever met, and believe me, I've met some fucked-up cases…. You walked into that bar, Tokyo Crow, with nothing but that knife you carry and you killed them all like it was a habit. And all the time, you had this little smile [2005, p. 166].

Undeniably, Kovacs is a protagonist firmly rooted in physicality whose frequent use of violence not only acts to subvert canonical cyberpunk, but also highlights and confirms his antiheroic identity.

The Paradox of Disposable Bodies

Through its extrapolated vision of transhumanism and technoscientific progress, the Takeshi Kovacs trilogy problematizes the concept of identity and further complicates the mind/body duality, thus highlighting the paradoxical nature of the narrative's protagonist. This complication emerges at the site from which Morgan's narrative departs from and radically subverts canonical cyberpunk's emphasis upon disembodiment.

Morgan's most significant contribution to the development of speculative fiction lies in his depiction of stack and sleeve technology. The stack is a small chip inserted in the upper spine shortly after birth that functions by recording and storing memories, experiences, and for what all purposes might be defined as the individual's consciousness. The stack does not represent a copy of the individual; rather, it is the individual, stored and digitized. The sleeve, on the other hand, refers to a commoditized body that is not born, but grown in an artificial womb and which can be tailored to suit individual specifications. Upon death it is possible to remove the stack and place it into another sleeve, thus granting individuals access to immortality.[20] Both sleeves and the original bodies are depicted as disposable, neither valued more highly than the other.[21] The possibility of transferring the individual from one body (sleeve) to another strongly resonates with existing transhuman theory (and goals) advocated by futurists such as Nick Bostrom, Ray Kurzweil, Max Moore, and Hans Moravec, who believe that "uploading" to either cybernetic bodies or virtual formats will inevitably lead to the emergence of a utopian social reality.

Cyberpunk's depiction of virtual reality and the possibility of disembodied existence can be interpreted as the sub-genre's most significant contribution to the development of speculative fiction. According to Frelik, canonical cyberpunk is characterized as "privileging the mind and reviling the body" and is essentially dominated by protagonists "seeking to escape embodiment" (2011, p. 185) for the freedom of cyberspace. This notion of disembodied existence inevitably evokes a sense of the Cartesian paradigm or dualism, which privileges the mind, or consciousness, over that of embodied existence. Here, mind and body are perceived as separate entities, suggesting that it is possible for the mind or consciousness to continue existing independent of the physical body (Howard, 2003). According to Hayles, this correlates strongly with the first fundamental perspective of transhuman theory, which "privileges informational pattern over material instantiation" to such an extent that "embodiment in a biological substrate is seen as an accident of history rather than an inevitability of life" (1999, p. 2).

While Morgan's trilogy does not appear to have a universal information network such as the matrix depicted in *Neuromancer*, virtual and computer generated realities are still prevalent. As Morgan states, however, the Takeshi Kovacs trilogy is "rooted deeply in physicality" (R. Morgan, personal communication, May 4, 2012). Further, where other cyberpunk protagonists expressed a subtle contempt for physicality and embodied existence, Kovacs, on the other hand, expresses a similar contempt for data-rats: he is "very much physical ... regardless of what physical flesh he happens to be wearing at the time" (R. Morgan, personal communication, May 4, 2012). Throughout the trilogy, as Frelik correctly points out, a "yearning for cyberspace" is depicted as either "a harmful addiction" or a monkish "pursuit practiced by few" (2011, p. 187), thus rejecting canonical cyberpunk's avocation for virtual reality and disembodied states of existence.

While retaining a focus on the embodied state and the significance of physicality, Morgan nevertheless detracts value from the body itself, evoking a paradox between embodiment and identity. Through the trilogy's depiction of stack- and sleeve-based technologies, physical markers such as sex, ethnicity, and even age become obsolete. Thus the physical appearance of the individual does not necessarily reflect their true—physical and ethnic—identity. In the first novel, Kovacs' observation of a "scattering of humanity" waiting for "friends or family to ride in from their altered carbon exiles" aptly reflects how the narrative's depiction of radical advances in technoscientific development problematizes the concept of identity:

> These people wouldn't recognise their loved ones in their new sleeves; recognition would be left to the homecomers, and for those who awaited them the anticipation of reunion would be tempered with a cool dread at what face and body they might have to learn to love [2001, p. 17].

Later, the separation between the body and physical identity is punctuated while Kovacs is waiting to enter Bay City Central[22] when he observes a "young black woman" and her two children ("also black") staring at the "stooped, middle-aged white man standing before them in tattered UN surplus fatigues" (2001, p. 273). He recognizes the situation as a family reunion: "The young woman's face was a mask of shock ... and the smaller child ... just didn't get it at all. She was looking right through the white man, mouth forming the repeated question *Where's Daddy? Where's Daddy*" (2001, p. 273). In this, the narrative reveals technoscientific development to have made physical identity—that is, identity informed by physical markers such as age, sex, ethnicity, or race—largely obsolete. Consciousness, it can thus be inferred, as the fundamental components of an individual's identity, exists as a dynamic entity, independent of the body, shifting to suit the situation by which it is confronted. The sense of centralized identity—one informed by both physical markers and external factors such as personal experience and socialization—is rendered illogical. In *Altered Carbon*, Kovacs confirms this when considering:

> As a child I'd believed there was an essential person, a sort of core personality around which the surface factors could evolve and change without damaging the integrity of who you were. Later, I started to see that this was an error of perception caused by the metaphors we were used to framing ourselves in. What we thought of as personality was no more than the passing shape of one of the waves in front of me [2001, p. 189].

However, this is not to suggest that identity is completely detached from the original, ethnically marked body, or that individuals have the capacity to change their physical appearance without a sense of alienation from themselves. In spite of his previous experiences being resleeved and training as an Envoy, even Kovacs sometimes experiences a sense of disconnection between his embodied state and identity, as evidenced in the first narrative, when he explains:

> As I dressed in front of the mirror that night, I suffered the hard-edged conviction that someone else was wearing my sleeve and that I had been reduced to the role of a passenger in the observation car behind the eyes. Psychoentirety rejection, they call it. Or just fragmenting.... For long moments I was literally terrified to have a detailed thought, in case the man behind the mirror noticed my presence [2001, p. 135].

The sense of alienation experienced by individuals upon entering a new sleeve is a psychological disconnection between an individual's original (ethnically marked) identity and current physical markers. This is expressed by the protagonist who frequently refers to his mixed Japanese and Hungarian origins, the former seemingly more influential in relation to physical appearance than the latter. However, as Frelik points out, Morgan constructs ethnic or cultural identity as "something mental, part of the personal data which can be carried between stacks and sleeves, even if or when it does not find its external expression" (2011, p. 177). In a number of ways this both reinforces and rejects the notion of Cartesian dualism. On one hand, Morgan presents the individual consciousness as having the capacity to exist independent of the original body while, on the other, it is also shown to be unable to exist outside the stack as a physical object. As a piece of technology, the stack represents a storage device that can be carried, removed, discarded, and destroyed and therefore a facet of physical reality. Even the virtual realities inhabited by the Renouncers[23] in *Woken Furies* still rely on the physical existence of the computers that support the metaphysical virtual realities they choose to inhabit. In both cases, individual consciousness does not exist independent of physicality, but only of the biological body. The computer, specifically terminals that support the virtual realities in which individuals and certain groups (such as the Renouncers) exist, and the stack, upon which individual consciousness is stored, are physical objects that serve as technological substitutes for the biological body. The paradox throughout Morgan's trilogy thus emerges through a disconnection between the body and identity. In spite of the emphasis placed around embodiment, or the body itself, the protagonist cannot be defined by his or her body. Or, more specifically, the protagonist lacks a physical identity through which he can be recognized and thus interpreted. While his mixed Japanese/Hungarian origins undeniably factor into Kovacs' personality as well as his psychological and ethnic or cultural identity, they are not necessarily expressed through his physical appearance. In all three narratives, Kovacs is seemingly detached from an identifiable, physical reference to his ethnic and cultural origins.

A further paradox emerges in relation to the disposability of the sleeve. Morgan envisions a highly technologized future social reality in which the body can be manufactured and has obtained the status of a commodity. The complication here emerges in relation to freedom, or the notion that individuals, irrespective of their status or situation, are the primary owners of their own physical bodies. According to Crawford Macpherson's account of possessive individualism, the individual is "essentially the proprietor of [his] own person or capacities, owing nothing to society for them" and that the "human essence is freedom from the wills of others, and freedom is a function of possession" (1962, p. 3). Throughout the Takeshi Kovacs trilogy, however, notions of freedom and possessive individualism are revealed to have become severely limited by the emergence of stack- and sleeve-based technology. As manufactured products, the technology depicted throughout Morgan's trilogy, especially the sleeve, have become highly commercialized and thus command high economic value. As a result, freedom (or more specifically possessive individualism, to borrow from Macpherson) can no longer be perceived as a basic right of birth to which all individuals can make claim as Hobbes and Locke would suggest. Instead, individual freedom and the concept of possessive individualism are reliant on one's economic status. The potential for emerging transhuman technologies to further exacerbate the disparity among individuals based on their ability to draw upon financial resources is an argument commonly voiced by critics of transhuman research and development such as Bill McKibben.[24]

Nevertheless, the paradox that emerges between humanist accounts of freedom/individuality and the existence of the commoditized body in an increasingly technologized social reality can be seen as underpinning the trilogy as a whole. In *Altered Carbon*, for example, Kovacs has been removed from storage and sleeved in the body of Detective Ryker, at the request of Laurens Bancroft.[25] Here, the restrictions placed upon the protagonist's freedom, individuality, and his capacity to act as a free autonomous agent are obvious. Firstly, Kovacs' ability to act is restricted by his contract[26] with Bancroft; secondly, the body in which he has been sleeved is not his own; rather, it has been provided upon a strictly temporary basis and subject to clauses detailed in a terms-of-release contract. Here, freedom is not a right, but something that can be given and reclaimed at the whim of other, more powerful individuals. As a result, technoscientific progress in Morgan's trilogy is shown not only to have the capacity to restrict human freedom, but to render notions such as possessive individualism all but obsolete.

In *Broken Angels* (2003), this is further displayed through the soul market, where stacks removed from individuals caught in the conflict on Sanction IV are collected, cleaned, and made available for purchase to interested parties. It is here that Kovacs and Mandrake executive Hand obtain the team that will support them in their effort to secure a Martian artifact. Individual candidates are uploaded into a virtual construct and interviewed, and if deemed to be in possession of the necessary skills each is given the choice either to provide support or be returned to the soul market, where they will have to wait to be purchased by other individuals or repossessed by the military. Unsurprisingly, it is an offer that none of the interviewees refuses, in spite of the fact that their existence is now subject to ownership.

Essentially, the paradox that emerges between the body, identity, and freedom throughout the Takeshi Kovacs trilogy has its origin in Morgan's extrapolated vision of the future in which science and technology have advanced to such a degree that notions of the body, identity, and subjectivity have become increasingly complicated. It is Morgan's vision of this technologized future social reality that also informs his unique reinterpretation of the transhuman.

Transhuman Dynamic

Morgan's vision of a technologized future informs a reinterpretation of the transhuman subject and raises questions relating to equality and disparity between individuals.

Unlike the narratives examined previously, Morgan's trilogy presents the reader with an image of a social reality in which the transhuman accounts for a majority of the population. Critical in his approach to and presentation of the changes informed by technoscientific progress, Morgan's trilogy does not depict a social reality in which inequality between individuals has been relieved through technoscientific progress. If anything, the Takeshi Kovacs trilogy offers a social reality in which the possibility of transcending the human condition through obtaining skills and abilities previously inaccessible to everyday individuals has further increased the disparity between socioeconomic groups. Throughout the narratives, however, the very concept of transcending the human condition is revealed to be a matter of degree, as there are a variety of transhuman figures, each having transcended the human condition differently and having obtained their own unique skills and abilities. Nevertheless, these skills and abilities stem from two primary sources: training and psychological conditioning, which, as a facet of experience and memory, become assimilated into the stack and thus account for a facet of the individual's consciousness, or augmentation applied directly to the body (sleeve).

As an advanced military unit, the Envoy Corps' primary concerns are war and the dynamics of armed and unarmed combat. In Morgan's vision of the future, however, the face of war has changed, especially in relation to the means and methods by which such conflicts are fought and won. The number of combatants one force is capable of deploying against another has become largely irrelevant, especially when considering that the vast majority of "military victories of the last half millennium have been won by small, mobile guerrilla forces" which can be directly decanted into "sleeves with combat conditioning, jacked-up nervous systems and steroid built bodies" (2001, p. 34). This process is not without complication, however, because these soldiers are now sleeved in bodies that are not theirs, have been placed on planets or in environments with which they may be unfamiliar, and are expected to fight strangers for causes they have "probably never even heard of and certainly don't understand" (2001, p. 34).

Irrespective of the fact that soldiers can be directly placed into jacked-up combat-ready sleeves, technology can only go so far. As Takeshi explains in *Altered Carbon*, "Neurachem conditioning, cyborg interfaces, augmentation—all this stuff is physical. Most of it doesn't even touch the pure mind, and it's the pure mind that gets freighted" (2001, p. 34). It was these complications, Takeshi says, that the Envoy Corps sought to address by overcoming both the human condition and the very technology by which its natural limitations were superseded. At the core of Envoy training is psychological conditioning and the implementation of "psychospiritual techniques that oriental cultures on Earth had known about for millennia," which have been structured into a "training system so complete that on most worlds graduates of it were instantly forbidden by law to hold any political or military office" (2001, p. 34). As a result of this extreme conditioning, Envoy personnel are able to achieve states of mental clarity and focus inaccessible to everyday individuals. Further, as combat conditions are dynamic, making it impossible for soldiers to anticipate the situation by which they will be confronted, the members of the Corps learn to forgo expectation and anticipation, theoretically making them prepared for anything.

From his training and experience within the Corps, Kovacs has gained skills and abilities that no ordinary human, augmented or otherwise, is capable of matching. One of the main attributes of Corps training is the acquisition of an eidetic memory, or total recall. As Kovacs explains to Bancroft during their initial meeting: "I work by absorption.... Whatever I come into contact with, I soak up, and I use that to get by" (2001, p. 34). For Kovacs, information can be as useful in combat and conflict as any weapon.[27] Another, perhaps more obvious ability gained through his training is lightning-fast combat reflexes. While Takeshi's aptitude for physical conflict is displayed throughout the trilogy, his reflexes are displayed in *Altered Carbon* during a confrontation with a man who blames Bancroft for his daughter's death: "The ex-tac spun on me without warning, and there was blind murder in his eyes and his crooked hands.... But you can't jump an Envoy—the conditioning won't let it happen. I saw the attack coming almost before he knew he was going to do it himself" (2001, p. 97).

The principle of Envoy conditioning is based around the deconstruction of the human condition. This is explained in *Broken Angels*, when Kovacs tells a fellow soldier that in the Corps they "push you to the wall, they unpick your psyche in virtual and they rebuild you with a whole lot of conditioned shit that in your saner moments you'd probably rather not have" (2003, p. 246). Through the application of psychospiritual techniques and combat-oriented philosophy, Corps training seeks to remove natural hard-wired responses to environmental or situational stimuli and predispositions. Envoys are trained to forgo the confidence other soldiers place in weaponry. Throughout the trilogy, the philosophical principles of Envoy training are revealed through Kovacs's former trainer Virginia Vidaura. In *Altered Carbon*, for example, Takeshi remembers her explaining:

> A weapon is a tool ... a tool for killing and destroying. And there will be times when, as an Envoy, you must kill and destroy. Then you will choose and equip yourself with the tools that you need. But remember the weakness of weapons. They are an extension—you are the killer and destroyer. You are whole, with or without them [2001, p. 137].

In *Broken Angels*, Virginia is shown giving a similar address. However, here she is instructing trainees to reject their misplaced concerns regarding the physical body, or more specifically, the bodies in which they are currently sleeved:

> Check functionality.... It's not injury you're concerned with, it's damage. Pain you can either use or shut down. Wounds matter only if they cause structural impairment. Don't worry about the blood; it isn't yours. You put this flesh on a couple of days ago, and you'll be taking it off again soon if you can manage not to get yourself killed first. Don't worry about wounds; check your functionality [2003, p. 263].

Irrespective of the Envoy Corps' implementation of psychospiritual conditioning or their soldiers' ability to access Zen-like states of focus, as a facet of the military whose primary concern is armed conflict, the success of Corps' soldiers inevitably derives from their will and capacity for violence. In *Altered Carbon*, Takeshi explains that to make an Envoy, "They burn out every evolved violence limitation instinct in the human psyche. Submission signal recognition, pecking order dynamics, pack loyalties. It all goes, tuned out a neuron at a time; and they replace it with a conscious will to do harm" (2001, p. 238).

Through a process of deconstruction during which natural responses and tendencies are removed while others are reinforced, the Envoy Corps is shown to have the capacity to produce transhuman individuals with abilities and skills that far supersede those of others. They are highly adaptable, merciless, and brutal. In spite of their superiority to others, however, Envoys, especially those who are discharged or choose to return to civilian life, inevitably come to question whether they are the same individuals they had been prior to Envoy induction. Ironically, even in a social reality predominately populated by transhumans, those who have gained the capacity to transcend the limitations imposed upon other individuals are still left carrying a sense of estrangement.

In the final installment of the trilogy, *Woken Furies*, Virginia expresses this sense of alienation, asking Takeshi: "Do you ever wonder ... if we're really human anymore?" In response, Kovacs says: "As Envoys ... I try not to buy into the standard tremble-tremble-the-posthumans-are-coming crabshit, if that's what you mean" (2005, p. 455). Although she admits that it is stupid, Virginia nevertheless goes on to explain that "sometimes I talk to Jack and the others,[28] and it's like they're a different fucking species to me. The things they believe. The level of belief they can bring to bear, with next to nothing to justify it" (2005, p. 455). Despite this, their displacement and superseding of the everyday individual carries with it a sense not of "belonging" but of "brutal power.... The liberating savagery that rose out of a bone-deep knowledge that you were feared. That you were whispered of across the Settled Worlds and that ever in the corridors of governance on Earth, the power brokers grew quiet at your name" (2005, p. 502).

Richard Morgan's Takeshi Kovacs trilogy borrows from and shares with movement-era cyberpunk a number of aesthetic, thematic, and ideological similarities. Morgan's implementation of various cyberpunk elements such as the cityscape, drug use, and petty criminality informs the appearances of the characters and the social reality in which they exist, while also reinforcing the protagonist's antiheroic identity and aids in demonstrating how speculative fiction has developed in response to the emergence of transhuman theory and technoscientific development. However, Morgan's greatest contribution to both speculative fiction and the paradoxical protagonist stems from his subversion of canonical cyberpunk's most recognized tropes, specifically virtual reality and disembodiment. In this, the Takeshi Kovacs trilogy returns focus to the body and rejects cyberpunk's advocacy of disembodied states of existence. This emphasis is primarily supported through the protagonist's use of violence and the visceral impact of the narrative as a whole. However, through its depiction of advanced technologies, which not only provide individuals with access to immortality but the freedom to choose their own physical appearances through the commodification of the body, Morgan problematizes the concept of identity and further complicates notions pertaining to mind/body dualism. In spite of the emphasis Morgan's trilogy places upon the body, its protagonist cannot be defined by his physical appearance or the ethnic or cultural factors that—while clearly informing a large part of the his identity and personal belief system—are often devoid of physical/aesthetic representation. Further, unlike canonical cyberpunk protagonists whose mode of action is limited to their capacity to manipulate the information networks in which they operate, Kovacs uses violence to achieve desired goals, thus affirming his antiheroic identity.

Seven

Genetic Fear in Richard Morgan's *Black Man*

Focusing on Richard Morgan's *Black Man* (2007), this chapter examines the use of the transhuman antihero to reflect the fear and anxiety surrounding the use of genetic technologies such as genetic engineering. Through its depiction of artificially created beings that inevitably come to be perceived by everyday individuals as nonhuman monsters, Morgan's narrative not only embodies much of the fear surrounding the use of genetic technologies but also moves to explore the moral implications as well as the possible socio-political consequences that may emerge from their use. However, as the artificially created beings of the narrative appear no different from ordinary individuals, *Black Man* reinterprets the contemporary monster mythology. Further, in drawing upon the nature-versus-nurture debate—specifically in relation to identity and the significance of factors such as genetics and socialization upon its development—the novel blurs the boundaries between human and nonhuman. It is this ambiguity that promotes not only the protagonist's antiheroic identity but also his paradoxical nature.

Fear of Genetic Technologies

Richard Morgan's stand-alone novel *Black Man* explores sensitive areas relating to the use of genetic technologies within humans, specifically genetic or biological engineering. To this end, the novel ultimately comes to embody many of the fears and anxieties surrounding the use of such technologies and the potential consequences that may emerge should they be implemented for the creation of artificial life.

At its most basic, genetic engineering refers to the direct alteration of an organism's genome using genetic technologies. Thus, a genetically engineered organism is one which has been created through the introduction of recombinant DNA. As one of several areas of technoscientific development that has the potential to offer individuals the means by which their physical and mental limitations might be overcome, genetic technologies, specifically those relating to genetic engineering, have become closely affiliated with the transhuman movement. As with other areas of technoscientific development affiliated with transhumanism, much of the focus surrounding genetic technologies stems from its potential application for the enhancement, or general improvement, of the human organism. According to Buchanan, Brock, and Daniels, genetic technologies will "empower human beings to cure and prevent diseases" and have the potential to offer individuals the ability to "shape some of their most important biological characteristics" (2000, p. 1). Irrespective of the potential benefits offered by genetic technologies, research and development in such areas remain controversial and a highly contested issue, one that is perhaps surrounded by more fear, anxiety, and stigmatization than any other within the fields of technoscience. According to Chris Gray, much of the controversy surrounding genetic engineering stems from the fact that it not only seems to foreshadow a human/transhuman divide, as will be discussed later in the chapter, but also represents the "most likely and certainly the most effective, way of using artificial evolution to produce intelligent nonhuman creatures" (2002 p. 118). The concept of "artificial" or designer evolution, to which Gray refers, seeks to reduce the risk of unstable variables which greatly impact upon species adaptation during the process of natural selection or evolution. Advocates such as Buchanan claim that designer evolution will be integral for ensuring the continuity of the human species, arguing that natural selection is flawed, near-sighted, and often provides only short-term fixes, rather than the best possible outcome for species in terms of increasing their survivability (2011, p. 28). Buchanan suggests that adaptations resulting from natural selection are not simply "nonconscious" but rather "downright unintelligent" and the organisms it produces are not "beautifully designed, harmonious, completed masterworks that will endure so long as we don't meddle with them" but "cobbled-together, unstable works in progress" whose progress is subsequently abandoned, often at a critical juncture (2011, p. 28).

Buchanan is not alone in his advocation for designer evolution. Futurist Max More believes that with a complete understanding of genetics, individuals will gain the ability to alter their appearances and radically improve their health and well-being in general (1993). For Ray Kurzweil, genetic technologies reflect one of several areas of technoscientific development that have the potential to provide individuals access to immortality (2009). If Kurzweil is correct, this would mark the realization of Victor Frankenstein's dream of not only gaining insight into the very secrets of life and death, but of discovering the means by which death might be overcome. Even renowned theoretical physicist Stephen Hawking warns genetic engineering will become integral to the survival of the human species as computer technology is evolving so rapidly that it might someday come to be recognized as the dominant species—albeit an artificial one—upon the planet (Walsh, 2001).

In spite of its potential applications, there are many who radically oppose genetic technologies. A common argument taken up by critics is that genetic engineering is, in effect, playing God, as outlined in the report *Splicing Life* (Abram et al. 1987), produced by the President's Commission for the Study of Ethical Problems in Medicine and Biomedical and Behavioral Research. There are other considerations, such as the potential creation of genetically engineered viruses or the militarization of genetic technologies in general. Protest against the implementation of genetic technologies is especially efficacious in relation to the alteration of the human genome. As Al-Rodham Nayef points out, one of the most common arguments deployed against the use of genetic technologies in humans is that "human nature is sacred and delicate and that it should not be tinkered with, particularly since the consequences of modifying the human form are unpredictable" (2011, p. 194). Further, Nayef claims that another significant focal point is the Frankenstein argument—a scenario wherein genetic modification leads to the creation of a "superior breed of humans," which would radically undermine the "worth and dignity of normal, unmodified humans" (2011, p. 195).

It is essentially the latter scenario that is the primary focus of *Black Man*. Set one hundred years in the future, Morgan's narrative confronts the reader with a social reality in which advancements in genetic technologies have led to the creation of several variations upon the human genome. Although the genetically modified beings presented in *Black Man*—often referred to as "variants" or, derogatorily, "twists"—do not reflect a "superior breed of humans" (2011, p. 195), they do possess skills and unique attributes unattainable by unmodified individuals.

That the existence of genetically engineered beings has the potential to undermine or devalue the "worth and dignity of normal, unmodified humans" (Nayef, 2011, p. 195) is aptly expressed by female protagonist, Sevgi Ertekin,[1] during her discussion with fellow detective Tom Norton[2] concerning the latter's reaction to Carl Marsalis, a thirteen[3] and the narrative's primary protagonist. It's only natural for an unmodified male to feel intimidated and uneasy around a variant thirteen, Sevgi explains, going on to say that, after all, "it's how they built them, it's what they're for. And your reaction—that's how they built you" (2007, p. 188). The only difference, however, is that where it took natural selection and biological evolution "hundred thousand generations" to put Tom together, it has taken human science less than a century to genetically engineer Marsalis and the rest of his kind (2007, p. 188). Nayef points out that while the use of genetic technologies may seem inconsequential when implemented upon an individual level, when deployed upon a broader social or even global scale, as depicted in *Black Man*, they would undermine the intrinsic value of the human organism as a whole (2011, p. 194). This sentiment is one shared by Francis Fukuyama, who argues that while anxieties concerning the unintended consequences are legitimate, the primary fear surrounding the use of genetic technologies (within humans) is that "biotechnology will cause us in some way to lose our humanity—that is, some essential quality that has always underpinned our sense of who we are and where we are going" (2002, p. 101).

Another concern surrounding the use of genetic technologies is the potential for the creation of new forms of inequality and disparity. According to Nayef, many fear that use of genetic technologies will "increase the gaps between the rich and poor and [...] more firmly solidify differences and inequalities across generations and cultures" (2011, p. 195). The potential inequality produced through the implementation of genetic technologies is something recognized by a number of critics. Elaine Graham, for example, argues that while it is impossible to ignore the potential benefits of genetic technologies, specifically in relation to health and medicine, it would be naïve to assume that such technologies should be free of commercial interest or financial investment (2002, p. 118). In fact, Graham goes on to argue that while even the most cynical critics may perceive research into genetics as little more than an egotistical pursuit of knowledge, there are others—though she does not stipulate who, it should perhaps be pointed out—who see it as little more than a quest for "lucrative financial benefits," one which "epitomizes the global trend of information as commodity, data that commands a high price" (2002, pp. 118–119). This argument is also explored extensively by Fukuyama, who warns that progress in the areas of biotechnologies, specifically genetic engineering, will inevitably lead to a future in which the human individual will have been altered beyond recognition and the emergence of a new "kind of eugenics, with all the moral implications with which that word is fraught" (2002, p. 72).

The potential forms of inequality that may result from the use of genetic technologies are both broad and numerous. Perhaps the most obvious, or at least one of the most widely discussed, is the possibility for exploitation. As Stephen Wilkinson points out in his examination of the growing "designer-baby" trend, in choosing the production of one individual over the other, individuals concerned in making such decisions are thus confirming that the existence of one is preferable or more valued—for whatever reason—than that of the other (2010, p. 2). Further, Wilkinson argues this affirmation leads to children, or individuals in general, being "wrongfully instrumentalized" and "treated as mere means rather than ends-in-themselves" or even perceived and "treated as commodities" (2010, p. 130).

In *Black Man*, the notion of exploitation, especially for economic purposes, and the treatment of genetically modified individuals as mere means, rather than ends in themselves, is described by Jeff Norton when he explains to his brother Tom that variants, with their unique attributes, were all designed to fulfill specific roles: "Spaceflight programmes wanted the hibernoids, the bonobos were patriarchal authority's wet dream of womanhood" (2007, p. 99). The bonobos were thus used as companions and sex workers. The thirteens, on the other hand, with their natural aggression and predisposition to violence, were produced to engage in war and conflict. As explained by the protagonist, Carl Marsalis, during their training as children, the young thirteens were often told that they were special because they had the capacity to do what the society that created them "no longer had the stomach for" (2007, p. 528). Ironically, however, with no wars left to fight and deemed too dangerous to live among the general population, variant thirteen, as will be explained later in the chapter, becomes subject to further inequality. This oversight, Jeff goes on to explain, is similar to that concerning the "bonobos and the hibernoids and every other misbegotten premature poke at reengineering last century's idiot optimist pioneers saddled us with. Guesswork and bad intentions" (2007, p. 99). In conclusion, Jeff claims that no one designed variants "because they thought they were giving it a better shot at life, liberty and the pursuit of fucking happiness. They were products, all of them, agenda targeted" (2007 p. 99).

That such oversights should occur coincides with existing concerns regarding the rapid progress being made in the fields of genetic technologies. As Gray argues, science's "ability to manipulate genes is rushing ahead of our understanding of what they do and how they do it" (2001, p. 114). This is a special concern when considering the impact upon the individuals who may be subject to genetic modification or engineering in the future, specifically children. As Fukuyama points out, "a child who is brought up a certain way can rebel later," but having a child genetically engineered is like giving her "a tattoo which she can never subsequently remove and will have to hand down not just to her own children but to all subsequent children" (2002, p. 94). Individuals or beings derived through genetic engineering are essentially predisposed to have specific attributes or reflect certain qualities. Thus it could be argued that genetic engineering in children reflects a violation of fundamental human rights, seeing it is not only non-consensual, but also has the potential to diminish a future individual's capacity for self-determination.

Although concerns regarding the potential exploitation of genetically engineered beings are not without merit in discussing the potential consequences of such technologies, far more recognized are issues pertaining to the potential for disparity between genetically modified and unmodified individuals. In Morgan's *Black Man*, the disparity separating unmodified humans and variants, specifically variant thirteen, has led to the latter being perceived as monsters.

(Non)human Disparity

Morgan's narrative depicts a not-too-distant future where progress in genetic technologies has resulted in the existence of several variations upon the human genome. Essentially, the narrative focuses on Carl Marsalis, a variant thirteen, which is described throughout the narrative as being the most dangerous and clearly the most feared and stigmatized of any variant. With their predisposition to violence and sociopathic nature, thirteens were designed for their potential military application, but a decline in military campaigns has made the purpose for the thirteens' continued existence questionable. Further, deemed too dangerous to coexist alongside unmodified individuals, the thirteens have been rounded up and sent to the colonies on Mars. Those who refused were detained in internment camps, and the few who escaped or fled were hunted down and incarcerated or executed. As Jeff Norton explains to his brother, the danger posed by variant thirteens is not only due to their predisposition to violence, but their refusal to cooperate with authority, compounded with their aggressive and unpredictable nature. Further, he explains, thirteen is a type of human that hasn't existed in over twenty thousand years and one that has little interest in anything other than "taking what they want, regardless of damage or cost" (Morgan, 2007, p. 102).

As a result of the fear and stigmatization surrounding variant thirteens, they have inevitably come to be perceived as the nonhuman other, or monsters, a perception that has been compounded by the Jacobsen report and the subsequent loss of their basic human rights. The similarities that might be drawn between variant thirteen and Victor Frankenstein's monster are obvious: both are artificially created beings, designed and brought to life through the implementation of technology and science; both are subsequently abandoned by those who created them; and both come to be perceived as monsters simply because of what they are, albeit for different reasons. More complex, however, are the allegorical and philosophical similarities shared between Morgan's *Black Man* (2007) and Shelley's *Frankenstein* (1818). This is especially the case in relation to each narrative's treatment and exploration of identity and the impact of external factors—such as the individual's experiences of social reality (in *Frankenstein*) and genetics (in *Black Man*)—upon its development.

Essentially, both *Frankenstein* and *Black Man* concern themselves with the possibility of using science and technology to create life and the potential consequences that may arise as a result. Where *Frankenstein* retained an individual focus, only ever hinting at the possibility of broader ramifications, *Black Man* moves to explore the potential consequences of life-creating technologies upon a global scale, paying particular attention to areas such as national and international politics and economic agenda. Both narratives feature protagonists who have come to be defined as monsters and thus alienated from the social reality in which they exist. However, devoid of the grotesque aesthetic affiliated with Frankenstein's monster, variant thirteens fail to evoke the same sense of visceral horror, yet are nonetheless feared, loathed, stigmatized, and perceived as monsters by everyday individuals.

Although all thirteens are considered monsters, for Carl Marsalis the hatred with which he is forced to exist is twofold. Early in the novel, it is explained that there is a "whole shifting topography of dislike out there for what Carl Marsalis was, and it touched on pretty much every level of human wiring" (2007, p. 11). As a result of his chosen vocation—hunting down and either detaining or executing other variant thirteens—there are individuals, both human and variant alike, who "condemned his professional existence as amoral" (2007, p. 11). This, he explains, is compounded upon an emotive level by the "generalized social revulsion that comes with the label turncoat" (2007, p. 12). Further, there was also "a rarely admitted but nonetheless giddy terror that he was, despite everything, still one of them" (2007, p. 12). The latter carries a dual meaning. On the one hand, there is the fear derived from unmodified humans who, in spite being aware of Marsalis's genetic status, are forced to acknowledge that he is human, perhaps largely due to thirteen's lack of the grotesque aesthetic so often affiliated with nonhuman monsters. On the other hand, however, the "giddy terror" to which he refers is evoked within his fellow thirteens whom he hunts down. In this respect Marsalis is not only perceived as a monster by ordinary humans, but also loathed by his fellow thirteens.

Aesthetically, variant thirteens are no different to unmodified individuals. Nevertheless, they are preconceived as monsters. While the differences between unmodified individuals and variant thirteens are described throughout the book, it is aptly expressed by Rovayo Yavuz,[4] who explains to detective Sevgi that while she doesn't want to sound like a human purity advocate, she has spent the last decade working around the internment camps, and as far as she is concerned, thirteen is the "closest thing to an alien race you're ever going to see" (2007, p. 277). That such differences separate thirteens from unmodified individuals is also acknowledged by the protagonist, who admits that, as a thirteen, he neither can nor should be recognized as a human (2007, p. 158). This is further reinforced by the South American crime lord whom Marsalis approaches while tracking a rogue thirteen. The criminal tells him that the color of an individual's skin is no longer relevant but it's never been a "race thing where thirteens are concerned ... more a species gap" (2007, p. 314).

The differences between variant thirteens and ordinary humans are not merely superficial, but engraved at the genetic level. This is aptly expressed by Marsalis when he explains to Sevgi and her partner Tom Norton that there is no reason Merrin's[5] actions or motivations should make sense to them because at a basic biological and genetic level he is nothing like them: "Down in the limbic system where it counts," Marsalis explains, "across the amygdalae and up into the orbitofrontal cortex, Merrin has about a thousand biochemical processes going on that you don't have ... of course" what he does "doesn't make sense to you" (2007, p. 162). This is reinforced when Sevgi and Tom question the haphazard trail of bodies—victims seemingly selected at random—left in Merrin's wake, believing that his behavior is typical of a serial killer. In response, Marsalis is quick to point out that they have no understanding of what they are dealing with: "You think because Merrin's killed a couple of dozen people, he's some kind of serial killer writ large? That's not what this is about" (2007, p. 216). Further, he goes on to explain:

> Serial killers are damaged humans. You know this.... They leave a trail, they leave clues, they get caught. And that's because in the end, consciously or subconsciously, they want to get caught. Calculated murder is an anti-social act, it's hard for humans to do, and it takes special circumstances at either a personal or social level to enable the capacity. But that's you people. It's not me, and it's not Merrin and it's not any variant thirteen. We're not like you [2007, p. 218].

In the same address, Marsalis stipulates that there are large psychological differences separating variant thirteens from unmodified individuals. For a variant thirteen, he contends, murder is not a symbolic act, as is often the case with humans, but rather a means to an end:

> We're the witches. We're the violent exiles, the lone-wolf nomads that you bred out of the race back when growing crops and living in one place got so popular. We don't have, we don't need a social context. You have to understand this: there is nothing wrong with Merrin. He's not damaged. He's not killing these people as an expression of some childhood psychosis, he's not doing it because he's identified them as some dehumanised, segregated extra-tribal group. He's just carrying out a plan of action, and he is comfortable with it [2007, p. 218].

This notion reinforces the comments made earlier by Sevgi during her initial examination of the bodies found aboard the ship upon which Merrin returned to Earth. A fellow officer suggests that the thirteen would have had to be insane in order to commit acts so heinous, and in response Sevgi concedes that there is a possibility that the rogue thirteen they are searching for has become psychologically unstable, if not prior to, then certainly following his arrival upon Earth, having just spent the last "several months completely alone in deep space ... apart from the sporadic company of fellow crewmembers revived long enough to carve edible meat from" (2007, p. 65). Nevertheless, she reasons, an individual wouldn't "have to be insane in order to do these things" but rather "just have a goal and be determined to attain it" (2007, p. 65). According to Sevgi, the scene aboard the ship, as grim and macabre as it may seem, does not reflect "symptoms of insanity" but only evidence of "great force of will. Evidence of planning and execution shorn of any socially imposed limitations" (2007, p. 65).

While it is not impossible for individuals to commit murder, as Marsalis points out, it is nonetheless an "anti-social act" that is "hard for humans to do," and irrespective of what they might believe "it takes special circumstances at either a personal or a social level to enable the capacity" (2007, p. 218). Essentially, it is their capacity to shuck "socially imposed limitations" (2007, p. 65), specifically in relation to violence, that has determined their nonhuman status and led unmodified individuals to perceive them as monsters.

While the variant thirteens depicted in Morgan's narrative share an affinity with Frankenstein's monster, it is revealed that, unlike the latter, variant thirteen is not completely artificial in origin. Instead it is explained throughout the narrative that thirteen is a breed of humans that died out over twenty thousand years ago, largely due to their inability to adapt to the demands imposed by the emergence of agriculture-based society. Unfortunately, however, in spite of their seemingly natural origins, the similarities between variant thirteen and the traditional monster, specifically artificially created beings such as Frankenstein's monster, but also those derived from myth and legend, were too obvious to ignore. This view is expressed by Nevant, a thirteen whom Marsalis had tracked and incarcerated some years prior to the events of *Black Man*, who explains to Marsalis that humans have been "desperately looking for witches and monsters ever since they wiped us out the first time around" but "now they've got us back," they don't really know how they should respond (2007, p. 282). This notion coincides with Jeffrey Cohen's statement that no monster, as an embodiment of social fear and anxiety, "tastes of death but once" (1999, p. 5).

Nevant goes on to explain that much of the fear and stigmatization by which variant thirteen is confronted stems from ordinary humans' inability to comprehend or in this case coexist alongside what they do not understand. According to Nevant, this is largely due to a propensity for absolutism, specifically in relation to belief and moral reasoning, which is as genetically coded into unmodified humans as a predisposition to violence is for variant thirteen (2007, pp. 282–283). Further, Nevant explains that humans lack rational perspectives because their beliefs and perceptions of the world are based on "knee-jerk" reactions (2007, p. 285), concluding that for humans there are "monsters, there is evil, and it's somewhere out there in the dark" (2007, p. 285).

More pragmatic in his perception of the fear surrounding variant thirteen, Jeff Norton states that while thirteens were unarguably superior in a hunter-gatherer context, they became obsolete simply because "they won't fucking do as they're told. They won't work in the fields and bring in the harvest for some kleptocratic old bastard with a beard" (2007, p. 264). As Jeff goes on to explain, it was ultimately their refusal to conform that led to variant thirteen's original demise, because those remaining, all the "wimps and conformists, band together under that self-same kleptocratic bastard's paternal hold authority, and we go out with our torches and our farming implements and we exterminate those poor fuckers" (2007, p. 264).

Irrespective of the cause or origins underpinning the fear surrounding variant thirteen, even Marsalis, in spite of being a thirteen himself, is unable to find logic in their continued existence, as revealed during his conversation with Onbekend[6]: "*there is no place for what we are any more....* They killed us twenty thousand years ago with their crops and their craven connivance at hierarchy. They won, Onbekend" (2007, p. 453). Further, he explains that the shift from hunter-gatherer to agricultural-based society was a logical one and that in the end ordinary humans won "because it *worked*. Group cooperation and bowing down to some thug with a beard worked better than standing alone as a thirteen was ever going to.... They hunted us down and they exterminated us, and they got the future as a prize" (2007, pp. 453–454).

The most telling account of the division existing between variant thirteen and unmodified humans is reflected toward the end of the narrative, during Marsalis's last conversation with Onbekend, whom he has mortally wounded in a firefight—during which their location has been surrounded by Bambaren's[7] men, who have been dispatched in response to Marsalis's presence. Just before he dies, however, Onbekend accuses Marsalis of being unable to understand, despite the current situation and the glaringly obvious juxtaposition of variant and human: "the two of us in here, all of them out there," while the "cudlips ... talk such a great fight about equality, democratic accountability, freedom of expression" (2007, p. 624). For Onbekend, democracy has failed and nothing has changed. Neither discrimination nor inequality has been eliminated, merely redirected, providing society a new focus for the projection of their fear and hatred. In the end, Onbekend concludes that humans have kept with the "same old agenda they've had since they wiped us out the first time around" (2007, p. 625).

Having been derived from genetic technologies, the variant thirteens presented in Morgan's narrative have come to be perceived by ordinary individuals as nonhuman, or monsters. To this end, they share an affinity with the monster depicted in Shelley's *Frankenstein* (1818). Whether their identity as monsters is deserved (especially when considering the fear and inequality with which they are confronted) is questionable. Unarguably, however, it is variant thirteens' capacity for violence that has determined their status as monsters and acts to reinforce the protagonist's antiheroic identity.

Violence

As a variant thirteen, Carl Marsalis is naturally aggressive and described as having a genetic predisposition to violence—however, his use of violence is largely pragmatic. Nevertheless, compounded by Morgan's highly visceral prose, violence not only determines Marsalis's antiheroic identity, but also works to ground the protagonist in physicality. Like Takeshi Kovacs, the protagonist of Morgan's earlier trilogy, Marsalis is largely defined by his body and physical ethnic markers; unlike Takeshi, who (in spite of frequent reference to his mixed Japanese and Hungarian ancestry) has the freedom to change his physical appearance at will, due to radical advances in science and technology, thus rendering physical markers such as age, sex, and ethnicity obsolete, Marsalis has a fixed, physical identity. Marsalis is of African descent, suggesting parallels between racial and genetic prejudice. This is most effectively illustrated early in the novel when, having failed to register with local authorities before conducting his investigation and attempting to detain a rogue thirteen, Marsalis is charged and placed in a Republican[8] prison where, for the first time, he encounters prejudice based not on genetics but ethnic markers. He describes being able to track his change in attitude toward the "antique racial epithets" still used within the Republic:

> *Nigger.* The first couple of times, it was disconcerting and almost quaint, like having your face slapped with a dueling glove. With time, it came to feel more and more like the verbal spittle it was intended to be. That his fellow blacks in general population used it of themselves did nothing to stem the

slowly awakening anger. It was a locally evolved defense, and he was not from here. Fuck these Republicans and their chimpanzee-level society" [2007, p. 129].

The association established between genetic and racial prejudice is later reinforced during Marsalis' conversation with Rovayo, who is also of African descent. When Rovayo questions the purpose of the Haag⁹ system, Marsalis explains that it was designed to take down thirteens, described as having an immune system twice as effective as those possessed by unmodified humans. Rovayo scoffs in response, before going on to inform Marsalis that "a couple of hundred years ago, they built a whole new type of bullet because they thought ordinary slugs wouldn't take down a black man with cocaine in his blood" (2007, p. 517). She claims that government officials first tied cocaine use to black communities, making it a "race-based issue. Then they reckon they need a bigger bang to put us down, because we're all coked up.... Welcome to the .357 magnum round" (2007, p. 518).

As with the Takeshi Kovacs trilogy, Morgan's emphasis upon physicality and the body is highlighted through the protagonist's use of violence. However, what comes to be revealed throughout the narrative is that in spite of variant thirteens' affinity with monsters, their use of violence is largely pragmatic, used only as a means to an end. For example, when Carl Marsalis is first introduced, he is depicted in a bar, asking questions regarding the whereabouts of the thirteen he is currently tracking, when an individual produces a knife and attacks. In response Marsalis defends himself by hitting him "with a tanindo move—palm-heel, twice" which "broke the man's nose, crushed his temple, sent him sprawling away from the bar to the floor" (2007, p. 14).

In the latter scene, Marsalis becomes aware of a girl who has slipped out during the commotion. Once outside, he finds her easily and follows her back to the house being used by the thirteen he is currently tracking. The moment he enters the residence, however, a firefight breaks out. Initially Marsalis attempts to negotiate and demands that the thirteen, Gray, put down his weapon and surrender. With Marsalis distracted, Gaby (the woman who had led him to the house) rushes for him, "hands up, fingers splayed like talons," and he shoots her (2007, p. 19). Marsalis then turns to Gray and fires, the latter stumbling "backward like a boxer taking heavy blows" (p. 19); Marsalis approaches the wounded thirteen, disarms him, and then shoots him "twice again in the chest" before watching him "carefully, gun leveled, until the life dimmed out of Gray's eyes" (2007, p. 19).

As Marsalis goes to leave, however, he finds Gaby, whom he had shot, wounded but still alive. He tells her that he is going for help before making his way to the door, where he pauses and "in the flood of light from outside … swiveled quietly and shot her once more, through the back of the head" (2007, p. 19). While the decision to shoot her might seem cold-blooded, it can also be interpreted as something of a kindness seeing that she had been tagged by a Haag gun, which would inevitably result in a long and painful death.

Although Marsalis' use of violence is selfish, it is not without purpose and, to some extent, justification. As a thirteen, Marsalis had originally been sent to the colonies on Mars, but gained a unique opportunity when he won the "lottery" that provided him with the luxury of being allowed to return to Earth. Still restricted by his genetic identity, however, Marsalis was still considered too dangerous to live alongside unmodified individuals and thus had few options. Before long, he was approached by UNGLA, a particular branch of the government that dealt with genetic variants, with an offer: he would be able to remain on Earth and have limited freedom in exchange for his services as a bounty hunter—tracking down and apprehending or, depending on the circumstance, executing other variant thirteens. The violence implemented by Marsalis is therefore not only sanctioned by UNGLA, and thus politically justified, but at an individual level, it is also a matter of necessity if he is to remain on Earth. In spite of being the only thirteen allowed to exist upon Earth outside the internment camps, the life Marsalis currently leads is not one he enjoys, something that comes to be revealed after he is arrested by local law-enforcements with whom he had failed to register, when he reflects upon a curious, yet unavoidable epiphany: "*I don't want to do this any more*" (2007, p. 25). This lends a sense of tragedy to the protagonist's existence, comparable to what is experienced by the monster in Shelley's *Frankenstein*.

As with a number of paradoxical protagonists examined in previous chapters, specifically Takeshi Kovacs, and Rorschach, Marsalis is also depicted engaging in violence for more personal, if not altruistic purposes. Toward the end of the narrative, for instance, Sevgi has been shot with a Haag gun and is admitted to the hospital, but nothing can be done. Believing that he is largely responsible, Marsalis remains at the hospital and is soon approached by Murat, Sevgi's father, who presents him with a syringe containing a drug commonly used in euthanasia and requests that Marsalis end his daughter's life. Murat tells him that he is unable to do it himself because he is a doctor and has thus signed an oath, but goes on to explain that "even if I had not taken an oath, I do not think I would be capable of ending my own daughter's life" (2007, p. 507). Just before the injection is given, Sevgi reassures Tom and her father, telling them that she knows they would have given her the drug, had she asked, but instead she had chosen Marsalis "because he can, that's all" (2007, p. 522). Further, she tells Tom and her father not to cry, but notices that the thirteen is the only one in the room with dry eyes: "His face was black stone as he prepped the spike, held it up one-handed to the light, while his other hand touched warm and callus-fingered on the crook of her arm" (2007, p. 523).

In another example of benevolent violence, just prior to her death, Sevgi tells Marsalis that if there was anyone she would like to have killed it would have been Amy Westhoff, who she believes had been responsible for the death of her former lover, Ethan. Ethan had been a thirteen, and Amy, jealous of his relationship with Sevgi, had informed the police, who, in turn, had gunned him down. After Sevgi dies, Marsalis thus arranges to meet with Amy in a café close to the hospital. When he asks, Amy denies having informed the police about Ethan and then questions what all this was about. In response, Carl tells her that he has a message from Sevgi that she was unable to deliver herself. When Amy asks what message, Carl shoots her:

> She flinched, yelped, reared back in the booth and looked down at her trouser leg. She pressed on her thigh with both hands. "What the fuck was that?"
> "That was a genetically modified curare flechette," Carl said coldly. "It's going to paralyze your skeletal muscle system so you can't breathe or call for help."
> Westhoff stared at him. Tried to get up from the table, made a muffled grunting sound instead and dropped back into her seat, still staring at him.
> "It's a vastly improved variant on natural curare," he went on. "You might call it the thirteen of poisons. I think you'll last about seven or eight minutes. Enjoy" [2007, p. 587].

Although Marsalis' capacity for violence might be the result of his genetic structure, or more specifically, his identity as a variant thirteen, it is often driven or motivated by emotional or personal factors.

Later in the narrative, for instance, Marsalis, driven by revenge, determines to hunt down and kill Onbekend, the thirteen who had tagged Sevgi with the Haag gun, those responsible for the latter's presence of Earth, and anyone else who gets in his way. He approaches Tom Norton and asks for support. When the latter asks if killing is all he can think about, Marsalis explains, "This is what's wired into me, it's what my body chemistry's good for. I am going to build a memorial to Sevgi Ertekin out of Onbekend's blood, and I will cut down anyone who gets in my way. Including you, if you make me" (2007, p. 528). Tom agrees to help, and together they follow the evidence left in Onbekend's wake, which inevitably leads them to Ortiz.[10] They approach Ortiz in a hospital, where Marsalis asks how it is that Ortiz came to be involved with Onbekend. Here, Ortiz reaffirms the link between variant thirteen and the monster when he tells them:

> It was he who came to me, here in New York one night, like a ghost through the security around my home ... like something I had summoned up. I should have known then, all those lessons our myths and legends scream at us, time and again. Never summon up what you cannot control [2007, p. 576].

In spite of Ortiz's cooperation, Marsalis tells Ortiz that he is still going to die. The latter responds by pointing out the irony of Marsalis having previously saved his life only to kill him. However, he goes on to say, it has "always been the double-edged blade that your kind offered us, from the very beginning. Variant thirteen, the avatars of purified violence, our saviours and our nemesis" (2007, p. 576). Marsalis then hauls "the COLIN director up onto his lap, locked an arm around the man's neck, positioned his free hand against the skull" (2007, p. 583). After breaking Ortiz's neck, Marsalis makes his way through the hospital, reflecting on the sirens sounding in response to Ortiz's death, which he perceives as "the wail of distressed cudlip society" (2007, p. 583). For Marsalis, this signifies a call to arms: "*Man of substance down. Rally, gather, form a mob. The beast is out*" (2007, p. 583).

Marsalis's reference to himself as a beast reaffirms the narrative's relationship with other works such as Shelley's *Frankenstein* (1818), inevitably positioning the reader to question, or at least consider, the inequality and prejudice experienced by minority groups—in this case, the thirteens. At the same time, however, this reference also reflects the protagonist's acknowledgment that, as a thirteen, he exists beyond the scope of human individuals, and therefore, irrespective of the causality by which his experiences of social reality are framed, he reflects something that is other and nonhuman—a monster that is not to be considered or understood so much as it is feared, stigmatized, and, if necessary, destroyed.

As a thirteen, Marsalis is described as being naturally aggressive and genetically predisposed to violence. Inevitably, it is variant thirteens' affinity with conflict and their capacity for violence that has led to the fear and stigmatization surrounding their existence. To unmodified individuals, variant thirteen reflects the nonhuman other, or monster. Essentially, it is this nonhuman status, compounded by a capacity for violence, that both determines and reinforces Marsalis's antiheroic identity. Further, it is this same capacity that underpins the protagonist's identity as a transhuman.

Better by Design

As with all the protagonists examined throughout this study, Carl Marsalis is essentially a transhuman, depicted as having skills and attributes unobtainable by ordinary individuals. While not to the same extent as Morgan's Takeshi Kovacs trilogy, *Black Man* depicts a social reality in which transhumans represent a not insignificant percentage of the total population. Unlike Morgan's previous trilogy, however, and a number of other narratives examined within previous chapters (such as Gibson's *Neuromancer*, Effinger's *When Gravity Fails*, or even Bester's precursory *The Stars My Destination*), *Black Man's* depiction of the transhuman is neither cybernetic nor wholly technological; rather, the transhumans depicted in *Black Man* are beings derived through the alteration and manipulation of the human genome. Each variant is described as having its own unique set of skills and attributes, as explained previously.

Like all variant thirteens, Marsalis is depicted as having skills and capacities that supersede the limitations imposed upon unmodified individuals. Compounded by a predisposition to violence, Marsalis, as with all thirteens, is naturally large, well-muscled, and capable of achieving feats of strength and speed that unmodified individuals would find impossible to match. This inhuman strength and speed allow Marsalis, and other thirteens, to implement a style of martial arts called Tanindo, or float fighting, which was derived from existing combat styles, yet developed on Mars, taking full advantage of the planet's lower gravity. Tom argues during a press release—in an attempt to cover up the presence of a thirteen (Marsalis) on Earth—that a martial-arts *"designed for a low-gravity environment isn't likely to be all that dangerous, or even useful, here on earth"* (2007, p. 243)—unless, of course, as Sevgi points out *"you're inhumanly strong and fast"* (2007, p. 242).

Piled upon their natural affinity for violence and enhanced strength and speed, variant thirteens are also equipped with "mesh," a system of internal nanobots that supports their already bolstered attributes, sharpens their combat reflexes and instincts, and aids in pain management. This is revealed early in the narrative during Marsalis's pursuit of Gaby, who he believes knows the location of the rogue thirteen, Gray, he had been pursing:

> With the combat, the mesh had kicked in for real. It flushed him now, warm as the sun, and the pain in his side dropped to memory and a detached knowledge that he was bleeding. His field of vision sharpened on the woman running from him, peripherals smearing out with the brightness in the air [2007, p. 15].

While it is not described as comprehensively, the "mesh" system might be interpreted as a precursor to the neurochem system employed by members of the Envoy Corps depicted Morgan's Takeshi Kovacs trilogy.

As with a majority of the protagonists examined throughout this study, the most obvious and telling depiction of Marsalis's transhuman attributes is reflected through his skills in physical combat. During the attempt made upon Ortiz's life, for example, Marsalis rushes in against three armed opponents with:

> sprinted steps and a whirl of *tanindo* technique. The blade of his left hand slammed in under the lead skater's chin.... The two of them went over together in a tangle of limbs. The spray gun dropped and skittered. Carl got on top of the skater and started hitting him in the face and throat.... The mesh strung moments apart like loops of cabling. Carl hacked down savagely with an elbow one more time and beneath him the lead skater went abruptly limp. As the tumbled wingman got almost back upright, Carl lunged, grabbed up the leader's electromag, clumsily left-handed, squirmed sideways, getting line of fire and emptied the gun [2007, p. 208].

It can thus be argued that many of the transhuman characteristics displayed by Marsalis, as with a number of other protagonists examined throughout this study, are defined, situated, and reinforced through his capacity for violence. Further, violence in this context acts as a marker, highlighting what is essentially the apparent physical superiority of transhuman individuals to unmodified humans. This is aptly reflected following the above scene. Here, eager to get on with the investigation into the recent, failed assassination attempt, Sevgi tells the attending officer that he is wasting their time and and detracting from their capacity to do real police work (2007, p. 212). In response, the officer argues that the real police work at hand concerns the fact that "this twist just killed two armed men in broad daylight, empty-handed, and he doesn't even appear to have a scratch on him" and that while it might be his paranoia, "something about that doesn't chime in time" (2007, p. 212).

The fact that that Marsalis, due to his genetic inheritance, is capable of killing two armed men without sustaining injury himself reveals what might be interpreted not only as the area of exploration upon which *Black Man* focuses, but also, as will be discussed in the following section, the essential paradox underpinning the narrative's protagonist.

Monsters: Born or Made

This section examines how variant thirteens' monster status reveals a paradox concerning the nature of violence and its relationship with human and nonhuman identities. Further, it will be shown how Morgan highlights the ambiguity of categorical identities (human/nonhuman/ monster) by exploring the significance of external factors such as genetics and socialization upon identity development.

Through its depiction of genetically engineered beings who have come to be identified by unmodified individuals as monsters, *Black Man* inevitably explores identity development, specifically the significance of biological factors such as genetics and external influences such as social-ization. However, when the variants depicted throughout the narrative act contrary to what is assumed to be their genetic and thus natural behav-ior, they evoke a paradox that, in consideration of Morgan's treatment of the nature/nurture debate, ultimately raises two questions: Are variants really the monsters unmodified individuals believe them to be, and is their monstrosity a product of genetic inheritance or something gained through socialization and their experience of the social reality in which they are forced to exist?

As previously explained, genetic variants like thirteens are feared and stigmatized by unmodified individuals, who identify them as nonhu-man or monsters. Thus, for a majority of individuals inhabiting the social reality described in *Black Man*, genetics are a clear indicator of individ-uality and for the most part, determine the actions undertaken by a spe-cific individual. Indeed, so great is this belief that laws have been created in order to protect unmodified individuals from genetic variants. The notion that aggressiveness and a predisposition for violence can be linked to genetics, however, is not without merit. Michael Rutter, for instance, points out that there is a "growing body of empirical evidence on the con-tribution of genetic factors to individual differences in antisocial behav-ior" (2008, p. 1). Viding and Frith, also suggest that the existing wealth of twin and adoption studies "confirms that individual differences in violent/ antisocial behavior are heritable" (2006). Although they stipulate that it is highly unlikely that "genes directly code for violence," there is growing evidence that "allelic variation is responsible for individual differences in neurocognitive functioning that, in turn, may determine differential predisposition to violent behavior" (2006).

Perceiving genes as definitive markers for certain characteristics, as depicted in *Black Man*, has a number of negative consequences, especially in relation to inequality and disparity. According to Chris Gray, if it were to be accepted that individuals are little more than their genetic inheritance, "we will have bled most initiative and choice out of the world" (2002, p. 125). Further, he contends that inequalities and prejudices that "people have struggled against for centuries, will become enshrined for all time by science" (2002, p. 125).

While identity (the characteristics or traits and the actions undertaken by an individual) might to some extent be influenced by genetic inheritance, there is equal evidence to support the contention that socialization, environment, and experience are just as, if not more, significant in identity development. According to Ramez Naam, it is impossible to accurately predict traits and characteristics within an individual because they "depend on a complex interaction of genes and environment" (2005, p. 153). Neither genetics, nor the environment in which the individual exists, she continues, "produce an effect in isolation" as both are required to "affect behavior" (2005, p. 153). Naam supports this argument by using intelligence as an example. While intelligence, specifically an individual's IQ, might, in some part, be determined by genetic inheritance, guaranteeing that the offspring of highly intelligent individuals might exhibit above-average IQ, to reach their full potential, they are going to require environments and to be confronted by "random life events just as exceptional as their genes" (2005, p. 157).

That Marsalis is a genetic variant is undeniable. Naam suggests that individuals who know they have been genetically designed "may feel deeply resentful, as if their lives have been controlled and scripted from the outset, leaving them no chance for individuality" (2005, p. 161). The sense of being forced to live what Naam calls "scripted" lives is seen when Rovayo tells Marsalis that she is half bonobo. Marsalis expresses disbelief, to which Rovayo replies by asking him if he knew what it felt like to be constantly "testing your actions against some theory of how you think you might be supposed to behave," wondering whether "every time you make a compromise … that's you or your gene code talking?" (2007, p. 392). In response, Marsalis simply nods and tells her "Of course I do. You just pretty much described where I live" (2007, p. 392).

If both genetics and environment are required to determine, though not always guarantee the characteristics and personality traits exhibited by an individual, the monster status placed upon variant thirteen becomes questionable, if not almost contradictory, specifically when considering the laws and legislations created to protect unmodified individuals. This ambiguity is expressed during Marsalis' conversation with Sevgi's father, Murat, who asks Marsalis if he is religious, to which the latter responds by pointing out that he is a thirteen and thus genetically incapable, due to thirteens' skeptical, cynical and pragmatic nature. Murat asks if he truly believes that his genetic heritage prevents him from being able to hold a belief, to which Marsalis responds by asking if there could be any other possible explanation. Murat tells him that when he was younger, "we were less enamored of genetic influence as a factor" (2007, p. 505). Further, he goes on to explain that his grandfather had been a communist and believed that you could make of an individual "anything you choose to. That humans can become what they choose. That environment is all. It's not a fashionable view any longer" (2007, p. 505). Marsalis counters that it is no longer fashionable because it's demonstrably untrue. And yet, Murat is quick to point out, variant thirteens have undergone extreme environmental conditioning, because those involved in the creation of the variant "did not trust your genes to give them the soldiers they wanted. You were brought up from the cradle to face brutality as if were a fact of life" (2007, p. 506). Murat thus asks: "Do you really believe you would have become this, that you were genetically destined to it, however you were raised as a child?" (2007, p. 506).

This issue is further reinforced during Marsalis' conversation with Bambaren, the South American crime lord to whom he explains that variant thirteens are "very convenient monsters" (2007, p. 314). Bambaren simply points out, "The human race has more than enough monsters as it is. There was [never] any need to invent new ones" (2007, p. 314). While this challenges the notion that variant thirteens are the monsters individuals perceive them to be, the most potent affirmation of the ambiguity underpinning thirteens' nature is again revealed by Bambaren:

> Look around you. This was once an earthquake-proof city built to honour the gods and celebrate life in games and festivals. Then the Spanish came and tore it down for the stone to build churches that fell apart every time there

was a minor tremor. They slaughtered so many of my people in the battle to take this place that the ground was carpeted with their corpses and the condors fed for weeks on the remains. The Spanish put eight of those same condors on the city coat of arms to celebrate the fact of those rotting corpses. Elsewhere, their soldiers tore nursing infants from the breast and tossed them still living to their attack dogs, or swung them by the heels against rocks to smash their skulls. You don't need me to tell you what was done to the mothers after. These were not demons, and they were not genetically engineered abominations like you. These were men. Ordinary men. We—my people—invented the *pistacos*[11] to explain the acts of these ordinary men, and we continue to invent the same tales to hide from ourselves the truth that it is ordinary men, always, who behave like demons when they cannot obtain what they want by other means [2007, p. 317].

In highlighting the savage and brutal nature of unmodified individuals, Bambaren inevitably challenges the perceived monstrosity of variant thirteens, arguing that they are no more deserving of such a title than ordinary human individuals. The latter point, however, comes to be contradicted towards the end of the narrative, during Marsalis's final confrontation with Onbekend. Dying, and with their location surrounded by Bambaren's men, Onbekend asks Marsalis if he knows how to breed a contemporary human from a thirteen. When Marsalis responds in the negative, Onbekend goes on to explain:

You domesticate them. Same thing they did with wolves to make them into dogs. Same thing they did with fox farming in Siberia back in the nineteen-hundreds. You select for fucking tameness ... for lack of aggression, and for compliance. And you know how they get that?... How you get a modern human. You get it by taking immature individuals, individuals showing the characteristics of fucking puppies. Area thirteen, man. It's one of the last parts of the human brain to develop, the final stages of human maturity. The part they bred out twenty thousand years ago because it was too dangerous too their fucking crop-growing plans. We aren't the variant, Marsalis—we're the last true humans. It's the cudlips that are the fucking twists [2007, p. 625].

When Marsalis points out that they had been designed, Onbekend tells him that humans had tried to contain them, but

we'll beat that. We will, we're fucking wired to beat it. We're their last hope, Marsalis. We're what's going to rescue them from the Ortizes and the Nortons and the Roths. We're the only thing that scares those people, because we won't comply, we won't stay infantile and go out and play nice in their plastic fucking world.... We're the long walk back to hunter-gatherer egalitarianism [2007, p. 626].

While this might be interpreted as little more than hyper-masculine posturing, it is not without credibility. Violence and aggression are not simply the means by which one demonstrates superior strength over another, but the catalyst for social, political, scientific, and philosophical progress. As Fukuyama points out, "Societies that face no competition or aggression stagnate and fail to innovate; individuals who are too trusting and cooperative make themselves vulnerable to others who are more bloody-minded" (2002, p. 98). Thus it can be argued that variant thirteens and perhaps the paradoxical protagonists in general—viewed as individuals who fail to comply with existing morals, who create unrest and to some extent evoke fear in ordinary individuals—are essential for ensuring social progression. Whether derived from their genetic heritage or the social realities in which they exist, what is evident is that it is inevitably variant thirteens' capacity for violence, something further bolstered by other attributes such as superior strength, speed, and immune systems, that contributes to both their transhuman identity and paradoxical nature.

Black Man embodies many of the fears and anxieties surrounding developments in areas such as genetic engineering by confronting readers with a social reality in which technoscientific progress has led to the creation of several variations upon the human genome. In spite of the number of variants, the narrative focuses upon variant thirteens, which, as a result of their natural aggression and predisposition to violence, have come to be perceived by unmodified individuals as monsters. Through the protagonist Marsalis, however, Morgan explores the inequality and disparity experienced by variant thirteen—at times alluding to racial prejudice—and ultimately comes to question the significance of genetics and other external factors such as socialization and individual experience in relation to identity development. In this respect Marsalis shares with the monstrous protagonist of Mary Shelley's *Frankenstein* both being feared and loathed, initially not for anything they have done, but simply because of what they are. However, just as Frankenstein's monster comes to adopt his own monstrous identity, so too does the protagonist of Morgan's narrative, as expressed through Marsalis' capacity for and implementation of violence. Whether this is the result of a genetic predisposition or the inequality and prejudice by which he is confronted, however, remains ambiguous, thus evoking a paradox that blurs the line between categorical identities such as human and monster.

Conclusion

This book has sought to show that the protagonists of much modern speculative fiction, from *Frankenstein* through to the work of Richard Morgan, can be described as "paradoxical" and that these protagonists are best described as antiheroes. Their paradoxical nature is shown to derive from the way in which they each represent various combinations or hybridizations of the human and the monstrous and/or the human and the transhuman, and their status as antihero is shown to also be derived from a paradox, inasmuch as these protagonists will use conventionally immoral or un-heroic deeds (such as killing and acts of terrorism) to advance heroic purposes such as the protection of freedom or the righting of great personal or social wrongs.

For the purposes of this study, the figure of the antiheroic transhuman is traced at least as far back in time as Mary Shelley's *Frankenstein* (1818). Although possessing strength, speed, and intelligence superior to that of ordinary individuals, the transhuman creature in *Frankenstein* is shown to be a kind and sensitive being, and it is only after being rejected and denied a place in society that the creature is forced to acknowledge (if never truly accept) a monstrous identity. While the violence implemented by the monster in its quest for revenge is inarguably immoral, it is difficult to perceive it as being without cause or provocation.

The paradoxical protagonist, as a being that has in some way transcended the human condition, has much in common with Frederick Nietzsche's Übermensch, described in *Thus Spake Zarathustra*, and these similarities were highlighted through an examination of three narratives: Stapledon's *Odd John* (1936), Sturgeon's *More Than Human* (1952), and Bester's *The Stars My Destination* (1956). While interpretations of the Übermensch may vary, what remains consistent is an emphasis upon transcending the human condition through self-overcoming, and in all three narratives the protagonist seeks to transcend their own limitations. John of *Odd John* overcomes his physical limitations through rigorous training and later attempts to transcend those imposed by society by establishing a colony where he and his fellow homo superiors are free to focus on spiritual and intellectual advancement. The various characters in *More Than Human* overcome their individual limitations by joining together to form a new being, described as the next stage in human evolution, *homo gestalt*. And in *The Stars My Destination*, Gully Foyle transforms himself from a less-than-ordinary individual to an eccentric billionaire with cybernetic implants and, toward the end of the narrative, a being with God-like powers. To realize these transformations, however, the protagonists in all three narratives engage in immoral and distinctly non-heroic behavior, including murder, theft, rape, distortion, genocide, terrorism, and incest.

Such actions may be morally reprehensible, but the social reality in which they are shown to exist has the capacity to position the reader to accept (though perhaps not condone) actions and ideologies they might otherwise condemn. This is aptly demonstrated in Alan Moore and David Lloyd's *V for Vendetta*, in which the protagonist, V, commits acts of terrorism—which include murder and the assassination of political figures, larceny, kidnapping and torture—in an effort to topple the fascist, ultra-conservative, totalitarian Norsefire Party, which demands total obedience of its citizens and oppresses core facets of democratic ideology, including freedom of speech.

As beings who have transcended the human condition, it is reasonable to question whether transhumans can be judged or understood in terms of normative moral and social convention. This issue is reflected in Alan Moore's and Dave Gibbons's *Watchmen* (1986–1987) in which Ozymandias, the world's smartest man, destroys New York, effectively killing millions, but at the same time preventing a nuclear holocaust. The moral ambiguity of Ozymandias' actions is reflected by Dr. Manhattan, a being with God-like powers, who explains to Ozymandias that he understands "without condoning or condemning," as human affairs are no longer his concern (1986–1987, p. 27).

In cyberpunk, the paradoxical protagonist is reflected through the cyborg, which Donna Haraway describes as a "hybrid" of machine and biology (1991, p. 149). Cyberpunk is heavily influenced by the punk counter-culture, as can be seen through the social realities in which the narratives are set and in the appearance of the characters—especially in relation to their affinity with body modification. While fulfilling the punk aesthetic's desire to shock in cyberpunk, body modification gains a level of functionality within cyberpunk that demonstrates the physical integration between biology and technology and explores ways this integration might allow individuals the capacity to transcend the human condition. Ideologically, the punk counterculture can be seen influencing the protagonists' attitudes. This is perhaps most evident in their nihilistic approach to the body, especially in relation to self-destruction and drug use, yet also contributes to their involvement in criminal activities. It is more often than not the protagonists' adoption of the punk ideology that affirms their antiheroic identity.

Richard Morgan's Takeshi Kovacs trilogy shares a number of aesthetic and ideological similarities with cyberpunk. Morgan's implementation of various cyberpunk elements (such as the cityscape, bodily augmentation, drug use and petty criminality) informs the appearance of the characters and the social realities in which the narratives are set, while also reinforcing the protagonists' antiheroic identities and demonstrating how speculative fiction has developed in response to the emergence of transhuman theory and technoscientific development. Morgan's largest contribution to the paradoxical protagonist and to speculative fiction stems from his subversion of cyberpunk's most recognized tropes (particularly virtual reality and the digitization of human consciousness). Unlike most cyberpunk protagonists, whose capacity for action is limited to their ability to manipulate the information networks in which they operate, Morgan's protagonist frequently implements violence to achieve his desired goals, thus affirming his antiheroic identity.

The parallel between the monster and the transhuman again arises in Richard Morgan's *Black Man* in which variant thirteen—an artificially created variant of the human genome—embodies many of the fears surrounding advances in genetic and biological technologies. Through its protagonist, Carl Marsalis, the narrative explores the potential disparity manifest between human and transhuman and comes to question the significance of genetics (specifically in terms of predisposition for certain tendencies) when compared to other external factors such as socialization and individual experience in identity development. While Marsalis' antiheroic identity is established through his use of violence, actions undertaken contrary to the supposed nature of variant thirteen evoke a paradox that, in considering the narrative's treatment of the nature/nurture debate, evokes two questions: are variant thirteens truly the monsters unmodified individuals believe them to be and is their monstrosity—typified by a predisposition to violence and their sociopathic nature—the result of genetic factors or other external influences? The reasons for this protagonist's violent actions remain ambiguous, evoking a paradox that further blurs the boundary between categorical identities such as human and monster.

These paradoxical protagonists, along with the social realties in which they exist, provides an alternative medium for the exploration of the dynamic and complex relationship between individuals, society, and technoscientific development. Further, such characters also offer new insight into the crisis of identity as well as the generalized fear and anxiety surrounding the emergence of transhuman theory and the possibility of transhuman individuals.

Chapter Notes

Introduction

1. By this I refer to those more traditional, human, antiheroic protagonists such as the unnamed protagonist of Fyodor Dostoyevsky's *Notes from Underground* (1864), Holden Caulfield of J.D. Salinger's *The Catcher in the Rye* (1951), and Randle Patrick McMurphy of Ken Kesey's *One Flew Over the Cuckoo's Nest* (1962). Victor Brombert's *In Praise of Antiheroes* (1999) makes an intensive examination of such characters appearing within literature from 1830–1980. Though Michael Woolf's "The Madman as Hero in Contemporary American Fiction" does briefly mention speculative fiction (or more specifically, science fiction) as a mechanism for social commentary regarding issues and concerns of modern social reality, the article fails to connect the significance between such commentary and the antihero. Nevertheless, Woolf examines a range of traditional antiheroic figures such as Word Smith from Phillip Roth's *The Great American Novel* (1973).

2. The terms technoscientific or technoscience are umbrella terms used to refer to interdisciplinary research in a variety of fields pertaining to both science and technology. However, with a specific focus on those areas related to transhumanism, the terms might best be interpreted as referring to specific areas of study such as: nanotechnology, biotechnology, specifically biological or genetic engineering, genetic research and technologies, cloning, cryonics, bionics, cognitive science, cybernetics, computer science, specifically virtual reality, and artificial intelligence and information technology.

3. The narratives examined throughout this study were selected because, more often than not, the social realities which they depict, along with the moral and social convention by which they are underpinned, are not dissimilar from the reader's own.

4. The singularity refers to a point in time when advances in technoscience reach such a point that they are capable of progressing at an exponential rate.

Chapter One

1. While the hybridized monsters depicted in mythology were wholly biological and often the results of an unnatural cross-species union, those of contemporary popular culture typically emerge from the integration of biology and technology.

2. A philosophical notion derived from Egyptian hedonism that advocates pleasure as the only intrinsic good and the one thing for which all individuals should strive. In this, life is described as fleeting and thus one must fulfill all earthly pleasures before his death. In Wilde's narrative, the idea of new hedonism has a profoundly destructive force on Dorian Gray, who becomes obsessed with his own youth and beauty, and in becoming aware of the power afforded by his attributes, seeks to indulge his darkest desires.

3. Here Dorian recognizes his own youth and beauty for the first time and acknowledges its potential power to influence and seduce.

4. Captain (Robert) Walton is an Arctic explorer, whose ship, bound for the North Pole, becomes trapped within the ice, making progress impossible. It is by chance that, while waiting for the ice to thaw, Walton discovers Victor, emaciated, exhausted, and near death. Victor is taken aboard and nursed back to health and later tells the captain of the monster he had created and the series of events that had led him to the Arctic.

Chapter Two

1. A facet of the eternal-return whereby the Übermensch would devolve (metaphorically) into man so that man, once more, must be overcome by the Übermensch.

2. In *Thus Spake Zarathustra*, Nietzsche evokes the metaphor of a bridge by which the "last man" and the Übermensch are linked. In this, he refers to the individual's embrace of the Übermensch and of his own down-going, having fulfilled his purpose: "I love those who do not seek beyond the stars for reasons to go down and to be sacrifices: but who sacrifice themselves to the earth, that the earth may one day belong to the Superman" (1961, p. 44).

3. In literal translation, *letzte mensch* refers to the "last man." In Hollingdale's translation of Nietzsche's narrative, however, the term appears as the "ultimate man" (p. 45). Again, however, in order to avoid ambiguity and so as not to subtract from Nietzsche's intention posed by the juxtaposition between the Übermensch and the *letzte mensch*, this study will employ the original German term of letzte mensch. The figures of Übermensch and the letzte mensch are juxtaposed so as to represented alternative evolutionary paths. The Übermensch reflects self-overcoming and the means by which the species might be advanced, as a whole; the letzte mensch, on the other hand, while promising the safety and security of routine, nevertheless leads to stagnation.

4. The metaphor can be interpreted thus: the seed is the individual's capacity for self-overcoming and creativity; the "highest hope" reflects the Übermensch as the individual's ultimate goal; the soil can be interpreted as the individual's capacity for the will to power, which is discussed later in the chapter. In this, he suggests that it is only through the will to power that the Übermensch might be cultivated, yet left too long, even this will fade before the individual's desire for safety and comfort and the fulfillment of his more base desires.

5. Again this metaphor alludes directly to the Übermensch. Here, Nietzsche suggests that in the transition from individual to letzte mensch, the individual will forgo notions of self-overcoming, sublimation, and the will to power, thus losing the capacity by which the Übermensch, as the individual's ultimate goal, might be achieved. Here, the bow refers to the individual, as self, while the string can be interpreted as the will to power. Simply, it suggests that the individual will, sooner or later, lose the capacity and desire to ascend beyond other individuals.

6. Used in its literary definition as a system or group whose components are so similar that it cannot be defined by its individual parts.

7. This can be identified as an allusion to Mary Shelley's *Frankenstein* (1818), in which Victor's monster finds shelter in a hovel adjacent a farmer's cottage. Here Victor's monster first encounters and comes to learn of the human world and, by copying, learns to speak and understand the dynamics of human relationships. In exchange, the monster sneaks out at night and completes odd jobs such as gathering or chopping fire wood.

8. The significance of this relates to body modification in the development of the cyborg, which is discussed in Chapter Five in context to the influence of the punk rock subculture in cyberpunk.

9. Both the optimistic and pessimistic arguments affiliated with the transhuman movement are defined in the introduction, yet will be brought into sharper focus in following chapters, which examine, more closely, the potential consequences of transhumanism and its impact upon social reality.

10. In relation to both biology and philosophy, Nietzsche's concept of the will to power might be interpreted as being a response to Schopenhauer's theory of the "will to live." According to Schopenhauer's theory, all living things are driven by a primordial will to live. Schopenhauer thus places an emphasis on the subconscious desire to avoid danger and to ensure survivability, if only for the purposes of reproduction. The concept of the will to live is largely Schopenhauer's criticism of Hegel's popularization of the Zeitgeist (translated as: spirit of the time or spirit of the age), which advocated the notion of society existing as a collective consciousness, informing dynamic facets including morality. Schopenhauer challenges this, arguing that individuals are selfish, motivated by their primal desires, largely the will to survive. Nietzsche refutes Schopenhauer's suggestion, arguing that living, or having the capacity to do so, is only a secondary aim—a necessary factor for ensuring the acquisition and preservation of power—in that what all living things truly desire is power. Nietzsche punctuates this notion by pointing out that all living things, humans especially, are often all too happy to risk their lives and forgo safety and security in pursuit of power and glory: a poignant argument, specifically in consideration of the history associated with warfare and human conflict.

11. Jisbella breaks Gully's habit of using the "gutter tongue" and teaches him how to speak proper English, as well as informing him of his ignorance and naivety in trying to destroy *Vorga*, explaining that his revenge would be more effective should he target the crew and captain (those who gave and carried out the order that effectively left him for dead) rather than the ship itself (1956, pp. 65–70).

12. *Morgenröte. Gedanken über die moralischen Vorurteile* in German, yet also translated as *The Dawn*, *Day Break*, and *The Dawn of Day*.

13. As with Nietzsche's perception of the will to power, as the central force driving all living things, morality, as will be explained in the following, is inexplicably linked to the natural world, rather than to metaphysical belief.

14. In *Human All Too Human*, Nietzsche accuses older philosophies of having "always avoided investigation of the origin and history of the moral sensations" (1872, p. 37). The issues are further compounded by religious or theological doctrines that advocate a system of morality untenable for everyday individuals. As a result, Nietzsche claims, a "false ethics is erected, religion and mythological monsters are then in turn called to buttress it, and the shadow of these dismal spirits in the end falls even across physics and the entire perception of the world" (1872, p. 37). That is to say, Nietzsche perceives the avocation of such moral systems, through religion and the continuation of outdated philosophies, as leading to an obscured perception of reality.

15. Nietzsche's cynical approach to moral theory inevitably lead to his positing it in a realm of subjectivity, arguing notions such as good and evil, as concepts underpinning moral conventions and customs, were simply matters of perspective. In *The Gay Science*, for example, Nietzsche ascribes morality to convention through metaphor: "Where the good begins.—Where the poor power of the eye can no longer see the evil impulse as such because it has become too subtle, man posits the realm of goodness; and the feeling that we have now entered the realm of goodness excites all those impulses which had been threatened and limited by the evil impulses, like the feeling of security, of comfort, of benevolence. Hence, the duller the eye, the more extensive the good. Hence the eternal cheerfulness of the common people and of children. Hence the gloominess and grief—akin to a bad conscience—of the great thinkers" (1882, p. 115).

16. Here used in accordance with Nietzsche's rejection of object metaphysics and the notion of "the thing itself."

17. A nuclear-powered marine vessel constructed by John and his fellow Homo Superiors, which they intend to use for transport to their island, to gather supplies, and to ferry other members of their species to and from the island when necessary.

18. A term used to describe the relationship between the individual members within the gestalt itself. "Blesh" is an amalgam of "blend" and "mesh."

Chapter Three

1. Here Delia is referring to the Violet Carson, an uncommon rose that V propagated during his time at Larkhill in the small garden allotted to him as a reward for his success in increasing the productivity of the facility's vegetable garden. The rose holds significance for two reasons. On the one hand, it is named after the actress Violet Carson, who is most recognized for her role in *Coronation Street*, a long-running English television drama. On the other, the rose later comes to be a grim calling card left near the bodies of those individuals who worked at the Larkhill facility.

2. Moore elaborates upon this during the interview, explaining that rebellion is a tradition featured in British comics and that there is a "strong strand of anarchy which runs through nearly all the important characters in British culture" (Mapstone, 2012).

3. The phrase frequently employed by critics exploring the potential justification of terrorist actions such McPherson (2007) and Nathanson (2011) is essentially a misquotation of "One man's terrorist is another man's freedom fighter," which first appeared in Gerald Seymour's *Harry's Game* (1975).

4. This refers to Guy Fawkes's failed attempt to destroy the House of Lords and the Houses of Parliament on November 5, 1605. Fawkes was discovered guarding 36 barrels of gunpowder, which he had planned on detonating at midnight.

5. Essentially, V's anarchic philosophy mirrors that of the narrative's author, Alan Moore, who explains that early in his career, he came to the conclusion that the only political ideology to which he could adhere was "an anarchist one" (Killjoy, 2009, p. 42). For Moore, "anarchy is in fact the only political position that is actually possible" (2009, p. 42). When confronted with the argument that an anarchist society would simply denote survival of the fittest, a situation in which "the biggest gang would simply take over," Moore defends his belief, explaining that this has already happened, that contemporary social reality reflects a poorly "developed anarchist situation" in which the "biggest gang has taken over and have declared that it is not an anarchist situation—that it is a capitalist or a communist situation" (2009, p. 43). Modern perceptions of anarchy, however, often coincide with lawlessness, political and social unrest, and violence. Ontologically, anarchy is simply derived from the Latin *an-archon*, meaning without leaders. With this in mind, Moore argues that if individuals were to look at nature, "without prejudice" they would find "that this is the state of affairs that usually pertains" (2009, p. 44).

6. Here, V alludes to Fitch, the detective charged with his investigation, aware that it would be only just that he should die by his hands.

Chapter Four

1. Perhaps the most recognized modern adaptation or interpretation of the superhero comic-book character can be identified as Tim Kring's TV drama series, *Heroes*. The series comprised four seasons that aired from September 25, 2006, until February 8, 2010.

2. This refers to the popularity generated by comic-book adaptations into movies and games, rather than the comic books themselves.

3. A multiverse, in the context of comic books, refers to the continuity of the social reality depicted in a given narrative, thus allowing for the possibility of multiple or alternative perspectives on the same character or reality.

4. The Cold War between America and the Soviet Union.

5. Nite Owl's personalized aircraft, named after Merlin's pet owl.

6. Sally Jupiter's real name is Sally Juspeczyk. She changed it to hide her Polish heritage.

7. Moloch, also known as Edgar William Jacobi or Edgar William Vaughn, was a criminal and one of The Comedian's enemies who later becomes a legitimate businessman (1986–1987, ch. 2, p. 21).

8. Here, The Comedian is referring to Ozymandias's plot destroy half of New York City.

9. The sense of inevitability and pessimism that prevails over the narrative, along with the complex patterns to which Dr. Manhattan refers, is compounded by a number of reoccurring motifs. The most predominant is the bright yellow smiley face badge worn by the Comedian. This seemingly light-hearted image stands in stark contrast to the social reality in which he exists.

10. Here Dr. Manhattan is referring to his ability to see time and the events of both the past and the future. His perception, however, is limited to the events of his own life.

11. Dr. Manhattan's ability to see the events of the past and future is clouded by a form of interference produced by tachyons (subatomic particles moving at faster-than-light speed), which were generated by Ozymandias to prevent Dr. Manhattan from discovering his plan (1986–1987, ch. 12, p. 11).

12. Essentially, *Tales of the Black Freighter* serves two purposes. First, in its depiction of a graphic novel within a graphic novel, it serves to highlight the narrative's role as metafiction. Second, it serves to illustrate the fallibility of individuals and their perceptions and how, irrespective of their intentions, they can be corrupted by circumstances.

13. Using the scene following the destruction of New York, when Nite Owl, Silk Spectre, and Dr. Manhattan confront Ozymandias, Nuttall attempts to illustrates Rorschach's ignorance, as well as his lack of concern for others, in stating: "Rorschach, being single-minded in his pursuit of justice (or his sense of it, at least), has no concern for what might happen if he reveals Veidt's conspiracy" (2009, p. 92).

14. Moloch the Mystic, or Edgar William Jacobi, was a former adversary of the Comedian, presumably killed by Ozymandias in an attempt to frame Rorschach and thus terminate his investigation into the Comedian's death.

15. This is an excerpt from the fictional account written by Hollis Mason documenting his experience as a masked crime fighter.

16. Dr. Manhattan's metaphorical role as a character warning of the potential dangers regarding nuclear weaponry and the militarization of applied science is evident toward the conclusion of the novel, where it is revealed that while unaware of Ozymandias's plan to destroy New York City and other major cities, it was Dr. Manhattan's scientific research that made such widespread chaos possible. Further, the name Dr. Manhattan, given to him by the U.S. government, is an allusion to the Manhattan Project, the group of individuals responsible for the creation of the atom bomb, which was deployed during the Second World War against Hiroshima and Nagasaki.

17. In Chapter Four, Dr. Manhattan explains, "They're shaping me into something gaudy and lethal" (1986–1987, p. 12). On the following page, Dr. Manhattan is shown destroying a tank, and the caption reads, "And here, demonstrating that a Patton tank poses no greater difficulty" (p. 13).

18. Often identified as a piece of folk wisdom handed down from Uncle Ben to the young Peter Parker (Spider Man), the phrase actually first appeared in the final panel of *Amazing Fantasy #15* and not as dialogue, as many claim.

19. Here, I refer not to the monster, as a symbolic manifestation or metaphorical corporeal being, but to actions that so transgress moral and social convention, such as Ozymandias's destruction of New York City in order to save the world, as to be identified outside the pale of what can be defined as human agency. This will be discussed further in following chapters.

Chapter Five

1. First published in English in 1994.

2. For the purposes of this study, punk refers to the music and fashion subculture that started toward the end of the 1960s with the formation of more alternative bands such as The Stooges (fronted by Iggy Pop) and The Deviants, yet would not be fully recognized until the mid–1970s with the debut of the Sex Pistols.

3. It should be noted that this specific style is one most often associated with the English punk subculture, which differed slightly from the American scene, where punk subgenres such as OI and Hardcore were more common. Here, violence among individuals was more common and thus hair was kept short, often shaven, and piercings and other adornments such as jewelry and accessories were kept to a minimum to avoid further injury.

4. Ratz is the bartender operating The Chatsubo, a bar frequented by the protagonist, Case.

5. An elective surgery wherein the brain is augmented through the implementation of a technological device, the function of which is similar to that of a computer.

6. In Effinger's *When Gravity Fails*, "daddies" and "moddies" refer to the components that are used in combination with the ports hard-wired into the brain. Both are used in different circumstances, or are implemented to the user's preference. "Moddies," for example, contain complete personalities, thus changing the user's perspective and personality to match a given persona, which can be based on other individuals or fictional characters, whereas "daddies" are basic add-ons that provide the user with specific knowledge. These can be as complex as an additional language or the accumulated knowledge from a given discipline or as basic as a user manual for one piece of technology. Unlike the other characters in the novel, Marid has double ports, allowing him to implement a "moddy" and a "daddy" simultaneously.

7. Bopper is the term used by Rucker to refer to the robots who had gained cognition and self-awareness through a form of natural selection, instigated by their creator Cobb Anderson. In *Software*, the boppers have developed a complex society upon the moon, which is necessary for low temperatures boppers in order to function.

8. In *Neuromancer*, Armitage offers to pay for the operation that would repair the damage preventing Case from accessing the matrix. Case is then employed by Armitage as a hacker. Armitage was a former Green Beret named Willis Corto who was severely injured both physically and psychologically during a mission. Armitage is the persona developed as part of an experimental psychological recovery therapy developed by Wintermute, the artificial intelligence program that Case and the rest of the team are trying to liberate from the corporate giant Tessier-Ashpool SA.

9. It should be noted, if only for the sake of clarity, that toward the end of the narrative, Wintermute, the AI held by Tessier-Ashpool, is shown as being responsible for its own emancipation, having successfully manipulated Case and Molly through Armitage, who, it is revealed, is little more than a proxy acting in accordance with Wintermute's desires.

10. Tessier-Ashpool SA is the corporate front of the Tessier-Ashpool family members, who have obtained a form of immortality through cloning.

11. In *Neuromancer*, ICE refers to the program or anti-hacking parameters protecting a specific system. Thus, Gibson's notion of ICE can be thought of as the firewalls protecting existing computer systems.

12. The construct is a copy of Dixie's personality and knowledge at the time of death. Dixie exists only in the matrix, as a disembodied consciousness, yet remains self-aware.

13. The bopper race, specifically the Big Boppers, desired to acquire and tape human brains, which they could use to control remote bodies and also as a means of acquiring knowledge and forcing another form of human evolution through an integration with an entity known as the One, a program that reads bands of solar radiation.

14. This reinforces the notion of the cyberpunk protagonist's subversion of technology as a weapon against itself. In this, the technology implemented by the protagonist is produced through the wealth of the very multinationals against which they struggle.

15. 財閥 (ざいばつ) literally translates to financial clique and refers to financial or industrial conglomerates within Japan.

Chapter Six

1. While the obvious correlation between the image described by Takeshi and Frankenstein's monster does not require pointing out, it is nevertheless important to recognize the link speculative fiction draws between technoscientific progress and the individual's capacity to create monsters, either of themselves or from others.

2. A young and talented computer hacker who aids Takeshi and his group throughout the events of *Woken Furies*.

3. A group of elite shock troopers who operate under the Protectorate—the major governing body that maintains peace upon human-populated planets. Envoys are highly trained, psychologically conditioned, emotionally blunted, and often physically augmented.

4. This refers to a military debacle in which Kovacs loses a number of friends and, following the Protectorate's attempted cover-up, his faith in both the Corps and the military in general.

5. A high-class brothel owned and run by Reileen Kawahara, a former acquaintance of Takeshi, whom he met during deployment upon another world.

6. The Protectorate is an interplanetary political/governmental system under which the Envoy Corps serve.

7. A soldier killed in battle whose stack was purchased by Takeshi and Hand—the corporate executive overseeing the operation—to support them in their mission to retrieve the alien artifact.

8. As the primary reason for Kovacs's investigation into Bancroft's death, Kawahara is depicted as the narrative's primary villain and in many ways can be interpreted as foreshadowing the larger oppressive hegemonic systems encountered in *Woken Furies*.

9. Command heads are individuals who have interfaced directly with command technology, which is implanted directly into their neuron receptors and allows them to establish communication with other technological artifacts and establish a personal Net interface, which functions as a method of communication between members of the team. The technology behind the command-head software is the direct result of the events which took place upon Sanction IV (*Broken Angels*) and is derived from the implementation of Martian-based technologies discovered aboard the ship claimed by Kovacs and his team.

10. A zone where autonomous machines, as part of an abandoned military research

project, have gained a firm foothold and pose a potential threat to future human inhabitants either within or around the area.

11. Hayles (*How We Became Posthuman*, 1999, p. 36); Bukatman (*Terminal Identity*, 1993, pp. 143–146); Graham (*Representations of the Post/Human*, 2002, pp. 194–195).

12. As will be discussed later, the emphasis Morgan places upon embodiment is largely the site from which the paradox concerning the mind/body duality and identity emerges.

13. With the notion of physical incarceration made redundant by stack- and sleeve-based technologies, criminals are instead sentenced to serve a number of years—depending on the severity of the crime—in storage, during which the sleeve is frozen and the stack removed.

14. In Morgan's trilogy, constructs take the place of virtual reality and support specific artificial environments.

15. The female sleeve was used because it provided a shock to Takeshi, thus limiting his ability to implement his Envoy conditioning. Further, it was also devoid of even the most basic neurachem: "No combat conditioning, no reflect of aggression. Nothing. Not even calluses on the young flesh" (2001, p. 150).

16. The Hendrix refers to the hotel in which Kovacs is staying, which is run by an artificial intelligence.

17. In this, Kovacs might be interpreted as having an affiliation with protagonists such as Rorschach of *Watchmen*.

18. The individual who oversaw Kovacs's release from storage.

19. Apex predator on Harlan's World.

20. While stacks are implanted within every individual and sleeves freely available, it is the economic elite or ruling class that has benefited the most from such technology. These individuals are often describes as "methuselahs" in direct reference to the biblical figure, the oldest individual depicted in the Hebrew Bible, who was said to have lived for 969 years.

21. This refers to personal or sentimental value or, more specifically, the relationship between the individual and his original body: that is, the body in which he was born. Economically, sleeves represent a much greater value.

22. The main facility that oversees resleeving.

23. A religious group that advocates uploading as a means of spiritual enlightenment and to reduce strain on planetary resources. Renouncers reject embodiment in favor of virtual environments that are supported through large, cybernetic, computer-based networks.

24. McKibben stipulates that the availability of transhuman technology will be consumer-driven and inevitably lead to further disparity within society and the existence of what he defines as a genetic divide (2003).

25. As mentioned previously, Bancroft has Takeshi released from storage in order to investigate what he believes to be his murder.

26. Takeshi's contract, it should be pointed out, can be terminated at any time should he stray beyond the parameters of their original agreement or should Bancroft be dissatisfied with the results. In this instance, Kovacs would be forced to return to storage, where he would have to wait out the remainder of his sentence.

27. The notion of information being used as a weapon or to suit a military-based agenda resonates with theories pertaining to postmodern war and technoscientific progress, specifically the emergence and progressive evolution of computer-based technologies (Gray, 1997, pp. 19–70).

28. Jack Soul Brasil and the other members of the Little Blue Bugs, the crime gang to which both she and Takeshi once belonged.

Chapter Seven

1. Sevgi is a detective working homicide at the COLINS agency, which, though this is not expressed clearly, operates under the direct control of the Rim-States government.

2. Tom is a fellow detective who is assigned as Sevgi's partner.

3. Thirteen is a hyper-masculine variant designed for conflict.

4. An officer who works on the tracts and thus has extensive knowledge of and experience dealing with thirteens.

5. A thirteen who escaped from the Mars colonies by stowing away aboard a shuttle bound for Earth. Unable to be cryogenically frozen, he was forced to cannibalize the other passengers in order to survive the journey.

6. Onbekend is another thirteen living on Earth. He is Merrin's twin brother and arranged for his escape from Mars so that he might use his twin's presence as a cover for the murder of a number of political and governmental officials.

7. A South American crime lord and half-brother to Onbekend and Merrin.

8. States throughout America that have become separated from the rest of the country. These form what the novel refers to as Jesusland, which is depicted as largely backward, with archaic ideological notions.

9. A weapon designed to kill variant thirteens, which delivers a biochemical payload that systematically destroys the immune system.

10. Executive of the COLINS agency for which Tom and his former partner, Sevigi, work. Following Marsalis's initial induction into the COLINS case, Marsalis saves Ortiz's life during an attempted assassination, but as a thirteen, he is naturally paranoid and believes that he was their intended target and not Ortiz.

11. The pistaco or pishtaco refers to the mythological figure/monster originating in South-America, specifically Peru. According to legend, the pistaco is a monstrous figure, man-like in shape and size, that preyed upon unsuspecting natives by killing them and robbing them of their body fat, which it would use for cannibalistic purposes or sell as Chicharrón.

Bibliography

Abram, M., et al. (1987). *Splicing Life: The Social and Ethical Issues of Genetic Engineering with Human Beings*. Retrieved October 10, 2012, from http://bioethics.georgetown. edu/documents/pcemr/splicinglife.pdf.

Annas, G., Andrews, L., and Isasi, R. (2002). *Protecting the Engendered Human: Toward an International Treaty Prohibiting Cloning and Inheritable Alterations*. Retrieved April 15, 2011, from http://www.geneticsandsociety.org/downloads/2002_ajlm_annasetal. pdf.

Baehr, T. (2006). "Time Warner Promotes Terrorism and Anti-Christian Bigotry in New Leftist Movie, 'V for Vendetta.'" Retrieved January 2, 2011, from http://www.wnd. com/2006/03/35299/.

Banks, I. M. (1987). *Consider Phlebas*. New York: Orbit.

Baudrillard, J. (1994). *Simulacra and Simulation*. Michigan: University of Michigan Press.

_____. (1998). *The Consumer Society: Myths and Structures* (Turner, C., Trans.). Nottingham: Nottingham University Press.

Bear, G. (1985). *Blood Music*. London: Gollancz.

Bester, A. (1956). *The Stars My Destination*. London: Gollancz.

Billow, R. (2010). *Resistance, Rebellion and Refusal in Groups: The 3 Rs*. London: Karnac Books.

Bock, G., and Goode, J. (1996). *Genetics of Criminal and Antisocial Behaviour*. Chichester, Sussex: John Wiley & Sons.

Bostrom, N. (1999). *The Transhumanist FAQ*. Retrieved September 2, 2010, from www.N. transhumanism.org/resources/faq.html.

_____. (2005). *A History of Transhuman Thought*. Retrieved January 1, 2011, from http:// www.jetpress.org/volume14/bostrom.html.

Britt, R. (2012). *Why Science Fiction Needs Violence*. Retrieved May 14, 2014, from http:// www.tor.com/blogs/2011/05/why-science-fiction-needs-violence.

Broderick, D. (2005). *Reading by Starlight: Postmodern Science Fiction*. London: Routledge.

Brombert, V. (1999). *In Praise of Antiheroes: Figures and Themes in Modern European Literature 1830–1980*. Chicago: University of Chicago Press.

Buchanan, A. (2011). *Better Than Human: The Promise and Perils of Enhancing Ourselves*. New York: Oxford University Press.

_____, Brock, D., Daniels, N., and Wikler, D. (2001). *From Chance to Choice: Genetics and Justice*. New York: Cambridge University Press.

Cadigan, P. (2002). *The Ultimate Cyberpunk*. New York: Ibooks.

Calluori, R. (1985). "The Kids Are Alright: New Wave Subcultural Theory." *Social Text*, 12, 43–53. Retrieved February 12, 2011, from http://www.jstor.org.ezproxy.library. uwa.edu.au/stable/466603.

Campbell, J. (1949). *The Hero with a Thousand Faces.* London: Fontana Press.

Camus, A. (1956). *The Rebel: An Essay on Man in Revolt* (trans. A. Bower). New York: Vintage, 1991.

Canguilhem, G. (1962). "Monstrosity and the Monstrous." *Diogenes,* 10(40), 27–42.

Cavallaro, D. (2000). *Cyberpunk and Cyberculture: Science Fiction and the Work of William Gibson.* London: Athlone Press.

Cervantes, M. (1605). *Don Quixote* (E. Grossman, Trans). New York: Ecco, 2003.

Choen, J.J. (1996). *Monster Theory: Reading Culture.* London: University of Minnesota Press.

Clark, A. (2004). *Natural Born Cyborgs: Minds, Technologies, and the Future of Human Intelligence.* New York: Oxford University Press.

Clarke, J. (2009). *The Paradox of the Posthuman.* Melbourne: VDM.

Coogan, P. M. (2003). *The Secret Origin of the Superhero: The Origin and Evolution of the Superhero Genre in America* (Doctoral dissertation, Michigan State University). Retrieved from ProQuest Dissertations and Theses. (AAT 3092128).

Dale, P. (2012). *Anyone Can Do It: Empowerment, Tradition and the Punk Underground.* Surrey: Ashgate.

Daniel, A. (1994). *Anti-heroic Literature.* Master's thesis, San Francisco State University.

Davis, J. (Producer), Schroeder, A. (Producer), and Trank, J. (Director). *Chronicle* [Motion picture]. USA: Davis Entertainment.

Deleuze, G. (1983). *Nietzsche and Philosophy* (H. Tomlinson, Trans.). New York: Columbia University Press.

Di Liddo, A. (2009). *Alan Moore: Comics as Performance, Fiction as Scalpel.* Jackson: University of Mississippi.

DiPaolo, M. (2011). *War, Politics and Superheroes: Ethics and Propaganda in Comics and Films.* Jefferson, NC: McFarland.

Dostoyevsky, T. (1864). *Notes from Underground.* Camberwell, Victoria: Penguin Books, 2010.

Dumas, A. (1844). *The Count of Monte Cristo.* Oxford: Oxford University Press, 2008.

Effinger, G. A. (1987). *When Gravity Fails.* New York: Arbor House.

_____. (1989). *A Fire in the Sun.* New York: Doubleday.

_____. (1991). *The Exile Kiss.* New York: Doubleday.

Egan, G. (1994). *Permutation City.* London: Orion.

Epstein, J. (1998). *Youth Culture: Identity in a Postmodern World.* Massachusetts: Blackwell.

FM-2030. (1989). *Are You a Transhuman? Monitoring and Stimulating Your Personal Rate of Growth in a Rapidly Changing World.* New York: Warner Books.

Foucault, M. (1974). *The Order of Things: An Archaeology of the Human Sciences.* London: Routledge.

Frelik, P. (2011). "Woken Carbon: The Return of the Human in Richard K. Morgan's Takeshi Kovacs Trilogy". In Murphy, G. and Vint, S. (Eds.), *Beyond Cyberpunk* (pp. 173–190). New York: Routledge.

Fukuyama, F. (2002). *Our Posthuman Future.* London: Profile Books.

_____. (2004). "The World's Most Dangerous Idea". Retrieved March 2, 2011, from http://www.foreignpolicy.com/articles/2004/09/01/transhumanism.

Gibson. W. (1984). *Neuromancer.* London: HarperCollins.

Goldman, E. (1972). *Anarchism and Other Essays.* Retrieved March 10, 2012, from http://theanarchistlibrary.org/library/emma-goldman-anarchism-and-other-essays.

González, M. (2010). "Sympathy for the Devil: The Hero is a Terrorist in *V for Vendetta.*" In Billias, N. (Ed). *Promoting and Producing Evil.* New York: Rodopi, 2010.

Graham, E. L. (2002). *Representations of the Post/human: Monsters, Aliens and Others in Popular Culture.* Manchester: University of Manchester Press.

Iannucci, A. (Interviewer). Moore, A. (Interviewee). (2008). *Comics Britannia*. Retrieved January 5, 2012, from http://www.youtube.com/watch?v=QX7ehbE1vc0&list=PLC D8A370BD4702DB9.

Gray, C. H. (1997). *Postmodern War*. New York: Guilford Press.

_____. (2002). *Cyborg Citizen*. New York: Routledge.

Grossman, L. (2006). "The Mad Man in the Mask." Retrieved January 2, 2011, from http://www.time.com/time/magazine/article/0,9171,1169899,00.html.

Haraway, D. (1985). *A Cyborg Manifesto: Science, Technology and Socialist-Feminism in the Late Twentieth Century*. Retrieved August 15, 2010, from http://www.stanford.edu/dept/HPS/Haraway/CyborgManifesto.html.

Harris, J. (2007). *Enhancing Evolution: The Ethical Case for Making Better People*. New Jersey: Princeton University Press.

HardTALK (Interviewer). Moore, A. (Interviewee). (2012). *Alan Moore Interview*. Retrieved from http://www.bbc.co.uk/programmes/b01fq32k.

Hannon, S. (2009). *Punks: A Guide to an American Subculture*. Santa Barbara: Greenwood Press.

Hayes, T. R. (2007). *The Rough Beast's Hour: The Rise of the Anti-hero*. Master's thesis, San Francisco State University.

Hayles, K. (1999). *How We Became Posthuman: Virtual Bodies in Cybernetics, Literature and Informatic*. Chicago: University of Chicago Press.

Held, J. (2009). "Can We Steer This Rudderless World? Kant, Rorschach, Retributivism and Honor." In Irwin, W. and White, M. (Eds.). *Watchmen and Philosophy* (pp. 19–31).

Heuser, S. (2003). *Virtual Geographies: Cyberpunk at the Intersection of the Postmodern and Science Fiction*. New York: Rodopi.

Hobbes, T. (1651). *Leviathan*. Retrieved January 15, 2011, from http://www.gutenberg.org/files/3207/3207-h/3207-h.htm.

Hock-Soon Ng, A. (2004). *Dimensions of Monstrosity in Contemporary Narratives*. New York: Palgrave Macmillan.

Howard, R. (2003). "Dualism." In Zalta, E. (Ed). *The Stanford Encyclopedia of Philosophy*. Retrieved March 15, 2012, from http://plato.stanford.edu/entries/dualism/.

Hudson, B. (2006). "Punishing Monsters, Judging Aliens: Justice at the Borders of Community." *Australian & New Zealand Journal of Criminology*, 39(2), 232–247.

Hurley, K. (2011). *God's War*. San Francisco: Night Shade Books.

_____. (2011). *Infidel*. San Francisco: Night Shade Books.

_____. (2012). *Rapture*. San Francisco: Night Shade Books.

Irwin, W., and White, M. (2009). *Watchmen and Philosophy: A Rorschach Test*. New Jersey: John Wiley & Sons.

Jameson, F. (1990). *Postmodernism or the Cultural Logic of Late Capitalism*. Durham: Duke University Press.

Jeffreys, S. "'Body Art' and Social Status: Cutting, Tattooing and Piercing from a Feminist Perspective." *Feminism & Psychology*, 10(4), 409–429. Retrieved March 15, 2011, from http://www.psy.dmu.ac.uk/brown/selfinjury/jeffreys.htm.

Jenks, C. (2005). *Subculture: The Fragmentation of the Social*. London: Sage Publications.

Johnson, B (Producer), Pfister, W. (2014). *Transcendence* [Motion picture]. USA: Alcon Entertainment.

Johnston, J. (2012). *The Prosthetic Novel and Posthuman Bodies*. Madison: University of Wisconsin.

Kadrey, R. (1988). *Metrophage*. Retrieved March 15, 2011, from http://www.voidspace.org.uk/cyberpunk/metrophage.shtml.

Kant, I. (1797). *The Metaphysics of Morals*. Cambridge: Cambridge University Press, 1998.

Kaufmann, A. (1974). *Nietzsche: Philosopher, Psychologist, Anarchist*. Princeton, New Jersey: Princeton University Press.

Kaveney, Roz. (2008). *Superheroes: Capes and Crusaders in Comics and Films*. New York: I.B. Tauris.

Kearney, R. (2001). "Evil Monstrosity and the Sublime." *Revista Portuguesa de Filosofia*, 65(1), 485–502.

Keller, J. (2008). *V for Vendetta as Cultural Pastiche*. Jefferson, NC: McFarland.

Kesey, K. (1962). *One Flew Over the Cuckoo's Nest*. New York: Viking Press.

Killjoy, M. (2009). *Mythmakers and Lawbreakers: Anarchist Writers on Fiction*. San Francisco: AK Press.

Kirby, V. (1992). *Telling Flesh: The Substance of the Corporeal*. New York: Routledge.

Klock, G. (2002). *How to Read Superhero Comics and Why*. New York: Continuum.

Klossowski, P. (1997). *Nietzsche and the Vicious Circle* (Smith, D, Trans). London: Athlone Press. (Original work published 1969.).

Knowles, C. (2007). *Our Gods Wear Spandex: The Secret History of Comic Book Heroes*. San Francisco: Red Wheel.

Kurzweil, R. (2005). *The Singularity Is Near: When Humans Transcend Biology*. New York: Penguin.

Lee, S., and Ditko, S. (2007). *Amazing Fantasy Omnibus*. New York: Marvel.

Lévi-Strauss, C. (1963). *Structural Anthropology*. New York: Basic Books.

Lingis, A. (1995). *Foreign Bodies*: New York: Routledge.

Lopes, P. (2009). *Demanding Respect: The Evolution of the American Comic Book*. Philadelphia: Temple University Press.

Lucchine, D. P. (2009). *Beneath the Mask and Spandex: Reviewing, Revising, and Reappropriating the Superhero Myth in Alan Moore's Watchmen*. (Master's thesis, Villanova University). Retrieved from ProQuest Dissertations & Theses. (AAT 1473018).

Lykk, N., and Braidotti, R. (1996). *Between Monsters, Goddesses and Cyborgs: Feminist Confrontations with Science, Medicine and Cyberspace*. London: Zed Books.

Lyles-Scott, C. (2007). *Heeding the Antiheroines' Call: The Rise of the Antiheroine in Literature and Popular Culture*. Florida: Florida Atlantic University.

MacCormack, P. (2012). "Posthuman Teratology". In Mittman, A., and Dendle, P. (Eds.). *The Ashgate Research Companion to Monsters and the Monstrous*. Surrey: Ashgate.

MacDonald, H. (2005). *A for Alan: The Alan Moore Interview*. Retrieved January 12, 2011, from http://web.archive.org/web/20070305213808/http://www.comicon.com/the beat/2006/03/a_for_alan_pt_1_the_alan_moore.html.

Macpherson, C. (1962). *The Political Theory of Possessive Individualism*. Ontario: Oxford University Press.

Magnus, B. (1986). "The Will to Power and the Übermensch". *Journal of the History of Philosophy*, 24(1), 79–98.

Mapstone, D. (Interviewer) (2012). *V for Vendetta: The Man Behind the Mask*. Retrieved from http://www.channel4.com/news/v-for-vendetta-the-man-behind-the-mask.

Marx, K., and Engels, F. (1885). *Capital*. Chicago: Encyclopedia Britannica, 1952.

Matthews, G, and Goodman, S. (Eds.). (2013). *Violence and the Limits of Representation*. Hampshire: Palgrave Macmillan.

McCaffery, L. (Ed). (1991). *Storming the Reality Studio*. New York: Duke University Press.

McHale, B. (1987). *Postmodernist Fiction*. London: Methuen.

McKibben, B. (2003). *Enough: Staying Human in an Engineered Age*. New York: Henry Holt.

More, M. (2010). *The Overhuman in the Transhuman*. Retrieved January 1, 2012, from http://jetpress.org/v21/more.htm.

_____. (1993). *Technological Self-Transformation*. Retrieved May 14, 2012, from http://www.maxmore.com/selftrns.htm.

More, T. (1964). *Utopia* (E. L. Surtz, Trans.). New Haven: Yale University Press.

Morris, T., Morris, M., and Irwin, W. (2001). *Superheroes and Philosophy: Truth, Justice and the Socratic Way*. Chicago: Open Court.

Moore, A., and Lloyd, D. (2005). *V for Vendetta*. New York: DC Comics.
_____, and Gibbons, D. (2005). *Watchmen*. New York: DC.
Moore, P. (2008). *Enhancing Me*. Chichester, Sussex: John Wiley and Sons.
Morgan, R. (2001). *Altered Carbon*. London: Gollancz.
_____. (2003). *Broken Angels*. London: Gollancz.
_____. (2005). *Woken Furies*. London: Gollancz.
_____. (2008). *Black Man*. London: Gollancz.
Murphy, G., and Vint, S. (Eds.). (2010). *Beyond Cyberpunk: New Critical Perspectives*. New York: Routledge.
Naam, R. (2005). *More Than Human*. New York: Random House.
Nathanson, S. (2011). *Terrorism and the Ethics of War*. Cambridge: Cambridge University Press.
Nayef, A. (2011). *The Politics of Emerging Stragegic Technologies: Implications for Geopolitics, Human Enhancement and Human Destiny*. Hampshire: Palgrave Macmillan.
Ndalianis, A. (2008). The *Contemporary Comic Book Superhero*. New York: Routledge.
Niall, S. (2007). *Monsters and the Monstrous: Myths and Metaphors of Enduring Evil*. Amsterdam: Rodopi.
Nietzsche, F. (1886). *Beyond Good and Evil: Prelude to a Philosophy of the Future* (H. Zimmern, Trans.). Retrieved April 15, 2011, from http://www.gutenberg.org/files/4363/4363-h/4363-h.htm.
_____. (1881). *The Dawn of Day* (J. Kennedy, Trans.). New York: Macmillan.
_____. (1889). *The Gay Science: With a Prelude in Rhymes and an Appendix of Songs* (W. Kaufmann, Trans.). New York: Vintage, 1974.
_____. (1887). *On the Genealogy of Morals* (W. Kaufmann, Trans). New York: Vintage.
_____. (1885). *Thus Spoke Zarathustra: A Book for Everyone and No One* (R. Hollingdale, Trans.). London: Penguin, 1961.
_____. (1999). *Thus Spoke Zarathustra: A Book for Everyone and No One* (T. Common, Trans.). Retrieved April 12, 2011, from http://www.gutenberg.org/files/1998/1998.txt.
_____. (1967). *The Will to Power* (W. Kaufmann, and R. Hollingdale, Trans.). New York: Random House.
Nuttal, A. (2009). "Rorschach: When Telling the Truth Is Wrong." In Irwin, W and White, M (Eds.). *Watchmen and Philosophy* (pp. 91–1001).
O'Hara, C. (1995). *The Philosophy of Punk: More Than Noise*. Edinburgh: AK Press.
O'Toole, S. (2004). *Cyberpunk Visions: Coping with Converging Technologies and Transformations of Human Freedom* (Doctoral dissertation, University of California, Davis.) Retrieved from ProQuest Dissertations and Theses. (AAT 3148489).
Person, L. (1998). "Notes Toward a Cyberpunk Manifesto." *Slashdot*: Retrieved February 10, 2011, from http://slashdot.org/story/99/10/08/2123255/Notes-Toward-a-Postcyberpunk-Manifesto.
Pitts, V. (2003). *In the Flesh: The Cultural Politics of Body Modification*. New York: Palgrave Macmillan.
Price, I. (2004). *Nietzsche's Zarathustra/Zarathustra as Abomination*. Unpublished doctoral dissertation). University of New Texas. Retrieved April 15, 2011, from http://repositories.lib.utexas.edu/handle/2152/2166.
Pohl, F. (1976). *Man Plus*. London: Gollancz.
Purkis, J., and Bowen, J. (1997). *Twenty-first Century Anarchism: Unorthodox Ideas for the New Millennium*. London: Continuum International.
Reichardt, J. (1991). "Artificial Life and the Myth of Frankenstein." In Bann, S. (Ed.), *Frankenstein, Creation and Monstrosity*. London: Reaktion.
Robichaud, C. (2009). "The Superman Exists and He Is American." In Irwin, W., and White, M. (Eds.). *Watchmen and Philosophy* (pp. 5–18).

Robinson, H. (2003). "Dualism." Retrieved March 10, 2012, from http://plato.stanford.edu/entries/dualism/.

Ross, A. (1996). *Strange Weather: Culture, Science, and Technology in the Age of Limits.* London: Verso.

Roth, P. (1973). *The Great American Novel.* New York: Holt, Rinehart and Winston.

Rotten, J. (1977). "God Save the Queen." On *Never Mind the Bollocks, Here's the Sex Pistols* (CD). London: Virgin Records.

Rucker, R. (1982). *Software.* New York: EOS.

_____. (1988). *Wetware.* New York. Avon Books.

_____. (2010). *The Ware Tetralogy.* Gaithersburg: Prime Books.

Salinger, J. D. (1951). *The Catcher in the Rye.* Boston: Little, Brown.

Saunders, B. (2011). *Do the Gods Wear Capes? Spirituality, Fantasy, and Superheroes.* New York: Continuum.

Schildkrout, E. (2004). "Inscribing the Body." *Annual Review of Anthropology,* 33(1), 319–344. doi: 10.1146/annurev.anthro.33.070203.143947.

Seymour, G. (1975). *Harry's Game: A Novel.* New York: Random House.

Shaviro, S. (2005). *The Pinocchio Theory.* Retrieved March 10, 2012, from http://www.shaviro.com/Blog/?p=116.

Shelley, M. (1818). *Frankenstein.* London: Penguin Classics, 1985.

Shelley, P. (1832). "On *Frankenstein.*" In Bloom, H. (Ed.), *Mary Shelley's Frankenstein* (pp. 64–66). New York: Bloom's Literary Criticism.

Shildrick, M. (2001). *Embodying the Monster.* London: Sage.

Silver, J., Wachowski, L., Wachowski, A., (Producers), and McTeigue, J., (Director). (2006). *V for Vendetta* [Motion picture]. USA: Warner Brothers.

Smith, M., and Morra, J. (2006). *The Prosthetic Impulse: From a Posthuman Present to a Biocultural Future.* Cambridge: MIT Press.

Sorgner, S. (2009). *Nietzsche, the Overhuman and the Transhuman.* Retrieved January 1, 2012, from http://jetpress.org/v20/sorgner.htm.

Sponsler, C. (1993). "Beyond the Ruins: The Geopolitics of Urban Decay and Cybernetic Play." *Science Fiction Studies,* 20(2), 251–265.

Suvin, D. (1979). *Metamorphoses of Science Fiction: On the Poetics and History of a Literary Genre.* New Haven: Yale University Press.

Stableford, B. (2006). *Science Fact and Science Fiction: An Encyclopedia.* New York: Routledge.

Stapledon, O. (1935). *Odd John.* Mineola, New York: Dover Publications.

Stephenson, N. (1992). *Snow Crash.* New York: Bantam Books.

Stevenson, R. L. (1886). *The Strange Case of Dr. Jekyll and Mr. Hyde.* London: Penguin Classics.

Sterling, B. (1985). *Schismatrix.* New York: Arbor House.

_____. (1988). *Mirrorshades: The Cyberpunk Anthology.* New York: Ace Books.

Stowe, H. B. (1852). *Uncle Tom's Cabin.* New York: Reader's Digest, 1992.

Sturgeon, T. (1953). *More Than Human.* New York: Random House.

Swanson, R. (1982). "The Spiritual Factor in 'Odd John and Sirius." *Science Fiction Studies,* 9(3), 284–293.

Thompson, I. (2005). *Deconstructing the Hero.* (Master's thesis, The University of New Mexico.) Retrieved September 11, 2011, from http://www.unm.edu/~ithomson/Hero.pdf.

Toro, G. D., (Executive producer), Hoban, S., (Producer), and Natali, V., (Director). *Splice* [Motion picture]. Canada: Dark Castle Entertainment.

Tsitsos, W. (1999). "Rules of Rebellion: Slamdancing, Moshing, and the American Alternative Scene." *Popular Music,* 18(3), 397–414. Retrieved from http://www.jstor.org/stable/853615.

Turner, T. (1995). "Social Body and Embodied Subject: Bodiliness, Subjectivity, and Sociality Among the Kayapo." *Cultural Anthropology*, 10(2), 143–170. Retrieved from http://www.jstor.org/discover/10.2307/656331?uid=3737536&uid=2129&uid=2&uid=70&uid=4&sid=21101348206143.

Viding, E., and Frith, U. (2006). "Genes for Susceptibility to Violence Lurk in the Brain." Retrieved July 7, 2012, from http://www.pnas.org/content/103/16/6085.full.

Vylenz, D. (Director) (2008). *The Mindscape of Alan Moore* (DVD). London: Shadowsnake Films.

Walsh, N. (2001). *Alter Our DNA or Robots Will Take Over, Warns Hawking*. Retrieved April 5, 2012, from http://www.guardian.co.uk/uk/2001/sep/02/medicalscience. genetics.

"When Fantasy Is Just Too Close for Comfort." (2007). Retrieved March 10, 2012, from http://www.theage.com.au/news/entertainment/when-fantasy-is-just-too-close-for-comfort/2007/06/09/1181089394400.html?page=fullpage.

Wick, I. (2006). *Monstrous Fictions of the Human.* (Doctoral dissertation, University of Wisconsin-Madison.) Retrieved from ProQuest Dissertations & Theses. (AAT 3234865).

Wilde, O. (1890). *The Picture of Dorian Gray.* London: Vintage Books, 2007.

Wilkinson, S. (2010). *Choosing Tomorrow's Children: The Ethics of Selective Reproduction.* New York: Oxford University Press.

Wojcik, D. (1995). *Punk and Neo-Tribal Body Art.* Mississippi: University of Mississippi Press.

Woolf, M. P. (1976). "The Madman as Hero in Contemporary American Fiction." *Journal of American Studies, 10,* 257–269.

Wright, P. (2001). *Comic Book Nation: The Transformation of Youth Culture in America.* Baltimore: Johns Hopkins University Press.

Young, S. (2006). *Designer Evolution.* New York: Prometheus Books.

Index